PQ- DWU -725

About Island Press

Island Press is the only nonprofit organization in the United States whose principal purpose is the publication of books on environmental issues and natural resource management. We provide solutions-oriented information to professionals, public officials, business and community leaders, and concerned citizens who are shaping responses to environmental problems.

In 2005, Island Press celebrates its twenty-first anniversary as the leading provider of timely and practical books that take a multidisciplinary approach to critical environmental concerns. Our growing list of titles reflects our commitment to bringing the best of an expanding body of literature to the environmental community throughout North America and the world.

Support for Island Press is provided by the Agua Fund, The Geraldine R. Dodge Foundation, Doris Duke Charitable Foundation, Ford Foundation, The George Gund Foundation, The William and Flora Hewlett Foundation, Kendeda Sustainability Fund of the Tides Foundation, The Henry Luce Foundation, The John D. and Catherine T. MacArthur Foundation, The Andrew W. Mellon Foundation, The Curtis and Edith Munson Foundation, The New-Land Foundation, The New York Community Trust, Oak Foundation, The Overbrook Foundation, The David and Lucile Packard Foundation, The Winslow Foundation, and other generous donors.

The opinions expressed in this book are those of the author(s) and do not necessarily reflect the views of these foundations.

About the Lincoln Institute of Land Policy

The Lincoln Institute of Land Policy, based in Cambridge, Massachusetts, is a nonprofit and tax-exempt educational institution established in 1974 to study and teach land policy, including land economics and land taxation. The Institute is supported primarily by the Lincoln Foundation, which was established in 1947 by Cleveland industrialist John C. Lincoln.

The Institute's goals are to integrate theory and practice to better shape land policy decisions and to share understanding about the multidisciplinary forces that influence public policy in the United States and internationally.

The Lincoln Institute seeks to improve the quality of debate and disseminate knowledge of critical issues in land policy by bringing together scholars, policy makers, practitioners, and citizens with diverse backgrounds and experience. We study, exchange insights, and work toward a broader understanding of complex land and tax policies. The Institute does not take a particular point of view, but rather serves as a catalyst to facilitate analysis and discussion of these issues—to make a difference today and to help policy makers plan for tomorrow. For more information: www.lincolninst.edu.

From Walden to Wall Street

From Walden to Wall Street

Frontiers of Conservation Finance

Editor
James N. Levitt
Assistant Editor
Lydia K. Bergen

LINCOLN INSTITUTE
OF LAND POLICY

ISLANDPRESS
Washington • Covelo • London

Library of Congress Cataloging-in-Publication data.

From Walden to Wall Street : frontiers of conservation finance / edited by
James N. Levitt.
    p. cm.
  Includes bibliographical references and index.
  ISBN 1-59726-030-4 (pbk. : alk. paper) — ISBN 1-59726-029-0
(cloth : alk. paper)
  1. Habitat conservation—North America—Finance. 2. Biological
diversity conservation—North America—Finance. I. Levitt, James N.
  QH77.N56F76 2005
  333.72—dc22

                                                              2005022607

British Cataloguing-in-Publication data available.

Printed on recycled, acid-free paper

Design by Linda McKnight

Manufactured in the United States of America
10 9 8 7 6 5 4 3 2

Contents

Foreword

James D. Range, Chairman,
Theodore Roosevelt Conservation Partnership

Americans have practiced conservation for centuries. From the Puritan's protection of the Boston Common in New England to the exemplary landscape stewardship practiced by George Washington and Thomas Jefferson in Virginia, conservation has been part of our culture since the founding of the nation. As a broad political movement, however, conservation started coming into its own and taking on a national character in the mid-nineteenth century. Among several conservation-related initiatives of the era, one of the most important was the effort mounted by sportsmen, in response to the ravages of commercial hunting, to establish seasons and bag limits as well as formal means of enforcing such restrictions. Their aim, concisely stated, was to sustainably manage wild game. That simple conservation philosophy, based on the belief that we Americans need to constructively restrain ourselves to ensure that resources like game animals will be available for future generations, became an important model for the subsequent management of natural resources throughout the country.

In the centuries since, the ideals of the American conservation movement have found their expression in numerous tangible ways. Much has been achieved during that time through the enactment of legal restrictions on the exploitation of natural resources. But the willingness of society to impose legal limitations on its use of land, water, fish, and game has been only a part of the story. In public, private, and philanthropic capacities we have repeatedly shown our willingness to commit our ingenuity and our money to the constructive conservation of our natural resources.

Indeed, the successful conservation of our nation's natural resources ultimately depends on the timely and adequate commitment of human and financial resources to get the job done. In America's free market economy, where citizens and policy makers balance the rights of property owners to utilize their private lands against the need to protect essentially public resources such as wildlife, conservationists often must bid against competing purposes to protect natural resources.

Fortunately, conservationists, ranging from local activists to U.S. presidents, have fought in the political arena to secure the investment of federal and state monies in the cause of protecting natural resources. At the same time, philanthropic enterprises such as local land trusts have sprung up, complementing and leveraging public investments to expand conservation efforts. Examples of conservation investments by the private, nonprofit, and public sectors are everywhere, in every state in the country.

Both in quantity and quality, much of our most significant conserved land is held by the federal government. The acquisition, maintenance, and management of these federal lands, including the national wildlife refuges, the national forests, and the national parks, were greatly advanced by President Theodore Roosevelt. The conservation work for which he laid much of the groundwork continues to this day and has required the public investment of tens of billions of dollars.

Our wide recognition of Teddy Roosevelt as this country's greatest conservation president is, in great measure, based on our understanding of his passionate love for the outdoors. Through his words and his deeds, Roosevelt was instrumental in defining the American sportsman/conservationist ethic that we know today. As a politician and national leader, Roosevelt understood that the conservation ethic must be backed up with adequate funding for resource management. He fought long and hard for the establishment of state and federal agencies that would set the standard for many decades to come.

Presidents and Congresses that followed built upon the foundation laid by Theodore Roosevelt and his associates. Teddy's younger kinsman, Franklin Roosevelt, signed into law in 1937 the Pittman-Robertson Act. With the enthusiastic support of hunters and anglers, this legislation continues to direct excise taxes on hunting and fishing equipment to pay for the conservation and sustainable management of game species. Since its passage nearly seventy years ago, this mechanism has provided more than $2 billion of funding for conservation.

In the 1970s and 80s, both Republican and Democratic presidents, working closely with Congress, established landmark laws that provided money for the regulation of toxic chemicals, the cleanup of hazardous waste sites, the construction of sewage treatment plants, and the control of non–point source runoff. Additional measures forced polluting industries to invest billions to pay for control technologies designed to reduce air and water pollution. These actions have directly benefited wildlife populations. In several cases, such as that of the American bald eagle and the wood duck, the combined effect of decades of conservation policy initiatives has allowed some wildlife populations to rebound to much more healthy levels in recent years.

In the mid-1980s, Congress agreed to invest additional resources in new Farm Bill conservation programs such as the Conservation Reserve Program and the Wetlands Reserve Program, which pay farmers and ranchers to conserve habitat and prevent erosion. Alongside Farm Bill measures, additional billions have been spent to protect wetlands and upland bird habitat on private lands by nonprofit groups like Ducks Unlimited and Pheasants Forever, often working in partnership with state governments and federal agencies such as the Department of Agriculture and the Fish and Wildlife Service.

Furthermore, the donation of billions of dollars worth of conservation easements has been encouraged through the federal tax code as well as through the purchase of development rights under the Farm Bill's Farm and Ranchland Protection Program. Groups like the Rocky Mountain Elk Foundation and land trusts across the country have ensured that conservation easements will continue to protect millions of acres of valuable open space and wildlife habitat. Such mechanisms are an essential part of our national conservation efforts. Without the commitment of such substantial financial resources, a great many farms, ranches, and other open spaces that provide critical wildlife habitat would be susceptible to economic pressures and risk being developed into yet more strip malls and clusters of oversized houses.

In recent decades, we have also witnessed the emergence of private companies, funded with private capital, that have made the restoration of ecosystem health an important part of their business. Sustainably managed forests and smart-growth oriented developments across the land offer tangible evidence that their efforts are having a substantial impact.

The history of conservation in America has shown that where the public recognizes a good cause, it can marshal the political will, the nonprofit passion, and the corporate focus to fund the work in a relatively straightforward way. But as times change, our funding methods can, and need, to change. While many investments in conservation continue to be well justified and will produce public benefits long into the future, record-setting annual federal deficits and massive accumulated national debts in recent years have put intense pressure on conservation budgets at the local, state, and federal levels.

Moreover, the expectations of the general public and of landowners are also changing. The idea, articulated by Nobel Prize–winning economist Ronald Coase and others, that the public can effectively negotiate and pay for clean air, clean water, and other environmental services, has gained acceptance. With increasing frequency opportunities to conserve and enhance critical open space and wildlife habitat are being realized at a financial cost.

When asked why he robbed banks for a living, the legendary outlaw Willie Sutton replied, "That's where the money is." Conservationists, many practiced at the art of raising money, now recognize that new and creative ways to fund conservation agendas will need to be identified in this politically polarized time. Where is, and where will be, the money to fund conservation initiatives in coming decades? There is a broad diversity of ideas being considered.

For instance, despite a very tight federal budget environment, Congress's appetite for enacting large, expensive infrastructure and subsidy bills has not diminished—today, it's where the money is. The Farm Bill provides billions in crop subsidies and farm-based conservation. The Water Resources Development Act and the Transportation Bill provide hundreds of billions for water projects and building roads and mass transit systems. These pieces of legislation provide billions in tax cuts, and all remain popular bills that are easily and regularly enacted and reauthorized. The challenge is to recognize the potential of these and similar large bills to fund new conservation work. Developing strategies that convince lawmakers that making conservation investments in the context of these bills is appropriate and necessary is a worthy goal. The good news is that conservationists have found that, in many diverse cases, these enormous federal spending bills do in fact provide meaningful opportunities to fund conservation efforts.

Complementing these potential sources of public-sector funding are important sources of nonprofit and private-sector conservation financing. Such sources provide capital for a variety of initiatives, including: limited development projects; the establishment of regional-scale wetland mitigation banks; the protection of working farms, ranches, and forests; and the establishment of new markets for ecosystem services such as water purification and air emissions reductions.

In sum, there is no shortage of creative proposals to fund the enormous conservation challenges that exist today and that will emerge tomorrow. Many focus on the unconventional use of large funding sources that have primarily nonconservation purposes. As the need grows and constraints on the federal budget grow tighter and tighter, conservationists will necessarily have to look to creative ways to fund worthy endeavors.

From Walden to Wall Street is a timely exploration of innovative ways to fund important conservation efforts. This book highlights how conservationists currently are finding funding success. In updating the public on the most recent efforts to secure new financing of conservation initiatives, it demonstrates that success is possible in this tough fiscal climate. If that is all this book does, it would be worth publishing. However, it provides a much more important service by stimulating further thought and discussion that I anticipate will lead to the next wave of innovative conservation funding strategies. By teaching us how to think about solutions to the next generation of conservation challenges, this book is planting the seeds of the next generation of successful conservation in America.

Preface

Genesis

The book you are now reading is the outgrowth of a spirited, wide-ranging series of discussions among senior North American conservation executives, field practitioners, and researchers. The Lincoln Institute of Land Policy convened this series of Conservation Leadership Dialogues (CLDs) in 2002, 2003, and 2004 to bring together exceptional talents from diverse organizations in the public, private, nonprofit, and academic sectors. Participants came from large and small operations scattered throughout the continent, including a small land trust in New Mexico, federal government agencies in the United States, an activist group with offices in British Columbia, a multinational timber investment organization based on the East Coast of the United States, and several of the continent's most distinguished universities.

These Lincoln Institute dialogues were convened for the purpose of considering some of the grand challenges and opportunities facing the land and biodiversity conservation community in North America. Our scope was broad and our time horizon was expansive. We were free, for example, to discuss the potential efficacy of very large scale initiatives that spanned national boundaries and cultural differences. We considered the possible impact of such initiatives throughout the course of decades and even centuries. After several sessions that brought into focus what might be accomplished in a broad range of disciplines and practice areas, we got down to business. We focused on a topic about which nearly every participant had a strong opinion and abundant experience: money.

More specifically, the first of the three CLDs, held at the Lincoln Institute's headquarters in Cambridge, Massachusetts, was focused on "Conservation in the Twenty-first Century." The invited participants addressed the challenge posed to them by keynote speaker E. O. Wilson, the celebrated biodiversity scientist. "We have entered the twenty-first century, the century of the environment," Wilson declared. "The question of the century is, how can we best shift to a culture of permanence, both for ourselves and for the biosphere that sustains us?"[1] One of the most compelling answers offered to his challenge was that we must find ways to dovetail the efforts of a multiplicity of North American landowners into landscape-scale initiatives that can sustain a full spectrum of species and ecosystems.

Responsive to the interest shown in landscape-scale initiatives, the second CLD, held in San Francisco in May 2003, focused on the great potential and significant hurdles faced by groups striving to launch such regional landscape-scale efforts.[2] At the end of a productive three days of field trips and structured discussions of the issue, participants reiterated their conviction that we should aim to sharply increase the pace of land and habitat conservation efforts in North America and around the world. They also expressed the unanimous view that in order to pick up the pace of conservation, the community must become more capable in conservation finance, thus facilitating the generation of new human resources, institutional resources, and capital resources. Toward that end, the group expressed a strong interest that the following year's CLD be devoted to innovation in conservation finance.

Accordingly, the 2004 CLD, convened in the spring of that year at Lincoln House in Cambridge, focused on the following challenge:

> How might the conservation community, by leveraging new and emerging institutional capacities and financing techniques, dramatically increase the level of financial resources per year that is annually dedicated to land and habitat conservation in the U.S.? Could we, over the next several decades, double or triple the level of capital funds devoted to conservation (i.e., build substantially on an estimated current level of $5 billion to $7 billion per year from public, private, and nonprofit sources)?

To address this challenge in a structured format, the authors prepared discussion papers focused on the following questions:

- What is the present institutional capacity for "doing" conservation finance, and how might that capacity be augmented in coming years to improve the "system of finance" serving land and habitat conservationist initiatives and organizations?

- What are the current and prospective supply and demand of human and financial resources available to meet conservation finance needs in the United States? How does the level of resources available now compare to perceived requirements in coming decades?

- What concepts, methods, and tools, involving the public, private, and nonprofit sectors, hold some promise for dramatically expanding the annual amounts of financing available for land and habitat conservation and stewardship?

At the conclusion of the conference, there was a strong consensus, among both discussion paper authors and other CLD participants, that the session had been highly productive and that we should share our ideas with a broader audience. We resolved to rewrite the essays based on comments made at the meeting and to compile the essays into a book—this book.

The authors and editors of *From Walden to Wall Street* have worked diligently to put together a volume that reflects both our passion for conservation and the professional practicality that is essential in the world of finance. Our considerations range from the musings of Henry David Thoreau—the personification of the "Walden" point of view—to the findings of Patrick Coady, a veteran of Wall Street and the World Bank, and one of this book's authors.

The resulting work brings together the thinking of sixteen sophisticated conservation finance practitioners who are, every day at their desks, inventing the future of their field. It is our sincere hope that such a compilation will be of considerable utility to a broad range of readers, including board members, executives, field practitioners, and financial officers of conservation organizations seeking to expand their own financial horizons; professionals serving (or hoping to serve) such organizations in their efforts to raise capital and operating funding, including investment bankers, commercial bankers, strategic consultants, lawyers, and accountants; professors, students, and academic researchers seeking to understand the ongoing maturation of the conservation field; policy makers and their staffs, scouting out new ways to achieve conservation goals of enormous significance to today's voters, their children, and generations to come; and interested members of the general public who are thinking through how to invest in the future of essential natural systems.

The Chapters of This Book

In chapter 1, I attempt to put innovation in conservation finance in a historical perspective. I point out that innovation in the field of conservation is a long-standing U.S. tradition, dating back to 1634 and the establishment of the Boston Common. As is evidenced by the chapters of my coauthors in this book, that tradition is still very much alive today.

Chapter 2 addresses the question of institutional capacity for "doing" conservation finance. Patrick Coady finds the existing state of affairs still in a formative stage. He provides a concise, compelling case for putting together several disparate components into a system of finance that can efficiently and effectively make financing available to worthy conservation initiatives. These necessary components of a conservation financing system, as Coady describes them, include project identification and preparation; provision of catalyst money; provision of bridge financing; provision of access to large, long-term financial instruments; and creation of new ownership models. Coady's insights are particularly valuable because they are based on a series of interviews that he conducted with senior conservation finance practitioners over the course of several years. Once such a system emerges, Coady believes, the process of getting deals done in the conservation field will more closely resemble that of the relatively efficient financial market that now serves private companies.

Chapter 3, prepared by Frank Casey from Defenders of Wildlife, is a much-needed effort to roughly size the supply and demand of capital required to complete an "ecologically and taxonomically comprehensive system of conservation lands" in the United States. Casey estimates that in the aggregate, across funding sectors and conservation methods, the total supply of conservation funding in the United States in 2003 was about $5.8 billion. Source sectors tallied in this estimate included federal and state government and nonprofit funding. Such funding included allocations for permanent land protection ($2.7 billion of the $5.8 billion total, including fee purchases and easements), nonpermanent conservation land "rentals," and cost-sharing programs that encouraged more sustainable production practices. Compared with the cost of assembling a comprehensive system of conservation lands (that is, the potential demand for conservation funding), Casey estimates an average annual funding gap of between $1.9 billion and $7.7 billion over a forty-year time horizon.

If, indeed, (1) a comprehensive and efficient system of conservation finance can be assembled throughout the coming decade, as Coady recommends, (2) current funding levels remain intact as a foundation for conservationists to build on, and (3) Casey's estimate of the funding gap is in the right order of magnitude, then a critical question comes into sharp relief: Can the conservation community come up with new methods for financing high-priority land conservation needs in the United States that will fill the conservation financing gap?

Like any good venture capitalist, the participants in the 2004 Lincoln Institute of Land Policy CLD understood that the odds of success improve with a diversified portfolio of innovative ideas. Fortunately, the authors of chapters 4 through 12 offer a wide range of creative ideas for increasing the amount of capital and operating funds available to the land and biodiversity conservation community. It is unlikely that each and every one of these ideas will substantially enlarge the pool of financial resources. But some of the concepts likely will thrive, perhaps dramatically. If even a few of the ideas suggested by the authors of chapters 4 through 12 achieve their full potential, the conservation-financing gap will narrow and perhaps disappear. Consider, for instance, the case presented in chapter 4 by Ernest Cook and Matt Zieper of the Trust for Public Land. They argue that if the conservation community in the United States can help to build policy frameworks for land conservation similar to the one that has been implemented in New Jersey, the potential exists for a fourfold increase in local government ballot measures for land conservation.

In addition to being enlarged, funding resources could be used with greater efficiency and effectiveness. Mary McBryde, Peter

R..Stein, and Story Clark explain in chapter 5 that the growth of interim financing mechanisms—particularly external revolving loan funds—can help to expand conservation financing potential. The authors emphasize that external revolving loan funds may enhance the effectiveness of local and regional conservation organizations both because they facilitate rapid responses to land conservation opportunities that suddenly come into the market and because the presence of a regional lending facility helps to sharpen strategic thinking about which projects have the highest priority.

In chapter 6, Ned Sullivan and Steve Rosenberg of Scenic Hudson offer several compelling case examples that demonstrate the potential of limited development strategies for bringing together financing from a variety of sources and sectors in order to realize important conservation and community development goals. The approach they discuss illustrates the enormous leverage that a strategic investment by a public agency or nonprofit organization can achieve, bringing substantial private investment dollars into areas that have been neglected for decades.

Kevin W. Schuyler, director of finance and investments at The Nature Conservancy, demonstrates in chapter 7 how the frontiers of conservation finance may be expanded by gaining access to well-established capital markets—markets that have private firms that grew from an idea in an entrepreneur's head into vital and far-flung organizations. In particular, Schuyler reviews the powerful potential of debt markets, convertible tax-exempt financing, emerging tax benefits, and private equity markets for conservation organizations with the institutional capacity to appropriately access them.

In chapter 8, Philip M. Hocker offers a lucid report on the growth of transferable tax credits for land conservation in Virginia and other states. Hocker's firsthand account of how the market for such credits is emerging in Virginia gives us a picture of what the sustained efforts of a small group of devoted conservationists can accomplish.

Similarly, Steve Weems's essay on the use of new market tax credits in a determined effort to conserve working forests gives us the clear sense that Yankee ingenuity is alive and well, and working for the good of both nature and a deep-rooted forest products industry in Maine. In chapter 9, he discusses the type of financial structuring that is required to realize such an initiative, as well as a sense for how broadly such approaches might be employed to protect working forestland, working farmland, and other valuable open spaces in years to come.

A particularly exciting opportunity for expanding financial resources for conservation, explains Adam Davis in chapter 10, is "mainstreaming environmental markets." Davis illustrates how private-sector firms, which can be capitalized with private equity and commercial debt, are breaking new ground by providing ecologically targeted, cost-effective wetlands mitigation banks. By offering ecosystem services that can be utilized by customers (for example, state departments of transportation) on an as-needed basis, such firms are providing significant public benefits.

Following up on Davis's discussion of wetland mitigation efforts now focused at the state level, Jeffery T. More reviews in chapter 11 the substantial opportunities for expanding federal conservation funding in conjunction with public infrastructure development. More points out that budgets for environmental mitigation and enhancement are now being considered in association with a wide range of infrastructure development efforts, including those administered by the U.S. Department of Transportation, the U.S. Department of Energy, and the U.S. Army Corps of Engineers.

Finally, in chapter 12, Robert Bonnie, who directs the Center for Conservation Incentives at Environmental Defense, considers the growth of conservation initiatives associated with the U.S. Department of Agriculture (USDA). In the past two decades, both the scope and the scale of conservation-related programs administered by the USDA's Natural Resource Conservation Service have grown substantially. The next farm bill, due in 2007, may well expand such efforts further, particularly in light of World Trade Organization negotiations to limit farm subsidy programs. Bonnie's article sheds light on what works and what can be markedly improved in the design and implementation of such programs.

In sum, the creativity and insight of the contributors to the book offer considerable reason for hope that, even in this era of widespread financial constraints, financial resources available to the U.S. conservation community could grow substantially, both in quantity and in diversity, for decades to come. The hard work of realizing such potential lies ahead for the current generation of conservation finance professionals and for generations of such professionals yet to emerge.

Acknowledgments

This book owes its existence to a great many people. Although insight and initiative have come from many sources, particular recognition is due to the following organizations and individuals.

First, the Lincoln Institute of Land Policy has set the table and sustained the entire Conservation Leadership Dialogue effort throughout its existence. Lincoln has, simply put, provided outstanding intellectual, financial, and physical support, from the first informal conversations about this process to the publication of this book. In helping to both conceive and implement the effort, my deepest gratitude goes to Armando Carbonell, senior fellow and cochair of the Institute's Department of Planning and Development. Carbonell's genuine interest and deep insight into land conservation—as well as his quick wit—have been of immeasurable value. Lisa Cloutier, the department's administrator, thoughtfully assisted Carbonell in seeing to countless substantive matters. Ann LeRoyer, the Institute's senior editor, has time and again offered her constructive comments, elevating the content of our published products and expediting the work. Rob Hoff, with great good humor and efficiency, captained a terrific logistics team of meeting planners that included Rie Sugihara, Helene Drew, and many others. Thanks to all of them, to Lincoln Institute former President H. James Brown, to staff members Dennis Robinson, Laurie Dougherty, Laura Mullahy, Ellen Cremens, and Ruth Terry, and to everyone else at Lincoln House for their unwavering support and goodwill.

At various stages along the way, money, logistical support, and intellectual stimulus also have been generously provided by the Kendall Foundation, the Doris Duke Charitable Foundation, and the Golden Gate National Parks Conservancy (GGNPC). Thanks to Ted Smith at Kendall, Mark Shaffer at Doris Duke, and Greg Moore at the GGNPC for those critical boosts.

For three years, the CLD series has benefited greatly from the advice of its steering committee. In addition to Armando Carbonell and myself, the committee has included Jean Hocker, president emeritus of the Land Trust Alliance and a member of the Lincoln Institute of Land Policy board of directors, and Nora Mitchell, director of the National Park Service Conservation Study Institute. Both Hocker and Mitchell have my profound appreciation for their common sense, their aspirations for excellence, and their friendship. Notably, Patrick Coady helped inspire us to tackle the subject of conservation finance and showed the way with his illuminating interviews of conservation finance practitioners.

The heart of the entire CLD process, certainly, is associated with the distinguished participants and invited speakers. Throughout the past three years, that group has included, along with myself, the following individuals: Bob Berner, John Bernstein, Robert Bonnie, Jessica Brown, Armando Carbonell, Douglas Carroll, Frank Casey, Douglas Causey, Story Clark, Patrick Coady, Philippe Cohen, Ernest Cook, Robert Cook, Gretchen Daily, Fred Danforth, Adam Davis, Julie Early, Jay Espy, Charles H. W. "Hank" Foster, Lynn Foster, Ralph Grossi, Jean Hocker, Philip M. Hocker, Reed Holderman, Jamie Hoyte, Ann Ingerson, Leonard Krishtalka, Nick MacPhee, Mary McBryde, Bob McIntosh, Nora Mitchell, Greg Moore, Jeffery T. More, Larry Morris, Bob O'Connor, Brian O'Neill, Matt Pearson, Bob Perschel, Jaime Pinkham, Glenn Prickett, Rosemary Ripley, Will Rogers, Steve Rosenberg, Keith Ross, Audrey Rust, Dan Sayre, Kevin W. Schuyler, Larry Selzer, George Smith, Ted Smith, Michael Soukup, Peter R. Stein, Ned Sullivan, Clare Swanger, Jeff Vonk, Wes Ward, Eric Washburn, Bill Weeks, Steve Weems, Rand Wentworth, Douglas Wheeler, E. O. Wilson, and Matt Zieper. To each of them, and especially to those who prepared chapters for this book, many, many thanks.

Appreciation is also due to all of those people with whom I have had a chance to work at Harvard's Kennedy School of Government and at the Harvard Forest and to all those who have offered encouragement and wisdom, including David Foster, John O'Keefe, Alan Altshuler, David Luberoff, Charles Euchner, Roger Kennedy, Gowher Rizvi, Marty Mauzi, Winthrop Carty, Philip Auerswald, Kara O'Sullivan, and Christine Marchand.

No book is produced without the seemingly endless efforts of editors, production personnel, and first-rate administrators, who keep the process running on an even keel. Jeff Hardwick, the editor for this book at Island Press, has done a wonderful job throughout. Two associates of mine, Anna Allen and Lydia Bergen, have helped keep the project afloat on a day-to-day basis and have been diligent beyond reason. My heartfelt thanks.

And finally, let me thank my wife, Jane, and our three children, Laura, Daniel, and Will. For the many days and nights that you let me type away on my computer, and for your unending love, support, and laughter, you have my devotion.

James N. Levitt
Belmont, Massachusetts
February 2005

Notes

[1] James N. Levitt, "Land and Biodiversity Conservation: A Leadership Dialogue," *Land Lines: The Newsletter of the Lincoln Institute of Land Policy*, July 2002, page 1. E. O. Wilson, quoted here, reiterated a theme he had articulated previously in several places, including an article entitled "The Bottleneck," prepared for *Scientific American*, February 2002.

[2] James N. Levitt, "Landscape-Scale Conservation: Grappling with the Green Matrix," *Land Lines: The Newsletter of the Lincoln Institute of Land Policy*, January 2004, page 1.

Chapter 1

Financial Innovation for Conservation
An American Tradition

James N. Levitt

Though I do not believe a plant will spring up where no seed has been, I have great faith in a seed. Convince me that you have a seed there, and I am prepared to expect wonders.

—Henry David Thoreau,
Faith in a Seed

Why do we invest in conservation? Why do human beings invest their time, energy, and financial resources in the protection of land, plants, and animals?

We invest in conservation because it is an expression of our faith in the future.

Conservation investment is an expression of our faith in the future of natural systems that are essential to life on Earth. It is an expression of our faith in the future of deeply loved natural wonders. And it is an expression of faith in the future of our families and communities, whose lives will be immeasurably enriched by the living world that we are striving to sustain.

We also invest in conservation-oriented projects with increasing frequency because we have faith that, well into the future, such projects can provide us with respectable and low-risk economic returns on principal.

Our faith in the long-term efficacy of our conservation investments can, of course, be severely tested. The first five years of the twenty-first century have not been encouraging ones for U.S. land and biodiversity conservationists. At the local, continental, and global levels, the need to pick up the pace of conservation efforts remains urgent. In my home state of Massachusetts, for example, given the rapid pace of land development, the window of opportunity for the conservation of large parcels of land may close in the next several decades.[1] On a continental scale, ecological forecasters can predict, with increasing levels of specificity, how the disruption of landscape-scale corridors over the next quarter-century will pose ever-greater threats to the amazing migrations of animals that travel thousands of miles each year to feed and reproduce.[2] Recent global forecasts are no more optimistic. An assessment, published in 2004 in the *Proceedings of the National Academy of Sciences*, predicts that as many as a quarter of all bird species on Earth may face extinction by the year 2100.[3] As technology and a growing global economy allow the spread of industrialization to every square kilometer of Earth's surface, habitat loss, compounded by pollution, human population growth, the spread of exotic species, and the landscape consequences of climate change, loom as increasingly important factors in discouraging dynamics.

The response of U.S. political leadership to such urgent reports, from state legislatures to international negotiations, appears to be tepid at best. At the state level, despite consistent voter approval of land protection ballot measures, several legislatures are cutting back on their commitments to conservation. In Maryland, for example, funding for Program Open Space, "the state's main program for conserving ecologically significant lands, threatened open spaces, forests and farmlands" was cut by 75 percent in 2004.[4] At the federal level, after increasing budgets in 2001 and 2002, the U.S. Congress has recently trimmed allocations for traditional sources of conservation capital, such as the Land and Water Conservation Fund,[5] in part because of growing federal budget deficits.

And, in contrast to its role as an international conservation and environmental leader throughout most of the twentieth century, the United States now has a conservation and environmental policy that is the object of pointed criticism from even our closest allies. As he prepared for his turn at presiding over the deliberations of the Group of Eight (G8) industrialized nations, British Prime Minister Tony Blair, in a prominent show of independence, commented on the U.S. refusal to take a leadership position on global climate change issues:

> We need to act now . . . Russian ratification of the Kyoto protocol means that we now have a new global treaty that is about to come into force. This is good news. But the level of change and ambition required will be far more than the Kyoto protocol is likely to provide. And with the United States, the world's largest emitter of greenhouse gases, refusing to sign up to the protocol, this makes measures we could secure through G8 even more vital.[6]

On the surface, then, the U.S. conservation outlook is not bright. However, if you look beneath this discouraging surface, you will find that a tremendous amount of initiative and innovative spirit is alive and well in the conservation community, both in the United States and internationally. Entrepreneurial-minded conservationists in the public, nonprofit, private, and academic sectors are keeping the faith, coming up with a broad spectrum of ways to address the challenges that face them in a range of relevant disciplines, including science, education, habitat protection, and stewardship. They are buoyed by the work of their colleagues and have an admirable capacity to forge ahead even in the face of budgetary constraints. Nevertheless, nearly all of these innovators have the same question at the end of the day: How are we going to pay for it all?

A thoughtful response to that question is the focus of this volume. The authors offer an array of highly inventive ideas for gaining access to financial resources in the public, private, and nonprofit sectors. Successful implementation of these ideas could significantly increase the flow of capital into land and biodiversity conservation in coming decades.

The work of these modern-day conservation innovators is very much in the American tradition. From the earliest days of English colonization of North America—nearly four hundred years ago—our emergent democratic culture has repeatedly come up with novel methods for finding the financial, human, and physical resources to protect open space and wildlife, even in times of deep national crisis. The stories of these innovations involve several of the most intriguing personalities in U.S. history. The list includes John Winthrop, Thomas Jefferson, Abraham Lincoln, Theodore Roosevelt, and Aldo Leopold. My own guess, strongly bolstered by the advances in conservation finance described in this book, is that this tradition of innovation in conservation finance will continue well into the future. Great women and men, as well as an army of unsung conservation heroes, are likely to innovate for many centuries to come, allowing the United States and the global community of nations to continue to face up to daunting challenges that threaten natural systems.

John Winthrop and the Boston Common in 1634: Self-Taxation for Land Protection

In the center of the city of Boston, Massachusetts, is a roughly fifty-acre patch of open space that has been called "sacred" and an "invaluable blessing"[7] by local residents. That space, the Boston Common, is the oldest public open space in the United States. Indeed, it is very likely the oldest *public* open space in the English-speaking world. At the time of the Boston Common's creation in 1634, there were other commons existing in England—for example, the New Forest created by William the Conqueror in 1079. Such places, however, were established and regulated by feudal authority. None had been established by a self-governing group of people by and for themselves.

What distinguishes the Boston Common as a public open space is the way the land purchase was financed and how the regulation of the new open space was established. That process was tightly intertwined with the emergence of autonomous local democracy in the New World. The Puritan residents of the town of Boston were participants in a unique experiment in which they asserted, because of the nature of the corporate charter under which they operated, the right to govern themselves. Their elected leader, John Winthrop (see figure 1.1), trained in the law at Cambridge University, was instrumental in devising a system in which local freemen (essentially, local homeowners who had taken an oath of loyalty) voted in town meetings on matters of importance to the town.

Early in the life of the community, the town was offered a piece of property by the Reverend William Blackstone. Blackstone

Figure 1.1.

John Winthrop, the first governor of the Massachusetts Bay Colony, helped devise a new form of local self-government in Boston. Using this early democratic form of government, the freemen of the town of Boston in 1634 taxed themselves to raise money to buy the open space that became the Boston Common. (Reproduced by permission of Harvard University Art Museums.)

had originally extended an offer to Winthrop's Puritan followers to come to the Shawmut peninsula, where an excellent source of fresh-water could be found. After four years of living among Winthrop's group, Blackstone decided to leave the area for Rhode Island and sought payment for his large parcel of land. What happened at that point is the subject of a 1684 deposition taken from John Odlin and several other elderly residents of Boston from then-governor Simon Bradstreet.[8]

The inhabitants of Boston, led by Winthrop, negotiated a sale price with Blackstone of thirty pounds. They agreed that each householder should pay at least six shillings for this purpose into a collection, with some households paying considerably more. The sum was collected and paid to Blackstone, who, in turn, sold to the inhabitants, their heirs, and assigns the rights to the land. The town then laid out a military training field and allowed cattle to graze on the property. Within twenty years, the Common was also used for recreation, when ladies and gentlemen would take their evening stroll. Land use regulations regarding the Common were self-imposed by town meeting members in the 1640s and 1650s, as they made rules, for example, regulating cattle grazing practices on the land, as well as forbidding home building on the land without the consent of a majority of the inhabitants of the town.

What is described here is a landmark in conservation finance and regulation: it is the first example that we know of in the English-speaking world in which a self-governing people agreed to tax themselves to raise money to purchase open space that would provide multiple public and private benefits. The newly purchased open space enhanced private wealth as individual householders grazed their cattle on the Common; the public as a whole benefited from the provision of a public training field for the militia, as well as the provision of a publicly accessible recreational resource.

What has been the return on this investment? Conventional time-value-of-money calculations are not relevant for a 371-year period, particularly when the direct and indirect benefits of the Boston Common have not been systematically compiled. Suffice it to say that Blackstone was paid thirty pounds for his land, which in Massachusetts in 1642 had an official value (at a rate of 4 shillings per bushel of wheat, and 20 shillings per pound) equal to that of 150 bushels of wheat.[9] In 2005, 150 bushels of wheat could be purchased, at about $3 per bushel, for $450 on Chicago commodities markets.[10] In contrast, the Boston Common today is of enormous civic and economic value, and is surrounded by many billions of dollars of real estate, ranging from multimillion-dollar residential condominiums to the Massachusetts State House.

What started in Boston in 1634, nearly four centuries ago, provides a precedent for the vast number of land conservation initiatives funded with the consent of taxpayers in the United States and around the world, which continue to this day. Considerable additional potential remains to be addressed. In chapter 4, Ernest Cook and Matt Zieper illustrate how, using policy frameworks such as the one now employed in New Jersey, local and state governments can build on the strong conservation financing levels already realized through conservation-oriented ballot measures at the local and state levels. Like the Boston Common, the value of such taxpayer investments is likely to be proven time and again in years to come.

Thomas Jefferson and the Natural Bridge in 1773: Personal Investment and Public Trust

Three years before he authored the Declaration of Independence, Thomas Jefferson, then a young lawyer, landowner, and entrepreneur, made a personal investment to acquire a natural wonder. The place he purchased from the Crown was in a remote location to the west of Virginia's settled communities. The parcel of land had on it a remarkable natural feature known as the Natural Bridge, a huge natural stone arch that spans a picturesque stream (see figure 1.2). Jefferson wrote about the Natural Bridge in his only book, *Notes on the State of Virginia*, calling it "the most sublime of Nature's works."[11] He sensed that the place could leave an indelible impression on visitors. Indeed, throughout his life, Jefferson consistently invited women and men to the site to impress them with the vast potential and awe-inspiring nature of the American land.

Jefferson did, on occasion, try to make a financial return on his investment in the Natural Bridge. In the early 1800s, he leased a portion of the property to entrepreneurs who used it to manufacture rifle shot and saltpeter; he also considered selling it to a man named William Jenkings in 1809. Nevertheless, in a letter to William Caruthers in 1815, Jefferson wrote that he had no interest

Figure 1.2.

Thomas Jefferson invested his own money to buy the Natural Bridge in Virginia. He viewed his ownership "in some degree as a public trust." His example set a very early precedent for the modern-day efforts of land trusts throughout the United States. (Reproduced by permission of Monticello and the Thomas Jefferson Foundation, Inc.)

in selling the Natural Bridge and that he had come to see his property "in some degree as a public trust." He emphasized that he would not permit it to be "injured, defaced, or masked from public view."[12] After changing hands several times following Jefferson's death, the land remains in private ownership today. At present, the site does not entirely conform to Jefferson's wishes: a wooden fence, for example, obscures the public's view from the top of the Natural Bridge. Nevertheless, the site, which has official status as a National Historic Landmark, does host a tourist destination complex that includes a hotel and conference center, several museums, and the Natural Bridge itself, billed as an "awesome natural wonder."[13]

In effect, Jefferson enunciated in 1815 an idea that twenty-first-century U.S. citizens still find intriguing—namely, that privately owned landscapes could provide public benefits as well as private financial return and personal enjoyment. The land trust movement, for example, has in recent decades used such a framework to help protect millions of acres from development.[14] In chapter 8, Philip M. Hocker gives a close-up account of how new financial resources, through the use of transferable tax credits, are being made accessible to landowners in Jefferson's Virginia (as well as other states, such as Colorado) who are prepared to put conservation easements on their land. Such programs help private landowners dedicate their property, at least in part, to provide public benefits. As we consider future public and private investments to provide essential ecosystem services and to protect the nation's irreplaceable land and biodiversity resources, we will do well to remember Jefferson's early example.

Abraham Lincoln and the Railroads in the 1860s: Transportation and Scenic Wonders

During his presidency, Abraham Lincoln was well aware of the multifaceted impacts that the completion of the Union Pacific railroad would have on the nation. In addition to a personal interest in railroads stemming from his experience as a lawyer for the Illinois Central in the 1850s, Lincoln received numerous communications during his term underscoring the importance of the transcontinental link. The president of Union Pacific wrote to Lincoln in 1863, emphasizing "the vastness of the enterprise, and its probable influence upon the political and commercial prosperity of the country."[15]

President Lincoln was also very likely impressed by the many paintings, photographs, and literary accounts of Western natural wonders that the new railroad would make accessible. Among such words and images, seen widely in Boston, New York and Washington, D.C., were Carleton Watkins's photographs, described by the *New York Times* in 1862 as "indescribably unique and beautiful."[16] The paintings of Yosemite by Albert Bierstadt, as well as the essays written by Fitz Hugh Ludlow that were published in *The Atlantic Monthly*,[17] probably also came to Lincoln's attention. The work of both men was sponsored, at least in part, by the Union Pacific, which in 1863 provided Bierstadt and Ludlow with free transportation to Yosemite. The railroad, which had five members of its board of directors[18] appointed by Lincoln himself, was apparently interested in promoting the wonders of the West to potential tourists, immigrants, and investors.[19]

It is not surprising, then, that when the idea of protecting the scenic wonders of Yosemite "for public use, resort, and recreation" was proposed by a transportation company executive in 1864, it found a receptive audience among Republicans in the Senate and the White House. Specifically, Israel Ward Raymond, an executive with the Central American Steamship Transit Company, wrote to John Conness, a Republican senator from California, in February of that year, urging the preservation of Yosemite Valley and the Mariposa Grove of giant sequoias. Attempting to resolve outstanding land claims, and apparently knowing that public accommodations would eventually have to be built at the site, Raymond proposed that a public land grant be made "inalienable forever but leases may be granted for portions not to exceed ten years."[20]

The proposal to commit public assets to the protection of "some of the greatest wonders in the world"[21] in the form of a land grant to the state of California eventually made its way to the president's desk. Lincoln signed it into law on June 30, 1864, in the midst of the greatest civil crisis in the nation's history. Just three days later, he signed the Pacific Railroad Act, granting additional land to the Union Pacific and Central Pacific to help finance the completion of the transcontinental railroad. The number of tourists traveling west by rail to see Yosemite and other well-promoted sites began to build as soon as the transcontinental railroad was completed (see figure 1.3), helping to build a hospitality industry that remains a mainstay of the California economy today.

In 1864, Lincoln approved the allocation of federal land resources—in essence, made a federal investment—in the protection of Yosemite and the completion of the transcontinental railroad. In doing this, Lincoln helped set in motion a chain of events that would culminate in the national parks movement. The creation of Yosemite was, for example, an important precedent for the establishment of the world's first national park at Yellowstone in 1872. Within a half century of Yosemite's creation, national parks had been established from coast to coast, often closely in conjunction with the expansion of the nation's railroad grid. And by the early twenty-first century, the national park idea had spread to virtually every nation on Earth. In the span of 136 years, from 1864 to 2000, nearly one billion acres of national parks were established across the globe—an area larger than that covered by the entire fifteen-nation European Community in the year 2000.[22]

In chapter 6, Ned Sullivan and Steve Rosenberg of Scenic Hudson describe their ambitious Long Dock Beacon initiative, located along the Hudson River, about sixty miles north of New York City. The project, on a brownfield site, will use money from private, nonprofit, and public sources for a thoughtfully designed complex, including a hotel and conference facilities and a spectacularly scenic public park along the Hudson River, nearby a world-class art museum and a planned environmental research center. Public access to the facility will be provided by rail, water, and highway. Like many other present-day social entrepreneurs striving to spark regional renaissance by combining community development with landscape conservation, Sullivan and Rosenberg are following a path that Abraham Lincoln helped to blaze.

Theodore Roosevelt and Pelican Island in 1903:
Leveraging Philanthropy to Protect Wildlife

Contrary to persistent public opinion, Theodore Roosevelt did not, as president, create the nation's first national park. As noted in the preceding section, that was accomplished in 1872, when Roosevelt was a teenager. Nor did Roosevelt establish America's first national forests. The first federal forest reserves were created by Presidents

11

Yo Semite Falls, 2,634 feet fall. Yo Semite Valley Route. (See page 193.)

Figure 1.3.

"Yosemite Falls" and the "Rail and Stage Route to Big Tree Groves and Yosemite," as depicted in Crofutt's *Trans-Continental Tourist's Guide*, published in New York in May 1871. In his preface to the third edition of his guidebook, George Crofutt proudly reported that the expanded volume now included "a map of the new route to Yo Semite Valley and the Big Trees." The fact that Crofutt was already in his third edition only three years after the railroad had been completed is evidence of how fast the transcontinental tourist business grew. (Courtesy of University of Nebraska Libraries.)

Benjamin Harrison and Grover Cleveland in the 1890s, several years before Roosevelt and his close associate Gifford Pinchot created the U.S. Forest Service, the storied agency that has managed the nation's forests for the past century.

Nevertheless, T. R., as he was known, was an enormously enthusiastic and inventive conservationist (see figure 1.4). One of his greatest conservation innovations was the establishment of the first national bird reservations. Roosevelt created fifty-one such sanctuaries by federal order "to preserve from destruction beautiful and wonderful wild creatures whose existence was threatened by greed and wantonness."[23] He noted in his autobiography that "the creation of these reservations at once placed the United States in the front rank in the world work of bird protection."[24] The first of those reservations, now part of the Federal Wildlife Refuge System, was created at Pelican Island, Florida, on March 14, 1903.[25]

Even with the executive power he commanded, Roosevelt had no federal appropriation to pay for wardens at the sanctuaries he was creating. He accepted the offer of independent philanthropists associated with several state Audubon societies and the American Ornithological Union to pay for wardens along a series of sites on the Florida coast. Paul Kroegel, warden at Pelican Island, was reportedly paid the princely sum of $1 per month for his work.[26] Tragically, in 1907 and 1908, two of Kroegel's associates, Guy Bradley and C. G. MacLeod, who were guarding other sites in South Florida and whose work was paid for by the philanthropists, were killed in the line of duty by poachers. The reaction to their deaths intensified national support for bird protection.

Roosevelt, himself a charter member of the Florida Audubon Society, expressed his gratitude for the ongoing financial and moral support for conservation that came from the philanthropic sector in general and from Audubon in particular. He wrote the following:

> It was the Audubon Society which started the movement for the establishment of bird refuges. The society now protects and polices about one hundred of these refuges, which, of course, are worthless unless thus protected.[27]

The U.S. tradition of public and nonprofit cooperation to conserve land and biodiversity—to express our collective vision and

Figure 1.4.

Teddy Roosevelt was an avid conservationist. He is shown here on a trip to Yosemite, where he conferred with John Muir. One of Roosevelt's greatest conservation innovations was to work, both politically and financially, with voluntary organizations such as the Florida Audubon Society to create, protect, and police the nation's first national bird sanctuaries. (Reproduced by permission of the Theodore Roosevelt Collection, Harvard College Library.)

faith in the future—continues to the present. In chapter 7, Kevin W. Schuyler describes the creative efforts of The Nature Conservancy (TNC) to raise funds from a broad array of sources, including commercial credit and equity markets, that it will use, frequently in conjunction with state and federal governments, to protect the world's "last great places." Often working hand in hand with public, private, nonprofit, and academic organizations to protect habitat critical to the survival of plants and animals worldwide, Schuyler's organization is working in the tradition of bird conservationists from more than a century ago. The leadership of TNC, as well as scores of other biodiversity conservation innovators, have the characteristic that T. R. described in his own contemporaries: "the precious gift of sympathetic imagination," giving them the ability "to see and to wish to preserve for their children's children, the beauty and the wonder of nature."[28]

The Fertile Mind of Aldo Leopold

As a graduate of the Yale Forestry School in the early twentieth century, Aldo Leopold was a member of the first generation of professional foresters trained in the United States. He joined the U.S. Forest Service in 1909, just four years after it had been created. In the early 1920s, as a Forest Service administrator based in Albuquerque, he proposed that a wilderness area be established in the Gila National Forest in New Mexico, in part because of his concern about the impact of automobiles on the quality of outdoor experiences. His proposal was eventually accepted by the Forest Service, leading to the establishment in 1924 of the first official wilderness area in the United States. That precedent helped lead to the formation of the Wilderness Society in the 1930s and the passage of the Wilderness Act in 1964.

Leopold's concern regarding the impacts of roads and mechanized infrastructure, and the need to mitigate such impacts, showed up in his writings throughout the rest of his life. He suggested, for example, that increasingly rare prairie wildflowers, often lost "where highway construction is destroying wild remnants," could, in fact, be propagated along the edges of such public roads. In addition, he suggested that private farmland could be enlisted in the effort to save prairie flora: "Any prairie farm can have a library of prairie plants, for they are drouth-proof [droughtproof] and fire-proof, and are content with any roadside, rocky knoll, or sandy hillside not needed for cow or plow."[29]

In the 1930s and 1940s, as he participated in and critiqued the policy experiments of the Dust Bowl era as a professor at the University of Wisconsin, Leopold articulated the perspective that conservation on private lands must complement public lands conservation work. He wrote the following:

> Let me be clear that I do not challenge the purchase of public lands for conservation. For the first time in history we are buying on a scale commensurate with the size of the problem. I do challenge the growing assumption that bigger buying is a substitute for private conservation practice. Bigger buying, I fear, is serving as an escape-mechanism—it masks our failure to solve the harder problem. The geographic cards are stacked against its ultimate success. In the long run, it is exactly as effective as buying half an umbrella. . . .
>
> The thing to be prevented is destructive private land-use of any and all kinds. The thing to be encouraged is the use of private land in such a way as to combine the public and private interest to the greatest degree possible. . . .
>
> This paper forecasts that conservation will ultimately boil down to rewarding the private landowner who conserves the public interest. It asserts the new premise that if he fails to do so, his neighbors must ultimately pay the bill. It pleads that our jurists and economists anticipate the need for workable vehicles to carry that reward.[30]

Fortunately, more than seventy years after Leopold's paper entitled "Conservation Economics" was first published, there is an active corps of jurists, economists, legislators, and conservation entrepreneurs that continue to heed his call for the design of "workable vehicles" for conservation in the public, private, nonprofit, and academic sectors. Among that corps are the following:

- Mary McBryde, Peter R. Stein, and Story Clark, who explain in chapter 5 how external interim financing provided by private and nonprofit organizations can play a critical role in the completion of land protection and stewardship projects across a landscape-scale array of public and private lands.

- Steve Weems, who in chapter 9 describes the use of recently developed techniques for the use of federal New Markets Tax Credits to advance sustainable working forestland initiatives on private land.
- Adam Davis, a leading figure in the global effort to mainstream environmental markets, who details in chapter 10 how private investment in ecosystem services such as wetland mitigation banks continues to show great promise.
- Jeffery T. More and Robert Bonnie, who, in chapters 11 and 12, respectively, consider opportunities for significantly expanding public investment in lands owned by individuals, families, corporations, nonprofit groups, tribal entities, and public organizations; if carefully crafted, such conservation investments can yield efficient, measurably effective benefits for the nation's farmlands and forestlands, as well as for property associated with the nation's energy, transportation, and water infrastructures.

No doubt, Aldo Leopold, with his probing mind and facility for critical thinking, would want to carefully investigate each of these approaches. Heartened by the intensity of effort, he would find a wealth of experimentation to inspect, problems to crack open, and opportunities to pursue in the early twenty-first century.

Our History and Our Future

As evidenced by the deeds and words of John Winthrop, Thomas Jefferson, Abraham Lincoln, Theodore Roosevelt, and Aldo Leopold, as well as their modern-day successors, investment in conservation is, in fact, a long-standing and deeply rooted American tradition. It is a tradition that has been advanced even in some of our (both literally and figuratively) darkest hours: in the midst of a bloody Civil War and in response to the rolling, choking clouds of the Dust Bowl era. The investments have yielded extraordinary results, ranging from our incomparable system of national parks to the extensive mosaic of protected lands that provides New York City with its drinking water.

Given the grand ecological challenges, budgetary constraints, and sometimes strident opposition[31] faced by conservationists in our own era, it is imperative that the tradition persist and flourish. Who will come up with the next big idea that will yield dividends for our children's children? What shape will landmark conservation innovations[32] take? The chapters that follow provide some strong leads. Nevertheless, the search for innovative approaches should be pursued far and wide, well beyond the pages of this book. Indeed, the work of the authors in this volume to identify new and effective ways to invest in the conservation of land and biodiversity—for the sustainable provision of renewable resources; for public and private recreation; for the ongoing supply of healthy soil, drinkable water, and clean air; and for the protection of the diversity of life on Earth—is but one indication of our faith in the future. A great diversity of seeds will be planted. Be prepared to expect wonders.

Note: The epigraph to this chapter is drawn from Henry David Thoreau, *Faith in a Seed: The Dispersion of Seeds and Other Late Natural History Writings*, edited by Bradley P. Dean. Washington, D.C., and Covelo, Calif.: Island Press/Shearwater Books, 1993.

Notes

[1] Massachusetts Audubon Society, *Losing Ground: At What Cost?* November 2003, available at http://www.massaudubon.org/news/index .php?id=19&type=news.

[2] See, for example, Jeff Wells, "Birds Are Losing Ground," *Seattle Post Intelligencer*, December 23, 2004, available at http://seattlepi.nwsource .com/opinion/204869_bird23.html.

[3] Çagan H. Sekercioglu, Gretchen C. Daily, and Paul R. Ehrlich, "Ecosystem Consequences of Bird Declines," *Proceedings of the National Academy of Sciences*, December 15, 2004, PNAS 2004 101, abstract available at http://www.pnas.org/cgi/content/abstract/101/52/18042?maxtoshow= &HITS=10&hits=10&RESULTFORMAT=&fulltext=birds&searchid= 1105371798451_4483&stored_search=&FIRSTINDEX=0&journalcode =pnas.

[4] Chesapeake Bay Foundation, "Take Action: 2005 Legislative Agenda," available at http://www.cbf.org/site/PageServer?pagename=action_action_ network_center_05_agenda_md.

[5] National Park Service, National Center for Recreation and Conservation, "Land & Water Conservation Fund: Current Funding for Grants," last

modified December 22, 2004, available online as of January 2005 at http://www.nps.gov/ncrc/programs/lwcf/funding.html.

[6]Tony Blair, "A Year of Huge Challenges," *The Economist*, January 1–7, 2005, page 44.

[7]Broadside in the collection of the Bostonian Society, Boston, Massachusetts (Doc 712, dated 1799).

[8]Nathaniel Brewster Blackstone, *The Biography of The Reverend William Blackstone and Ancestors and Descendents*. Homestead, Fla.: 1974, available at http://www.dangel.net/AMERICA/Blackstone/REV.WM.BLACKSTONE.html.

[9]Louis Jordan, "Commodity Money: An Introduction," Coin and Currency Collection, Department of Special Collections, Hesburgh Library, University of Notre Dame, available at http://www.coins.nd.edu/ColCoin/ColCoinIntros/Commodity.intro.html. The article notes, "On September 27, 1642 the General Court went further by establishing standard prices for specific farm products that could be used as commodity money to pay taxes. A bushel of wheat was valued at four shillings (4s)." Note also that prior to the late twentieth century, there were 20 shillings per British pound.

[10]Bloomberg.com, "Commodity Strategists: Wheat May Rally, Bank Says," January 25, 2005, available at http://www.bloomberg.com/apps/news?pid=10000081&sid=ayJRU7fG0qZU&refer=australia. The article reports, "Wheat prices in Chicago fell to $2.9475 a bushel on Jan. 20 [2005], the lowest closing price for a most-active contract since May 6, 2003."

[11]Thomas Jefferson, *Notes on the State of Virginia*, published 1781–1782, available online at http://etext.lib.virginia.edu/etcbin/toccer-new2?id=JefVirg.sgm&images=images/modeng&data=/texts/english/modeng/parsed&tag=public&part=5&division=div1.

[12]Thomas Jefferson letter to William Caruthers, March 15, 1815, cited in "Jefferson and the Natural Bridge," available at www.monticello.org/reports/interests/natural_bridge.html.

[13]For more information on the facilities now at Natural Bridge, see www.naturalbridgeva.com.

[14]For further discussion, see James N. Levitt, editor, *Conservation in the Internet Age*. Washington, D.C.: Island Press, 2002, pages 288–291.

[15]John Dix letter to Abraham Lincoln, November 23, 1863, transcription available from the U.S. Library of Congress, http://memory.loc.gov/ cgi-bin/query/r?ammem/mal:@field(DOCID%2B@lit(d2818400)).

[16]The *New York Times* quote is cited by Maria Morris Hambourg in "Carleton Watkins: An Introduction," in Douglas R. Nickel, *Carleton Watkins: The Art of Perception*. San Francisco: San Francisco Museum of Modern Art, 1999, page 10. Hambourg cites as her source: "as quoted in the *North Pacific Review*, vol. 1, no. 5 (February 1863), page 208, courtesy Peter Palmquist."

[17]Fitz Hugh Ludlow, "Seven Weeks in the Great Yo-Semite," *The Atlantic Monthly*, vol. 13, issue 80 (June 1864).

[18]See, for example, C. S. Bushnell to Abraham Lincoln, October 8, 1863 (recommendations for directors of Union Pacific Railroad), Library of Congress collection, available at http://www.cprr.org/Museum/Lincoln_Papers_LOC.html.

[19]For further discussion, see Levitt, editor, *Conservation in the Internet Age*, pages 26–27. Levitt cites the following as sources regarding Bierstadt and Ludlow's patronage by the Union Pacific: Joshua Scott John, "All Aboard: The Role of the Railroads in Protecting, Promoting and Selling Yosemite and Yellowstone," master's thesis, University of Virginia, 1996, available at http://xroads.virginia.edu/~ma96/railroad/home.html; and Alfred Runte, *Trains of Discovery: Western Railroads and the National Parks*, Fourth Edition. Boulder, Colo.: Roberts Rinehart Publishers, 1998.

[20] Alfred Runte, *Yosemite: The Embattled Wilderness*. Lincoln: University of Nebraska Press, 1990 (chapter 2, page 4 of 10 ff.), reproduced online and available at http://www.cr.nps.gov/history/online_books/runte2/chap2.htm.

[21]Ibid.

[22]James N. Levitt, "Conservation Innovation in America: Past, Present and Future," *Occasional Paper Series* (OPS 02-03), Institute for Government Innovation, John F. Kennedy School of Government, Harvard University, December 2002, page 7.

[23]Theodore Roosevelt, *An Autobiography*, 1913. Included in Theodore Roosevelt, *The Rough Riders, An Autobiography*. New York: Library of America, 2004, page 682.

[24]Ibid.

[25]For further Fish and Wildlife Service information on Pelican Island and its history, see http://pelicanisland.fws.gov/history.html#immigrant.

[26]National Wildlife Refuge Association, "Paul Kroegel and America's First Wildlife Refuge," *Blue Goose Flyer*, Summer 2003, available at http://www.refugenet.org/New-Centennial/CentStory3.html.

[27]Theodore Roosevelt, *A Book-Lover's Holidays in the Open*, 1916, available at http://bartleby.school.aol.com/57/10.html.

[28]Ibid.

[29]Aldo Leopold, "Roadside Prairies," originally prepared (but unpublished) between 1938 and 1942; available in Aldo Leopold, *For the Health of the Land: Previously Unpublished Essays and Other Writings.* Washington, D.C.: Island Press, 1999, page 139.

[30]Aldo Leopold, "Conservation Economics," *Journal of Forestry*, circa 1934, reprinted in Susan Flader and J. Baird Callicot, editors, *The River of the Mother of God and Other Essays by Aldo Leopold.* Madison: University of Wisconsin Press, 1991, pages 193–202.

[31]See, for example, Texas Republican Party, "1994 State Republican Party Platform," pages 5–6, cited by the Texas Center for Policy Studies, The Texas Environmental Almanac, 1995, available at http://www.texascenter.org/almanac/Land/LANDCH3P2.HTML. The party platform adopted in 1994 is reported to have included the following plank. "The Party understands that government ownership of land is an ideal of socialism. We affirm our belief in the fundamental constitutional concept of a person's right to own property without government interference. We decry the vast acquisition of Texas land by conservancy groups and government agencies. We call on our State Legislators to reclaim lands under federal control and return them to the people of Texas. We also affirm that groundwater is an 'absolute ownership' right of the landowner."

[32]For more on the characteristics of "landmark conservation innovations," see Levitt, "Conservation Innovation in America," pages 4, 5.

Chapter 2

Conservation Finance Viewed as a System
Tackling the Financial Challenge

Patrick Coady

Steve McCormick, president of The Nature Conservancy, offered his view of the tough choices facing the conservation community at the 2003 Land Trust Alliance Rally in Sacramento. Here's what he said:

> I believe we are at a crossroads. . . . The choice is this: We can go down one road that is, essentially, a continuation of where we have come from. For sure, this route will see some improvement, and certainly more success. But, frankly, my sense is that although we will accomplish more of some very good things, the aggregate of our results will still be on the margin. We will experience massive loss of land: precipitous declines in open spaces, greenbelts and viewsheds; virtual elimination of large intact functioning natural landscapes—prairie systems, desert oak woodlands—and dramatic conversion of farm and ranchlands. These consequences—some lands conserved, most lost—are a straight-line trajectory of where we are today. The other road is a lot steeper. Much more challenging, harder to navigate, even perilous in some stretches. The end point less sure of attainment. But, if we take it, it can lead to what I believe are truly transformational, and far more profoundly beneficial consequences.

From my vantage point, with the commitment of what has been my whole professional career, I think we have to take the harder route.[1]

McCormick's message was well received by his colleagues in the land and biodiversity conservation community. Despite many hard-won successes, there is a growing realization that efforts to preserve open space are falling behind. Studies across the country forecast that the next twenty-five years will offer us the last chance to save critical open space. To preserve comprehensive networks of areas of biological importance and to mitigate growing development pressures, financial resources for open space conservation need to be increased. To find new resources, the conservation community needs to both build on existing financial approaches and discover new ones.

Ultimately, the issue is how to increase and diversify appropriate long-term ownership and stewardship resources and organizational models. Historically, various federal government programs have provided the principal source of financing and the most significant ownership vehicles for preserving open space. In recent decades, state and local governments have assumed larger roles in providing financing and stewardship resources for managing conservation land. The growing use of conservation easements held by nonprofit land trusts and comparable organizations has, in the past twenty years, provided another significant mechanism for achieving land protection. Still, if we were to rely on these now well-established means of financing and managing land protection projects, we would likely face an inadequate supply of funds and management capabilities, provided through slow, deliberate, and unpredictable processes.

The transformation of the conservation financing landscape must take place across the board, in small organizations as well as large ones. It is true that conservation organizations exist that can mobilize the resources to see a big land conservation project to a successful conclusion, and there are land conservation opportunities that ultimately get done because the failure to act is broadly understood to be unacceptable. But many organizations and projects suffer for the lack of financial resources themselves, as well as the

23

absence of readily accessible professional capability that can help identify and deliver financial resources in a timely, efficient, and effective manner.

Many smaller and less experienced land trusts and conservation organizations are compelled to try to get their projects done by competing for what appears to be a limited pool of public and foundation sponsorship and financial resources. Their project advocates often have no training or experience in finance, and their organizations do not have the wherewithal to help them acquire the tools and the skills to put together comprehensive project acquisition and finance plans. What is needed in the field of land conservation is something that growing commercial businesses can almost take for granted: a "system," or web of resources, both human and financial, that organizations can call on, and learn to depend on, to help them gain access to the financial resources they need to get their jobs done.

Looking at a System of Finance

Despite the fact that a wide variety of financing sources and techniques are used by conservation organizations, there remain important gaps in the arsenal of funding mechanisms available for the preservation of open space. To fill those gaps, the conservation community needs to think of financing as a system that encompasses various steps along the way, beginning with "origination" and concluding with "closing the deal."

To work effectively and efficiently, the system requires adequate human and financial resources. In the presence of such resources on a consistent and widespread basis, the practice of conservation finance is likely to continue its evolution, moving from more disparate, localized efforts to initiatives that are characterized by collaborative organizational partnerships that are increasingly organized on regional, national, and international scales.

To accomplish this transition certain bottlenecks and gaps in the system of conservation finance need to be addressed. We can substantially improve the methods we use to realize conservation finance opportunities at many steps along the way, from project initiation to deal closing.

Project Identification, Preparation, and Origination   The idea that a particular property can and should be protected can come from a

great number of sources. An individual whose life is closely connected with a certain place may make that land's protection a personal passion. A property may come to the attention of a conservation organization opportunistically—for example, in the course of a dinner conversation with the neighbor of a local landowner who is preparing to retire. Alternatively, the need for and feasibility of protecting a given parcel may emerge as part of regional or landscape-scale priority-setting process. In any case, the early-stage work that needs to be done just to prepare to raise the money to do the deal can take extensive amounts of time, effort, and money.

Such early-stage preparation is often speculative, involving a high degree of risk. To get a deal ready for review, a finance plan must be prepared that covers the following: deal structure (e.g., who will grant the easement, who will hold the easement, and who will underwrite deal financing); financial mechanisms to be used (e.g., what combinations of public grants, private grants, debt financing, and tax credit mechanisms will be used); and a timeline for project completion. Lacking such plans, many worthy projects fail to proceed to the next stage or, alternatively, do proceed without the benefit of the appropriate resources and tools.

In the world of commercial finance, commercial and investment banks may share the risk of early-stage deal preparation by offering potential clients a suite of services that go under the rubric of "deal origination." That is, they will assist potential clients with strategic advice on how to structure a deal and how to raise the required capital from a variety of sources. Although a handful of firms offer such services in the conservation world, most land protection projects are prepared or originated within a given conservation organization, often by volunteers or young professionals who have scant training in the preparation of a finance or development plan. Even finding the financial resources that can fund this essential preparatory work can be a daunting task.

Provision of Catalyst Money   Public sector and philanthropic sources of conservation capital see a steady stream of proposals for funding. For example, federal programs that offer conservation funding are typically vastly oversubscribed. The challenge facing managers of conservation financing programs is how to pick out the most promising prospects from the field. Such funders, for good reason, may be hesitant to be the first mover on a project. They may hold back to see if someone else (or some other group of potential backers) steps forward first.

In the business world, there are early-stage financers (e.g., so-called angel investors and venture capital organizations) that are in the business of making lead investments in promising young companies. These early-stage investors are often compensated for the high degree of risk associated with such investments by high rates of return on successful deals. Conservation organizations seeking funds to complete complex conservation deals often struggle to find early-stage investors for high-merit, low-visibility projects. Such early-stage financing, once obtained, can give substantial credibility to an effort and, in effect, become the cornerstone of the project's financial plan.

Provision of Bridge Financing   Even with a carefully prepared financial plan and a boost from early-stage funding, most land conservation projects take months or years to pull together. Bridge financing (that is, most commonly, a short- or medium-term loan that can carry a project until sufficient long-term financing is obtained) can be key to the ultimate success of a land conservation deal dependent in the long term on, for example, a competitively obtained federal government grant. In business, such bridge financing is often arranged by commercial and investment banks to qualified customers, allowing such customers to develop nascent markets for their goods and services until they are large enough that the customers can obtain more permanent debt or equity financing.

Addressing the need for bridge financing, several new local and regional revolving funds have recently been created (see chapter 5). Such funds are a logical response to the evident need in the conservation field. They are, however, generally small and do not take any significant underwriting risk. Larger, risk-oriented, national revolving funds—which could have a significant impact on small and large conservation initiatives around the nation—generally exist only within the very largest conservation organizations and are typically reserved for internal use.

Provision of Long-Term Financing   At present, long-term financing for conservation projects usually comes in the form of grants and gifts from public and philanthropic sources: this is supplemented by the tax credit benefits provided by a variety of state and federal government programs. Such financing typically does not require the project to provide an ongoing return to investors. This is in sharp contrast with most commercial financings, which are expected to repay the debt or equity investor (be it an individual, a bank, or an investment fund) with a market rate of return.

By comparison, a new generation of conservation projects that are associated with recurring revenue streams have been successfully implemented in recent years. For example, in chapter 9, Steve Weems describes a project that, with the help of federal new market tax credits, conserves working forestland in Maine and provides a respectable ongoing return to project investors. Similarly, Adam Davis outlines in chapter 10 several new ways to "mainstream environmental markets" by capturing a financial return on the ecosystem services provided by a given landscape (e.g., commercially financed wetlands recovery projects that mitigate the impact of nearby road construction projects). By providing ongoing sources of revenue, such projects gain access to commercial sources of long-term debt and equity.

Similarly, large conservation organizations with stable balance sheets and reliable prospects for recurring revenues from members, grantors, and endowment investments now have access to markets more commonly used by universities, hospitals, and other large nonprofit organizations (e.g., see Kevin W. Schuyler's report on the recent efforts of The Nature Conservancy to expand its capital frontiers in chapter 7).

These success stories are both instructive and heartening, but most conservation organizations have little know-how or wherewithal to gain access to the enormous pools of capital available in conventional capital markets. Expanding these organization's access to long-term financing from banks and from institutional and global capital markets could be a challenge for years to come.

Closing the Deal and Following Through   As already noted, access to new forms of financing may require new deal structures and permanent ownership models. To "close" on conservation easement deals, conservation organizations and intermediaries have had to invent novel ways to share project benefits with new groups of stakeholders. For example, Phillip M. Hocker in chapter 8 considers the structural complexities of transferring, in a suitable and timely manner, Virginia state tax credits associated with land conservation easements. Similarly, groups such as The Conservation Fund are partnering with public agencies and for-profit timber investment firms to protect and sustainably manage vast holdings of forestland in northern New York and New Hampshire.[2]

Internationally, global investment organizations are getting into the act. To cite one highly creative example, Goldman Sachs recently structured a deal in partnership with the Wildlife Conservation Society (WCS) that effectively converts distressed debt into an enormous conservation asset, encompassing 680,000 acres of ecologically significant forestland in Chilean Tierra del Fuego.[3] Now that the property is under WCS stewardship, Chilean and U.S. advisers are thinking through ways of creating ecologically sustainable enterprises, such as ecotourism and high-end fly-fishing ventures, that are both ecologically sustainable and contribute to the local economy and community development. The new enterprises that emerge from this process are likely to inform an ongoing, multilateral give-and-take among conservationists around the world, in which North Americans have as much to learn from their international colleagues as they have to teach.

The exploration of novel ownership structures needed to close on innovative sources of conservation finance is ongoing and holds significant potential, but will require legal, financial, and management expertise. Creating such new ownership models will be difficult, but it is essential to the expansion of the system of conservation finance in the United States and internationally.

Addressing the Gaps

The gaps identified above can be addressed in a number of ways. A discussion of these approaches follows.

Encouraging Research and Development in Conservation Finance

If the conservation community is to significantly expand its supply of capital throughout the next several decades, it will have to thoughtfully support and pursue financial innovation. Innovation of financial products requires time, personal and organizational focus, and budgetary support. An interesting idea can be carried only so far before it needs sustained effort. Fashioning legislation and structuring capital market arrangements requires persistent and expensive professional attention. In short, the community, through various channels, must dedicate resources on an ongoing basis to research and develop new financial tools, mechanisms, and permanent funding sources, as well as to use existing sources and mechanisms more efficiently. Foundations with an interest in pioneering new approaches to achieve measurable conservation objectives would be logical sponsors of these efforts.

Building Human Resources and Organizational Capacity   Across the system of conservation finance identified in this chapter, from deal origination to closing, there are consistent shortfalls in the individual and institutional capacity to do necessary finance-oriented work. Major conservation organizations and the larger land trusts do employ some people who are prepared to do this work, but often in inadequate numbers. The situation is even less auspicious throughout most of the land trust community, where the median annual organizational budget is in the tens of thousands of dollars and staff is largely volunteer. If the pace of land conservation is to be accelerated, human and organizational capacity in finance must be improved.

Several paths to improve human and organizational capacity in conservation finance are evident. The first is to work to increase funding for relevant curriculum development and professional training, both within individual organizations and across the conservation movement. Although the Land Trust Alliance and other organizations do offer some training in these fields, much more could be done, particularly with regard to the type of advanced conservation finance methods discussed in this book. It is important to note that once trained, conservation organizations will have to offer competitive compensation and benefit packages to retain talented individuals. Greater capacity building and training in the area of conservation finance will pay a dividend, giving conservation organizations the ability to do increasingly large and complex transactions.

In addition to greater training, public, nonprofit, and private organizations should consider gathering into new organizations the financial talent that can provide specialized, third-party finance-related services to conservation organizations. Although several such service providers are now hard at work (e.g., as described in the reports on "conservation intermediaries" included in chapter 5), the field is relatively undeveloped. Specialists who are expert in new conservation financing techniques, such as the use of new market tax credits (see chapter 9) or mitigation banking (see chapter 10), are likely to find a number of ready takers for their services.

Enhancing Collaboration Across Landscapes   As experience has shown in several regions of the nation, including the Greater Yellowstone ecosystem, the Chesapeake Bay, the Northern Forest, and the Carolina lowlands, planning and implementing conservation programs across a landscape scale can yield multiple benefits. Such benefits include the establishment and professional management of landscape-scale conservation finance facilities, such as the regional external revolving loan programs described in chapter 5.

Landscape-scale conservation initiatives also have the benefit of facilitating the emergence of a cadre of land conservation professionals that can be instrumental, for example, in project origination, complex financial structuring, and the establishment of new corporate entities capable of implementing new long-term ownership models. In New England, for example, the creation of a number of new corporate entities designed to hold and manage working forestlands has been facilitated by a regional focus, throughout the past two decades, on issues related to the future of the Northern Forest. Individuals with years of experience in those highly charged discussions are stepping forward to help form and lead financially sophisticated projects that are protecting vast expanses of northern woodlands.

Enhancing Collaboration Across Organizations   As demonstrated, for example, by Kevin W. Schuyler in his essay on "expanding the frontiers" of conservation finance (see chapter 7), several of the largest conservation organizations in the nation have assembled the financial resources, staff, and know-how to navigate a wide spectrum of financial markets and funding mechanisms in the private, nonprofit, and public sectors. Organizations such as The Nature Conservancy, the Conservation Fund, and the Trust for Public Land (the so-called Big Three) are, in this and other capacities, playing critical leadership roles in the land conservation community. Their vitality, and their willingness to cooperate among themselves and with other conservation organizations, is of great importance to the development of human resources and organizational capacity throughout the conservation community.

Certainly competition among organizations can be a healthy and necessary practice. However, shaped by their individual business model and organizational goals, these organizations sometimes compete unnecessarily with one another and with other conservation organizations, driven by the underlying fear that the acquisition of financial resources for open space protection is a zero-sum game. Rather than simply redistributing slices of a pie that has a fixed size, greater cooperation and collaboration among conservation organizations, particularly in sharing best practices and expertise in the field of conservation finance, may help to "expand the pie" of resources available to the entire community.

Expanding the Diversity of Capital Sources   If the conservation community is to achieve its goal of doing more and doing it more quickly, then it must develop new, more diverse capital sources. A discussion about how a new set of institutions and financial sources could be used for conservation follows.

Foundations and Individual Donors

The primary sources of nongovernmental funds for land conservation in the United States today are charitable foundations and a few wealthy individuals. And many foundations interested in land conservation view requests for grants for open space protection as a bottomless pit, preferring to leverage their resources by helping to build conservation organizations or revolving fund mechanisms.

The current levels of charitable support provided by foundations and individuals are significant, but they are inadequate to the enormous conservation challenges ahead. Clearly, efforts to grow the ranks of such donors are critical: the financial resources provided by charitable contributors will continue to be of great importance to land conservation efforts. Such sources, however, pale in size compared with the commercial finance resources available for land development activities in the United States.

Foundations have traditionally been a catalyst for innovation in conservation finance and are likely to play a strong role in supporting efforts to spur conservation finance innovation on an ongoing basis. Some of the areas where foundations are having important impacts in the field of conservation finance include program-related investments, revolving fund creation and operations, direct support for landscape-scale conservation fee purchase and easement acquisition, organizational capacity building, and training.

New Sources of Bridge Financing

At the moment, most land conservation bridge financings involve modest amounts of money, and the financings are consummated only when take-out financing and a permanent owner have been identified. If the pace of land conservation is to be increased, then land conservation organizations will have to better compete for deals with commercial developers that have full access to banks and capital markets. Accordingly, conservation-bridge financiers will have to be enabled by their funders to take on greater risk with greater funding capacity.

One idea that merits exploration is the creation of conservation-bridge financing facilities designed to be operated for five to ten years by a small team of financial experts. The team, which would spread risk among a portfolio of financings, would be prepared to commit to important projects that did not yet have permanent ownership and take-out commitments in place.

Capital Markets and Bank Financings

In recent years, capital debt and equity markets have emerged as a major potential source of capital for working forestland, limited development, and other conservation-related deals that can yield ongoing revenue streams. A growing number of investment managers have shown interest in owning properties that can yield, for example, revenue from timber operations. Payment for ecosystem services such as the preservation of critical watersheds can also protect wildlife habitat.

In addition, large conservation organizations with very strong balance sheets, such as The Nature Conservancy, have had early success in gaining access to commercial debt markets to raise capital for a variety of land protection projects.

Conservation-related capital market and bank financings are not easy. They require significant upfront costs to cover, for example, property appraisal, management plan development, conservation easement organization, and professional tax planning assessments. A finance professional may have to devote several years to the development of a financial plan to fit the particular circumstances of a given project.

A number of interesting approaches and instruments might provide meaningful sums of money for this genre of conservation finance. Ideas of interest include various partnership structures, tax-exempt bond financings, real estate investment trusts, and collateralized bank loans.

When considering such opportunities, be aware that most key innovators are unlikely to come, at present, from the ranks of conventional commercial finance practitioners—people who are encouraged to work on deals that have a fee potential of more than $1 million and that can be completed in less than a year. Complex and novel conservation-oriented deals will require the attention of individuals (both from commercial and investment banks, and from financially sophisticated nonprofits) willing to persist for several years to pull together high-risk transactions. Once such pioneers have set precedents, other financial professionals are likely to follow.

Limited Development Opportunities

Although pristine wilderness land remains to be protected in the United States, many key battles for open space will be in areas that are now—or will soon be—threatened by residential or commercial development. Such areas include both exurban and rural locales targeted for year-round settlements or seasonal, recreation-oriented developments. Individuals and organizations that can proficiently guide limited development schemes, accommodating both development and the sustained protection of critical natural systems and amenities, will be in great demand.

33

At present, there are only a few conservation organizations set up to work with developers or property owners to realize both conservation and development objectives (e.g., see chapter 6, which offers an account of how Scenic Hudson spearheaded a limited development effort on the waterfront in Beacon, New York). Other conservation organizations find it difficult to lead limited development efforts, both because of a lack of qualified staff and because such efforts cut into the ethic of the organization. What may be needed are new profit-driven organizations with green mandates. Such green developers could provide leadership in situations where it would be better to save critical parcels in a limited development effort than to risk losing an entire area to development.

Commodity Markets for Ecosystem Services

The idea that the services provided by the natural environment are free is rapidly disappearing. Early "cap and trade" systems deployed in the United States, for example, put a marketable value on reduced sulfur dioxide emissions from power plants. These markets for environmental goods closely resemble markets for more tangible commodities, such as pork bellies or wheat. Similarly, important new work is helping to establish values for such environmental services as watershed protection, flood control, carbon sequestration, and air quality enhancement (e.g., see Adam Davis's discussion of the emerging market for wetland mitigation banking in chapter 10). As the value of such ecosystem services are quantified in orderly markets, ecosystem service producers (e.g., entrepreneurs who create wetland mitigation properties) will be able to gain access to commercial and institutional markets for long-term debt and equity financing, just as soybean and orange juice producers have done for decades.

Summing Up: The Need to Innovate and to Think Big

Individuals engaged in conservation finance tend to focus on the development of specific financial instruments and methodologies, rarely pausing to step back and look at the larger picture. Given the enormous need for additional conservation capital in the coming decades, it is important to appreciate that there are considerable opportunities for significant innovation throughout the entire system of conservation finance, from deal origination to the development of new forms of long-term ownership. In addition to nurturing innovative approaches to conservation finance in existing organizations, the conservation community needs to think about creating "new and big" financial institutions that are empowered to tackle conservation challenges in novel and significant ways.

If innovation is successfully encouraged across the entire system, a much more productive conservation finance community could emerge. That community should be capable of weaving together a variety of financial instruments and facilities to support a great many ambitious projects from conception to completion. Such an augmented system of finance would yield a broad array of benefits to public, private, and nonprofit interests dedicated to a high quality of life on Earth, wondrous in its variety.

Note: This chapter reflects the results of a series of interviews with conservation leaders, particularly those involved in conservation finance. The discussions were informed by a number of sources, including Coady's service as U.S. executive director of the World Bank from 1989 to 1993, where he was involved in many environmental policy issues, such as the formation of the $1.3 billion Global Environmental Facility; as a senior fellow at Conservation International from 1993 to the present; and as the current managing director of Coady Diemar Partners, an investment banking firm with offices in New York and Washington, D.C.

Notes

[1] Steve McCormick, "Conservation at the Crossroads" (remarks by Steve McCormick, president and chief operating officer, The Nature Conservancy, at the Land Trust Alliance Rally, September 13, 2003, Sacramento, California), available at http://nature.org/pressroom/files/land_trust_alliance_speech.pdf.

[2] See The Conservation Fund, "Northern Forest," available at http://www.conservationfund.org/?article=2249&back=true; see also Office of the Governor [of New York, George Pataki], "Governor Announces Historic Conservation Deal Completed," July 1, 1999, available at http://www.state.ny.us/governor/press/year99/july1_99.htm.

[3]For more on the Goldman Sachs/Wildlife Conservation Society partnership in Tierra del Fuego, see http://www.gs.com/our_firm/our_culture/ social_responsibility/tierradelfuego/. See also Ruth Bradley, "Saving a Unique Landscape," in *bUSiness Chile*, AmCham Chile (The Chilean American Chamber of Commerce), November 2004, available at http://www.amchamchile.cl/UserAmcham/business_cover_story.html.

Chapter 3

Contours of Conservation Finance in the United States at the Turn of the Twenty-first Century

Frank Casey

The Conservation Challenge

The United States faces a serious challenge with respect to land and biodiversity conservation. Despite our nation's economic prosperity, our wild heritage is increasingly at risk. For example, as of 2000, approximately one hundred species had become extinct and one third of our native species of vertebrates, flowering plants, and invertebrates were of conservation concern.[1] Furthermore, about one half of our natural community types are at similar risk, and twenty-seven ecosystems have declined by 98 percent since European colonization.[2] The number of threatened and endangered species increased more than sevenfold between 1976 and 2004, from 174 to 1,265.[3] Each of these alarming trends is, at present, being exacerbated by ongoing landscape fragmentation and habitat loss in the United States.

Significant conservation efforts exist in the form of regulatory controls and voluntary incentive measures. Voluntary measures include land acquisition and rentals, easements, cost-share practices, safe harbor agreements, and tax relief. Both regulatory and voluntary methods provide tools for stabilizing and improving the habitat of endangered and threatened species. However, even though all approaches and programs are critically important, they are clearly not keeping pace with the problem.

The location of at-risk species and habitats is extremely important with respect to determining what levels of conservation finance, in whatever form, will be required. Of the species that are imperiled, threatened, or endangered, 40 percent are not known to exist on federal lands. Likewise, 67 percent of the *populations* of these at-risk species are not known to live on federal lands.[4] This means that state and privately owned lands will be pivotal in conservation efforts. Furthermore, agricultural and forestry lands will be the dominant targets for conservation activity. Private cropland, pastureland, and rangeland account for about 48 percent of the land in the lower forty-eight states; private forestlands make up 22 percent. Thus, nearly 70 percent of the land available for conservation is in some type of private agricultural or forestry use. Because of diverse agricultural land use and ownership patterns, a menu of incentive strategies in addition to land acquisition will be required to attain conservation objectives. Such a diverse conservation strategy will have implications for the types and levels of conservation financing needed.

An ecologically and taxonomically comprehensive system of conservation lands will require, for the most part, inclusion of those private lands at lower elevations that have historically been the most productive for human use and the least protected.[5] The conservation of lands in inhabited areas will not only affect the level of financing required, but will also partially determine which financial instruments will be the most effective and efficient. As the intensity of human use increases for particular areas, so will the opportunity cost of land conservation.

Estimated Demand for Conservation Financing

In order to put the current supply of conservation financing into perspective, we first estimate the potential demand for its use based on one particular conservation goal: the protection of a viable, representative, and redundant network of ecosystem types in the United States. Conservation of a network of ecosystem types would not only have biodiversity benefits, but would also be compatible with a multitude of other goals currently associated with conservation funding.

As a first approximation to determine the land needed for a complete conservation network, we look to previous estimates, which suggest that nearly 25 percent of land in the coterminous United States would be necessary for a comprehensive system of habitat conservation areas.[6] We estimate about one half of the land area in this system to be in private hands. In terms of actual area, this yields an approximation of 1.9 million square kilometers, of which about 957,000 square kilometers (95.7 million hectares) are in private ownership. These estimates are for a network that would encompass all natural community types and all at-risk species, including those not yet listed as threatened or endangered. In this sense, our estimate represents the habitat portion of an overall biodiversity conservation policy, not simply an endangered species program.

The costs of conservation are approximated using three financial mechanisms: (1) fee-simple purchase, (2) easement, and (3) rental of lands not already in conservation status (see table 3.1).

Table 3.1.

Estimated Relative Costs for a Comprehensive National System of Habitat Conservation Areas (in Billions of Dollars)

Cost	Fee-Simple Purchase	Conservation Easement	Land Rental Agreement
Annual cost in year 1	7.7	5.4	0.3
Annual cost in year 30	18.2	12.7	21.2
Annual management cost in year 1	0.1	0	0
Annual management cost in year 30	5.1	0	0
Cumulative cost throughout 30 years	427.9	256.8	252.0
Average annual cost throughout 30 years	14.6	8.56	8.4
Cumulative cost throughout 40 years	488.4	256.8	502.0
Average annual cost throughout 40 years	12.2	6.42	12.55

Source

Mark J. Shaffer, Michael Scott, and Frank Casey, "Noah's Options: Initial Cost Estimates of a System of National Habitat Conservation Areas in the United States," *BioScience* 52:5 (May 2002).

Cost estimates are based on two major assumptions. First, it will take three to four decades to protect a comprehensive, nationwide set of habitat areas once they are identified. Thus, we prorate the amount of land brought into conservation status throughout a thirty- to forty-year period. For the thirty-year period, we base cost estimates on an annual addition to the system of 3.3 percent of the currently unprotected land area necessary for biodiversity conservation. This amounts to protecting approximately an additional 3.2 million hectares per year (somewhat less for the forty-year period). Second, we assume that the bulk of private lands necessary for a comprehensive system are located predominantly in rural areas and would be available for purchase or rental at average market prices; for purchased land, management costs are included.

As table 3.1 illustrates, the estimated annual average cost throughout the thirty-year period would be $14.6 billion[7] for fee simple purchases (including ongoing management costs), $8.56 billion for easements, and $8.4 billion for land rentals. The cumulative cost throughout thirty years would range from $252 to $428 billion, depending on the land acquisition tool used. Extending to a forty-year time horizon, fee-simple purchases and management costs would decrease to $12.2 billion per year, easements would decrease to $6.42 billion per year, and land rentals would increase to $12.55 billion per year. The major implication for conservation finance for the longer term is that fee-simple purchases would incur recurrent management costs only at the end of the selected purchase period (estimated at $5.1 billion per year), but annual land rental costs would continue to increase with inflation beyond the estimated $12.55 billion per year. Thus, throughout the longer term, it would make more sense to compare the current level of conservation financing with expenditures for fee-simple purchases and easement options.

The Contours of Conservation Finance

Current levels of conservation finance provide significant funding for multiple forms of land protection and use through various incentive instruments. The size of the conservation finance pie for land acquisition has been growing in the past few years and is estimated to have reached a total of about $2.7 billion in 2003, not including temporary land rentals (see table 3.2). This represents a

Table 3.2.

Estimated Levels of Conservation Finance, 2003 (in Millions of Dollars)

Instrument	Federal	State and Local[1]	Private[2]	Total
Purchases/easements	898 (Non-Ag)/ 500 (Ag)[3]	1,039.8	266	2,703.8
Land rentals	1,684[4]	2.88	N/A	1,686.88
Cost-share practices	1,173[5]	205	N/A	1,378
Total	4,255	1,247.68	266	5,768.68

Sources

[1] Defenders of Wildlife, *Conservation in America: State Government Incentives for Habitat Restoration: A Status Report* (Washington, D.C.: Defenders of Wildlife, 2002).

[2] Trust for Public Land and Land Trust Alliance, *Americans Invest in Parks and Open Space: Land Vote 2003* (Washington, D.C.: Trust for Public Land and Land Trust Alliance, 2004).

[3] Ann Ingerson, *Conservation Capital: Sources of Public Funding for Land Conservation, Focus on the Eastern United States* (Washington, D.C.: The Wilderness Society, 2004), available at http://www.wilderness.org/Library/ Documents/ConservationCapital.cfm.

[4] United States Department of Agriculture, Farm Services Agency, "Conservation Reserve Program Overview," in *CRP: Planting for the Future* (Washington, D.C.: United States Department of Agriculture, 2004).

[5] Sustainable Agriculture Coalition, "FY 05 Agriculture Appropriations Chart." Mimeo. (Washington, D.C.: Sustainable Agriculture Coalition, 2004.)

$600 million increase compared with 2001 levels and includes federal, state, and local government contributions and contributions by the private sector. And the $2.7 billion is actually somewhat of an underestimate, because it does not include the numerous expenditures by small land trusts. For 2003 purchases and easements, the federal government accounts for nearly 52 percent of the $2.7 billion, with state and local government furnishing 38 percent and private sources (mostly land trusts) the remaining 10 percent. However, these estimates do not include the contribution of landowner tax benefits received from conservation efforts at any level of government.

A closer look at the source and application of 2003 conservation financing yields some interesting insights. At the federal level (see column 1, table 3.2), nonagricultural federal land acquisition (purchases and easements) programs in 2003 were funded at about $898 million.[8] This is approximately a 36 percent increase over 2001 expenditure levels, a year for which comparable data are available. Federal funding for conservation easements on agricultural lands in 2003 was close to $500 million, making a total of $1.4 billion of federal funding for purchases and easements.

Federal agricultural land rentals through the U.S. Department of Agriculture's Conservation Reserve Program (USDA/CRP), which provides temporary conservation benefits, reached more than $1.625 billion in 2001 and expanded to about $1.785 billion in 2003.[9] The three federal land set-aside strategies (acquisition, easements, and rentals) accounted for about $3.2 billion in 2003, but more than half went to nonpermanent USDA/CRP land rentals. It is interesting to note that in 2007 approximately one half of the contracts for land in CRP (16 million acres) will be up for reenrollment, with another 6 million acres in 2008.

Conservation financing for the cost sharing of more sustainable production and conservation practices can significantly contribute to multiple objectives associated with resource protection. Federal cost-share programs averaged about $175 million per year from 1996 to 2001, but authorized funds in the 2002 Farm Bill increased significantly, to about $1 billion a year through 2012. Authorized financing of federal cost-share programs in 2003 was approximately $1.173 billion.

Not including all federal land set-aside programs, total federal conservation funding amounted to more than $13.1 billion from 1996 to 2001. In this same period, federal cost-share programs accounted for about $2 billion of this funding. Direct effects on wildlife and wildlife habitat were minimal, however, with only about 4 percent of total federal funding going to them.

Like the federal conservation program, state conservation programs also offer fee-simple purchase, easement, and land rental programs. Combined, these programs have historically averaged about $1.043 billion per year.[10] This was probably the case in 2003 and beyond. Throughout the five election periods from 1998 to 2002, ballot initiatives were passed to fund $23 billion in bond measures for land acquisition.[11] Because most bond measures run for twenty years, this means a commitment of nearly $1 billion a year. This $1 billion in bond-funded acquisition programs, therefore, represents about 96 percent of total state funding for permanent land set-asides. The purposes of these conservation programs vary a great deal, however, from open space to farmland protection to recreation to ecosystem restoration. Funding through state and local ballot initiatives has been highly volatile.[12] In addition to land set-aside programs, state conservation financing for cost-share conservation programs in fiscal year 2001 exceeded $205 million. Financing was probably at the same level in 2003.

The private nonprofit sector has also invested substantial amounts in land conservation. From 1991 to 2000, the combined efforts of the Conservation Fund, The Nature Conservancy, The Trust for Public Land, and Ducks Unlimited have provided more than $266 million annually for fee-simple purchases and easements. This estimate for private, nonprofit sector contributions is low, given that expenditure data for purchases and easements by numerous local land trusts are not available. We assume that for 2003 the private nonprofits listed above continued to expend at least $266 million, not including the contribution of smaller, private land trusts.

Across all sources of financing (federal, state, and nonprofit), the first rough estimate of the extent of conservation financing for permanent land acquisition (fee-simple purchases and easements) is $2.7 billion per year, not including investments by local land trusts. If the nonpermanent federal CRP land rental program is included, then the total annual allocation increases to a little more than $4.49 billion. Of this amount, federal financing represents about 70 percent of the total. Temporary land rentals through CRP represent about 40 percent of total annual financing for land set-asides. Thus, it is evident that temporary protection is the focus of our nation's current conservation efforts on private lands. Total federal and state financing for cost sharing more sustainable production practices and resource conservation is estimated at about $1.38 billion for 2003. Across all funding sectors and conservation strategies, the 2003 total conservation financing is estimated to be about $5.769 billion.

Figures 3.1 and 3.2 summarize the totals for 2003 conservation financing by source and incentive mechanism, respectively.
With regard to financing source, the federal government accounted
for 74 percent of the total, followed by state and local contributions
at 21 percent and private sources at 5 percent (see figure 3.1). Of the
total conservation financing, 47 percent came in the form of land
purchases and easements, 30 percent was allocated to land rentals,
and 23 percent was assigned to cost-share practices (see figure 3.2).
The allocation of 2003 financing across incentive mechanisms illustrates that nearly 53 percent of the total was applied to nonperma-
nent conservation measures (land rentals and cost shares).

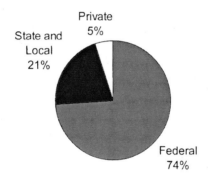

Figure 3.1.

Percentages for 2003 conservation financing by source. (Based on table 3.2.)

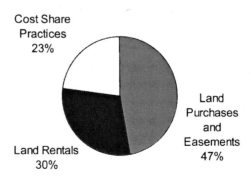

Figure 3.2.

Percentages for 2003 conservation financing by incentive mechanism. (Based on table 3.2.)

The Gap Between Supply and Demand

Given the estimated costs associated with funding a comprehensive system of lands for conservation purposes and the amount of financing currently available, some general bounds can be placed on the current gap between supply and demand. Including the federal CRP land rental program, total 2003 conservation expenditures for land set-asides were estimated at $4.5 billion. Taking the average forty-year time horizon cost estimates discussed in table 3.1, this means that there is an annual funding gap of between $1.92 billion (easements) and $7.7 billion (land purchases). The actual gap is smaller, because 2003 expenditure data do not account for land purchases or easements by local land trusts. Still, the finance gap is, no doubt, significant. If 2003 cost-share amounts are added in, then the funding gap decreases, to about $550 million per year under the easement option and to $6.33 billion per year under the land purchase option.

It is possible that the United States can at least partially close the estimated funding gap. On the demand side, surveys by the American Farmland Trust in 2001 indicated that 80 percent of U.S. residents said they valued land for the habitat it provided, thus providing evidence that taxpayers would be willing to increase either federal or state conservation funding. Furthermore, 63 percent said they would be willing to forgo part of a federal income tax rebate if the money were put toward protection of waterways, wetlands, and wildlife habitat. Finally, 60 percent said that they were willing to pay higher property or sales taxes to help ensure safe drinking water, and 40 percent would pay more taxes to protect scenic farmlands. To the degree to which each of these goals is compatible with ecosystem restoration and other conservation objectives, it signals a willingness on the part of the general public to pay more for the benefits that natural ecosystems and habitats provide.

On the supply side, rural landowners have demonstrated a willingness to participate more in conservation programs. The American Farmland Trust reports that nine out of ten farmers and ranchers offering to preserve open space by selling development rights are rejected, due to inadequate funding.[13] Furthermore, across all USDA nonacquisition resource conservation programs, the estimated total backlog of funding requested by landowners and operators for 2001 was about $1.66 billion. Defenders of Wildlife estimates that the total unmet demand for the Farm and Ranch Land Protection and Wetland Reserve Programs from 1996 to 2001 was about $921 million.[14]

Despite the general stated willingness of taxpayers to fund land conservation and the general willingness of landowners to "supply" conservation lands, there is always a great deal of uncertainty in the medium term regarding conservation program consistency, especially at the federal level. For example, in order to pay for drought and hurricane disaster relief in agricultural areas in 2004, nearly $3 billion in agriculture-related conservation programs was cut. Vagaries such as this in conservation financing will probably result in funding gaps that are both variable and significant.

Challenges, Opportunities, and Conditions for Expanding the Level of Conservation Financing

Estimates for the annual shortfall in expenditures to conserve a comprehensive network of ecosystem types run from approximately $1.92 billion to $7.7 billion per year throughout the next forty years (not including cost-share funds). This assumes, however, that the level of conservation funding attained in 2003 continues into the future. Depending on national economic and political conditions, this assumption may or may not be realistic.

What are the challenges and opportunities associated with closing the finance gap? Through public bond issues and surveys, U.S. residents have shown a willingness to provide conservation financing at significant levels. Similarly, rural landowners and residents have shown a willingness to participate in programs that set aside land for conservation purposes.

The challenges to and opportunities for success can be viewed within the context of three fundamental issues. The first issue is, How effective are the currently available funds in meeting land conservation goals? Are agencies strategically targeting conservation funds? Until these questions are answered, the size of the funding gap will remain unknown. A major challenge will be to generate better and more consistent data on annual conservation expenditures from all sectors across various incentive mechanisms.

Records of expenditure data at the state and local levels are especially poor. Records of programmed monies and actual project expenditures at the federal level are also problematic.

Targeting funds to defined conservation priority areas will help increase effectiveness. States, with the assistance of the federal government, are now developing comprehensive habitat conservation strategies that will serve as targeting mechanisms for the more effective use of conservation dollars. In addition, there is an urgent need to develop evaluation and monitoring programs—and the appropriate indicators—to measure the effectiveness of national and local land conservation programs. This will assist in developing ways to increase the economic efficiency of conservation efforts and help decrease the gap between funding supply and demand.

The second issue is, How economically efficient are the various incentive mechanisms in meeting conservation goals? Do some incentive mechanisms make better use of public or private dollars than others do? Which conservation incentive instruments lead to increased effectiveness: fee-simple purchases, easements, cost-share assistance, or tax relief? Given that land conservation must respond to the multiple goals of private landowners, incentive mechanisms may have to extend beyond fee-simple purchases or easements. Creating a national conservation fund that incorporates a menu of incentive measures, however, will be a challenge.

The third issue is, Given the large sums of publicly available financial resources for conservation, what are the equity implications for selecting certain projects over others? As long as enrollment criteria for public conservation programs remain complicated, participation may be limited to those who can most afford the time and money needed to apply. The development of fair criteria for distributing conservation funds to those that will use the funds effectively is essential.

At a macroeconomic scale, there are obvious challenges or threats to maintaining even current 2003 conservation financing levels into the future. These include the growing federal deficit and the threat of program cutbacks, the uncertain financial situation in some states and their ability to continue their own conservation programs, competition from other social investments (i.e., air pollution control, transportation, education, and so on) for scarce dollars, and the increasing reliance on the private sector to provide public goods. On both the local and the national scale, additional pressure will be put on conservation programs to demonstrate, and perhaps quantify, the economic (market and nonmarket) benefits of their efforts. Illustrating these benefits will provide the land and biodiversity conservation community not only the opportunity to maintain current funding levels, but perhaps expand them as well.

The importance of the private landowner in future conservation efforts will also provide both challenges and opportunities. With respect to challenges, compensation rates for purchases, easements, or rentals will certainly increase as the population grows. Furthermore, it will be challenging to find ways to expand conservation lands and at the same time allow for some compatible productive uses. This will call not only for flexibility in the terms of conservation instruments, such as easements, but also provide the opportunity to develop new incentive instruments and partnerships to reach conservation goals.

In addition to concerns about the adequacy of the "amount of pie" available for conservation purposes, there are also questions related to the *biological effectiveness* of current levels of conservation finance, the *economic efficiency* of the conservation instruments used, and the *social equity* associated with the distribution of public conservation resources. A detailed analysis of these factors is not possible here; nevertheless, these concerns point to the fact that the distribution of the pie is just as important as its overall size. With respect to biological effectiveness, more rigorous strategic planning of conservation investments is required. Additionally, much work needs to be done to compare the economic efficiency of various incentive tools (purchases, easements, cost-share assistance, and tax relief) to meet conservation objectives. Because nearly 88 percent of conservation funding comes from public funds, the equitable distribution of conservation projects is of interest to taxpayers and legislators.

Other chapters in this book explore innovations in financing mechanisms for land conservation. In examining these options, it is important to look at each one's potential to be effective, efficient, and equitable, and what the trade-offs are among the options.

Notes

[1] Bruce A. Stein, Lynn S. Kutner, and Jonathan S. Adams (eds.), *Precious Heritage: The Status of Biodiversity in the United States* (New York: Oxford University Press, 2000).

[2] Reed Noss, Edward T. LaRoe, and J. Michael Scott, Endangered Ecosystems (Biological Report 28) (Washington, D.C.: U.S. Department of the Interior, 1995); and Mark T. Bryer, Kathleen Maybury, Jonathan S. Adams, and Dennis H. Grossman, "More Than the Sum of the Parts: Diversity and Status of Ecological Systems," in Stein et al., *Precious Heritage*.

[3] United States Fish and Wildlife Service, "Species Information: Threatened and Endangered Plants and Animals," available at http://endangered.fws.gov/wildlife.html.

[4] Craig R. Groves, Lynn S. Kutner, David M. Stoms, Michael P. Murray, J. Michael Scott, Michael Schafale, Alan S. Weakly, and Robert L. Pressy, "Owning Up to Our Responsibilities: Who Owns Lands Important for Biodiversity," in Stein et al., *Precious Heritage*.

[5] J. Michael Scott, "Gap Analysis: A Geographic Approach to Protecting Biological Diversity," *Wildlife Monographs* 123:1–4 (1993).

[6] Mark R. Shaffer, J. Michael Scott, and Frank Casey, "Noah's Options: Initial Cost Estimates of a System of National Habitat Conservation Areas in the United States," *BioScience* 52:5 (May 2002).

[7] Figures cited are in nominal dollars, inflated at 3 percent per annum. They are not adjusted to reflect "constant dollar" amounts.

[8] Ann Ingerson, *Conservation Capital: Sources of Public Funding for Land Conservation, Focus on the Eastern United States* (Washington, D.C.: The Wilderness Society, 2004), available at http://www.wilderness.org/Library/Documents/ConservationCapital.cfm.

[9] United States Department of Agriculture, Farm Services Agency, "Conservation Reserve Program Overview," *CRP: Planting for the Future* (Washington, D.C.: United States Department of Agriculture, 2004).

[10] Defenders of Wildlife, *Conservation in America: State Government Incentives for Habitat Restoration: A Status Report* (Washington, D.C.: Defenders of Wildlife, 2002).

[11] Land Trust Alliance, *Voters Invest in Open Space: 2000 Referenda Results* (Washington, D.C.: Land Trust Alliance, 2001); and Trust for Public

Land and Land Trust Alliance, *Americans Invest in Parks and Open Space: Land Vote 2003* (Washington, D.C.: Trust for Public Land and Land Trust Alliance, 2004).

[12]Conservation funding for land set-asides from state and local ballot measures totaled $5.2 billion in 1998, $1.8 billion in 1999, $7.8 billion in 2000, $1.8 billion in 2001, and $6.1 billion in 2002.

[13]American Farmland Trust, *Protecting Our Most Valuable Resources: Results from a National Public Opinion Poll, 2001* (Washington, D.C.: American Farmland Trust, 2001).

[14]Lisa Hummon and Frank Casey, *Federal Conservation Incentives: Programs, Status, and Trends, 1996–2001, Conservation Economics Working Paper No. 1* (Washington, D.C.: Defenders of Wildlife, 2004).

Chapter 4

State and Local Government Funding of Land Conservation
What Is the Full Potential?

Ernest Cook and Matt Zieper

In recent years, growing attention has focused on the amount of money that state and local governments are spending to acquire and protect open space. In urban communities, governments use the money to expand park and greenway systems, in exurban communities to protect scenic and watershed areas, and in rural or wilderness areas to preserve agricultural land and wildlife habitat. In some cases, acts of the legislature make this funding available. Other times, funding is derived from an initiative process: proponents gather signatures to place a measure on the ballot, bypassing the legislature. Often, this new government funding involves a two-step process of legislative action that refers a measure to the ballot for voter approval.

Since 1996, the Trust for Public Land and the Land Trust Alliance have been tracking the ballot measure phenomenon. Accurate data therefore exist for initiatives and referenda, particularly in the five-year period from 1999 through 2003, when the two organizations had honed their methodology. There is no comparable source of data for conservation funding created solely through legislative action. But we are also familiar with all major legislation at the state level that funds land conservation as well as legislative trends at the local level.

From 1999 through 2003, voters have approved an estimated $19.2 billion in new state and local government funds for land conservation through ballot measures alone. The local government share of that was $8.8 billion. Does this amount represent the full potential for conservation finance in the United States? This chapter posits that the answer to this question is a resounding no. There is considerable evidence of a long-term upward trend in state and local government spending for land conservation that seems likely to continue. But even more important, states could adopt conservation policies and spending programs modeled on those of New Jersey, which would generate a huge wave of new local government spending on land conservation.

If every state in the United States of America had the "policy framework" for land conservation that has been pioneered by New Jersey, local government ballot measures for land conservation would have been nearly four times as high in this same five-year period—increasing from $8.8 billion to $33 billion. We have not yet developed a methodology for deriving the full potential of state government spending.

Trends in Conservation Finance

In many respects, conservation finance on a significant scale—in the sense of state and local government spending to acquire or protect parks and open space—dates back to the 1960s. That was the decade when New Jersey first offered a statewide "Green Acres" conservation finance bond to its voters for approval (1961) and when the country's first dedicated tax at the local government level for land conservation was instituted in the city of Boulder, Colorado (1967).

Conservation finance gathered steam in the following years. Many states launched major conservation initiatives. Some notable examples include Maryland's Program Open Space, funded by a real estate transfer tax (1969); Michigan's Land Trust Fund, backed by revenues from oil and gas leases on state lands (1976); the creation of a lottery in Colorado (1980); California's $776 million Proposition 70 general obligation bond (1988); a ten-year commitment by the Florida legislature to bond $300 million per year (1990); and a thirty-year dedication of $98 million in sales taxes per year to create the Garden State Preservation Trust in New Jersey (1998).

At the local government level, conservation finance measures often gained a foothold in well-heeled resort communities, upscale suburbs, or liberal strongholds, and then spread to other parts of a state. For example, the creation of "land banks" on Martha's Vineyard and Nantucket led to demands by Massachusetts mainland communities for similar legislative authority. After Boulder set a precedent in Colorado, other local governments in the Denver metropolitan area followed suit. The two least affluent counties in that region have adopted an open space tax: Adams County in 1999 and Arapahoe County in 2003.

The job of land conservation is a job that is never done. Typically, state and local governments do not enact a conservation finance measure, spend the money—and then stop protecting land. Instead, they renew their finance programs, often at a higher level of spending. Meanwhile, new jurisdictions are constantly joining in. On a collective national scale, the overall result seems destined to be inexorable growth in state and local government spending on land conservation.

What is driving the growing public investment in land conservation? Several trends seem to be at work.

- *Use of land conservation to manage growth, often as an alternative to regulation.* As the U.S. population continues to grow and as new development typically takes a less dense form than older development, more and more open land is being consumed. Oregon-style growth boundaries have never gained favor in the United States. But hundreds of communities are using land conservation to steer development away from sensitive areas. Paying landowners to protect open space is a market-based incentive that does not give rise to controversy and that appeals to voters and elected officials across the political spectrum.
- *Growth of the land trust movement.* Behind almost every conservation finance measure is one or more local, regional, or national conservation organizations. As land trusts multiply and become more sophisticated, they become increasingly involved in conservation finance measures.
- *Matching funds that stimulate local finance measures.* Since the mid-1990s, several states (including Florida, Georgia,

Massachusetts, and Utah) have created or expanded programs that require a local match. Some counties have also created innovative matching funds for their municipalities. Examples include Wake County, North Carolina; and Dutchess County, New York.

- *Expanded authority for local governments to dedicate funds for land conservation.* In New Mexico, counties were not permitted to bond for land conservation until a state constitutional amendment was passed in 1996. In Ohio, a new law in 1998 gave counties the authority to raise sales, use, or property taxes to pay for conservation easements. In Massachusetts, a new state program gives all municipalities the right to levy a property tax surcharge dedicated to land conservation, historic preservation, and affordable housing. Since 2000, nearly one fifth of the state's cities and towns have adopted the surcharge.

- *Growing popularity of programs to purchase development rights.* Most of the privately owned open space in the United States is in some form of agricultural use: farming, ranching, or forestry. Often, the goal of a conservation program is to keep this land in its existing use (and on the property tax rolls) rather than acquiring it outright for public ownership and use.

- *Concern about water supplies.* As new roads and buildings reach farther into rural areas, pristine watersheds that were once taken for granted now need conscious efforts to protect them. Local governments in all parts of the country have increased funding for land conservation in the past decade for this purpose. Examples include San Antonio, Texas; Carroll County, Georgia; Mecklenburg County, North Carolina; and New York City.

None of these trends seems likely to abate in the foreseeable future. Our conclusion is that state and local spending on land conservation in the United States today has far to go to reach its full potential. We predict that existing programs will be renewed and expanded, while new programs come on line—just as we have seen throughout the past ten years.

But what is the full potential for state and local government funding? To address that question, this chapter closely examines the case of New Jersey, which of any state in the nation is clearly the closest to achieving full potential. We distill a set of "best practices" from the New Jersey example and calculate their impact if applied in other states. Using a set of fairly conservative assumptions, we conclude that local government spending in the United States would increase approximately fourfold if the other forty-nine states adopted the "New Jersey model." In the five-year period from 1999 to 2003, that would have meant an increase in spending authorized through ballot measures from $8.8 billion to $33 billion. The additional $24 billion in this period would have enabled much greater advances toward important conservation goals.

For a variety of reasons, the methodology we use to analyze local ballot measures does not apply to state funding programs. For example, the ballot measure history of the states throughout 1999 through 2003 included in LandVote, an annual compilation of open space ballot measures published by the Trust for Public Land and the Land Trust Alliance, has too few data points to provide a reliable sample. So this chapter focuses only on the full potential of local governments to fund land conservation. As will become clear, local governments cannot achieve their full potential alone: strong partnerships with state funding programs are essential.

New Jersey: The Unrivaled Leader in Local Conservation Finance

From 1999 to 2003, New Jersey was home to nearly one quarter of the open space ballot measures that were voted on in the country (see figure 4.1). According to LandVote 2003, during that time 187 of the 834 conservation finance measures on the ballot were in New Jersey.

A Tale of Two States: New Jersey and New York   New Jersey is head and shoulders above all other states in terms of local conservation finance activity. Since 1987, all twenty-one of New Jersey's counties—from urban Hudson County to rural Sussex County—have created a special dedicated fund for land conservation. These "open space trust funds" are financed through an annual property tax levy. In addition to these county funds, nearly two hundred of New Jersey's municipalities have also adopted a dedicated property tax for open space. Collectively, local governments in New

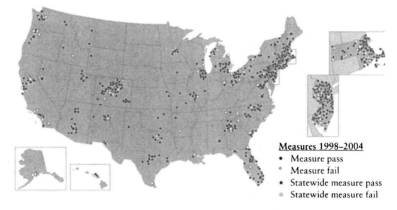

Measures 1998–2004
- Measure pass
° Measure fail
* Statewide measure pass
☆ Statewide measure fail

Figure 4.1.

Location of conservation finance ballot measures in the United States: 1998–2003. (Source: Trust for Public Land and Land Trust Alliance, *Americans Invest in Parks & Open Space: LandVote 2003*, February 2004.)

Jersey generate more than $200 million per year in support of land conservation.

The picture in neighboring New York is quite different. At the county level in New York, only one of New York's fifty-eight counties has a dedicated tax for open space. Three other counties do provide some degree of regular funding for land conservation through their annual budgets, but the amounts are modest compared with New Jersey, and the spending is vulnerable to annual budget decisions.

At the municipal level, the contrast between New York and New Jersey is equally stark. Fewer than a dozen municipalities in New York have a dedicated tax for open space. And five of those are exceptional cases: wealthy resort communities in the Hamptons/Peconic region of Long Island to whom the state legislature granted special permission to levy a real estate transfer tax. Rather than using dedicated taxes, municipal governments in New York tend to rely on voter-approved general obligation bonds for land conservation. Even so, in the five years between 1999 and 2003, only 32 municipalities in New York approved open space debt or new taxes, compared with 173 in New Jersey (see table 4.1).

Table 4.1.
Open Space Ballot Measures 1999–2003

	Number of Municipalities	Number of Municipalities Passing Open Space Measures
New York	1,547	32
New Jersey	566	173

Sources

TPL LandVote Database (www.landvote.org); New Jersey State League of Municipalities (http://www.njslom.org/types.html); New York Office of the State Comptroller (http://www.osc.state.ny.us/localgov/munilist.pdf).

Looked at another way, fewer than 5 percent of New York municipalities dedicated funds for open space in this period, while more than 30 percent of New Jersey's municipalities took action.

Why Is the Conservation Finance Landscape in New York So Different from New Jersey?

One might offer several hypotheses to explain why open space spending is so popular in one state compared with the other. We will examine—and dismiss—a few of them before offering our explanation.

Hypothesis #1: New York Voters Won't Support Conservation Finance Measures

Based again on LandVote data for the years 1999 through 2003, New Jersey has a high record of success in ballot measures for open space. Voters approved 86 percent of all local government (county and municipal) open space measures in New Jersey, compared with a national average of 80 percent. But the data from New York is actually stronger. When New York voters have the chance to vote on an open space ballot measure, their record of support is outstanding. Between 1999 and 2003, voters approved 34 of 38 local ballot measures (89 percent). On the most recent statewide measure in New York to include funds for land conservation—the $1.75 billion Clean Air, Clean Water Bond Act of 1996—New Yorkers also showed a propensity to endorse land conservation, with 57 percent voter support. So an absence of voter enthusiasm does not seem to account for the relative paucity of local government open space funding in New York.

Hypothesis #2: New York Is a Poor State That Can't Afford Open Space Spending According to the U.S. Census Bureau, 1999 median household income in New Jersey topped the United States at $55,146. New York was nineteenth at $43,393, so the average household is appreciably less well off than in New Jersey. But even looking at wealthier areas of New York, there is no consistent spending on land conservation. In the well-to-do downstate region of the Hudson Valley and Long Island, there are seven counties where median household income levels top $50,000, yet none has passed ballot measures or dedicated taxes for open space other than Suffolk County. Furthermore, many areas of New Jersey with lower incomes have enacted open space trust funds, including Hudson County at $40,293 and Cape May County at $41,591. So income levels do not explain the very different patterns evident in the two states.

Hypothesis #3: New York Is Less Urbanized and Has Less Sprawl and Therefore Has Less Need to Protect Open Space New Jersey is the nation's most urbanized state, with 96 percent of its population living in what the Census Bureau defines as urban areas. Sprawling growth and diminished open space/farmland have been common for decades in many parts of New Jersey. Although New York is a much larger state with many rural areas, it does have significant areas experiencing sprawl and loss of open space. But areas of New York that are comparable to New Jersey have not responded with similar funding for land conservation. Some people point to Nassau County, Long Island, as the epitome of sprawl. Home to Levittown and similar post–World War II housing developments, the county is almost fully "built out." Yet neither the county nor any of its towns has a dedicated open space tax, although the county had its first-ever open space bond measure on the November 2004 ballot that was approved by voters.

The preceding hypotheses do little to explain why local governments in New Jersey and New York differ so much in their participation in conservation finance ballot measures or their proclivity to dedicate taxes for open space. We believe the primary reason that New Jersey and New York differ so sharply is that each state has a very different state policy framework in support of land conservation.

The New Jersey Model

New Jersey's success is a direct reflection of a policy framework—a set of policies—that encourages broad participation by local governments in dedicating taxes for open space by passing conservation finance ballot measures. The elements of this policy framework are as follows:

- New Jersey grants local governments the authority to establish a dedicated fund for open space using the property tax.
- In addition, the state makes a substantial and reliable annual investment in providing matching funds, which is a compelling incentive for local governments to tax themselves for land conservation.
- Finally, New Jersey presents its spending proposals for land conservation at all levels of government to its voters: this has created a political culture that supports public investments in land conservation funds.

This combination of policies has provided local governments the opportunity and the incentive—as well as the political backing—to become full partners with the state in promoting land conservation.

Enabling Authority for Local Governments to Establish a Dedicated Open Space Tax   In 1989, New Jersey passed legislation that enabled all local governments—counties and municipalities—to establish "open space trust funds" that were paid for with a modest increase in the property tax. The referendum process established the funds, requiring a simple majority to pass. Today, all twenty-one counties and nearly two hundred municipalities have established an open space trust fund by referendum, with ten counties having approved at least one subsequent tax increase.[1] Morris County tops the list with twenty-eight municipalities having their own open space tax, followed by Bergen County, with twenty, and Hunterdon and Monmouth Counties with fifteen apiece (see table 4.2).[2]

Table 4.2.

New Jersey County Open Space Taxes: County Tax Rates and Adoption Dates

County	Date of Approval or Increase	Rate (cents/$100)	Revenue Raised (2002)
Warren	1993/1999/2002	6 cents	$4,878,931
Morris	1992/1998/2001	5.25 cents	$27,888,486
Burlington	1996/1998	4 cents	$11,191,009
Somerset	1989/1997	3 cents	$12,113,460
Middlesex	1995/2001	3 cents	$18,270,453
Monmouth	1987/1996/2002	2.7 cents	$16,000,000
Salem	2002	2 cents	N/A
Mercer	1989/1998	2 cents	$5,606,658
Atlantic	1990/1998	2 cents	$5,014,625
Gloucester	1993/2000	2 cents	$3,002,960
Sussex	2000	up to 2 cents	$2,204,694
Hunterdon	1999	1–3 cents	$5,278,000
Union	2000	1.5 cents	$6,959,156
Bergen	1998/2003	1.5 cents	$5,404,355
Ocean	1997	1.2 cents	$6,252,000
Passaic	1996	1 cent	$3,129,426
Camden	1998	1 cent	$2,344,411
Cape May	1989	1 cent	$2,369,000
Cumberland	1994	1 cent	$513,844
Essex	1998	1 cent	$5,316,636
Hudson	2003	1 cent	N/A

Source

New Jersey Department of Environmental Protection (http://www.state.nj.us/
dep/greenacres/coprograms.htm) and New Jersey Division of Local Government
Services (http://www.state.nj.us/dca/lgs/taxes/02_data/02taxmenu.shtml).

A successful referendum enables the local governing body to levy a tax annually, in any increment, up to a ceiling specified in the ballot question (e.g., up to 2 cents per $100 of assessed valuation). These ballot measures are technically "only advisory" in nature, but in practice, local governments adopt open space taxes equal to the maximum allowable levy. The local governing body may change the amount of the annual levy through passage of a new ballot measure.[3]

Although the idea of dedicating a portion of a local government tax for open space protection seems simple enough, in other states it is not common. It is often difficult to accomplish (requiring a charter amendment or supermajority vote) or is not even permitted by the state constitution or statute.

Those states that do allow a dedicated tax for open space often use the sales tax, the real estate transfer tax, or something even more specialized. The sales tax can be awkward because it typically adjusts by large increments, it can be controversial, and it may raise more money than a community is currently seeking. The real estate transfer tax and other specialized taxes generate opposition from representatives of those narrow sectors of the economy that feel the brunt of these taxes. In contrast, the property tax usually adjusts in very small increments, and its base is quite broad, thus raising a fair amount of money without generating too much pain for anyone.

In New Jersey, the referendums on open space property tax increases always take place in a November election. This almost always ensures a high turnout, which means that a broad spectrum of voters will decide the matter, and there is much less danger that a small opposition group will engineer a defeat.

In all respects, the structure set forth in New Jersey's enabling legislation has proven to be ideal: (1) it provides authority to all levels of local government to create a dedicated open space fund, (2) enactment through referendum requires a simple majority at a November election, and (3) the use of the property tax allows for modest and completely flexible increments of adjustment.

Reliable State Matching Funds The enabling legislation may provide the "how," but it is the remarkable set of state financial incentives offered by New Jersey that provides much of the "why."

Any jurisdiction that adopts an open space trust fund and submits an open space plan that the state approves is virtually assured of receiving substantial "Green Acres Planning Incentive" matching funds. After state approval of the open space plan, a local government can acquire lands identified in its plan without having to file grant applications for each parcel. Eligible local governments may receive grants for as much as 50 percent of a project's costs.

Permanent funding for New Jersey's Planning Incentive Grant program, and the whole range of the state's land conservation programs, was secured in November 1998, when voters approved (by a 2 to 1 margin) a constitutional amendment that dedicated $98 million a year from the state sales tax throughout a period of thirty years for land conservation, farmland preservation, and historic preservation. By bonding against a portion of this revenue stream, the state will be able to invest nearly $200 million per year in the decade between 2000 and 2009.

Despite the significant level of funding from the state, the popularity of local open space trust funds is so high that eligible projects exceed the available funding for Green Acres. For this reason, the Department of Environmental Protection recently added a new source of support to local governments for meeting their land conservation goals. Through New Jersey's Environmental Infrastructure Financing Program (EIFP), local governments may borrow money from the state. The EIFP is a low-cost (currently one-quarter market rate) loan program that is available to provide financial assistance for projects that protect or improve water quality, which is typically the case with land conservation projects. In recent years, the EIFP has become an important resource for open space preservation in New Jersey.[4]

The Trust for Public Land frequently conducts public opinion surveys in local communities to evaluate voter interest in increasing government funding for land conservation. The opportunity to receive matching funds is almost always one of the most important considerations in deciding to support a local measure. In a national poll conducted for TPL by the Mellman Group and American Viewpoint in 1999, the promise of a state matching grant increased support among likely voters for a 1 percent increase in the local property tax from 46 to 55 percent.[5]

New Jersey's "Political Culture of Conservation"   The extensive use of the ballot box to consider land conservation funding in New Jersey has undoubtedly been at least partly responsible for the state's highly motivated electorate and highly responsive public officials. In 1961, New Jersey created the Green Acres program to preserve New Jersey's natural, historical, and cultural heritage. From 1961 to 1995, voters overwhelmingly approved nine separate state bond issues, generating $1.39 billion for the state's Green Acres and Farmland Preservation programs.[6] Then, in 1989, the enabling legislation for local open space trust funds unleashed a torrent of more than 250 ballot measures, in every county in the state, with a success rate that historically has exceeded 80 percent. In years when a state open space funding program is on the ballot, many voters have the option to approve three separate funding measures at the same election through a state bond, a county trust fund tax, and a town or borough trust fund tax. And usually they say yes to all three.

Placing funding decisions before the voters makes land conservation funding part of the political discourse. Voters want to know how the money will be spent, and government officials explain why the money is needed. When voters approve a measure—as they usually do in New Jersey—government officials are rewarded and encouraged to think about renewing or increasing the funding, when the appropriate time comes. After a piece of land is purchased, the new owner typically places signs on the property identifying the funding source, so New Jersey voters also see the tangible reward for their tax payments.

The frequency and success rate of ballot measures for open space funding in New Jersey have educated the voters and motivated its elected officials, creating a political culture that favors land conservation. This culture set the stage for passage of a remarkable 1998 state constitutional amendment championed by Governor Christine Todd Whitman, which dedicates nearly $100 million per year, for thirty years, in support of land conservation and parks, farmland preservation, and historical preservation. The goal of that measure is to protect 50 percent of the state's remaining privately owned open land.

Is New Jersey a Special Case?   As described in the preceding comparison of New Jersey and New York, New Jersey is the wealthiest and most densely developed state in the country. Framed by the major cities of New York and Philadelphia, New Jersey has been battling metropolitan sprawl from both directions for decades. When the New Jersey model is used in other parts of the country, does the amount of local government funding dedicated to land conservation similarly increase?

Our research shows that states in other parts of the country that have a policy framework similar to New Jersey's are the most active in dedicating local funds for land conservation. States that lack elements of this structure accomplish much less. Furthermore, there is ample evidence that people of widely different politics, incomes, and races will support new government spending for land conservation when given the choice.

Outside of New Jersey, Florida and Colorado are the two states with the most active history of voter-approved funding for land conservation in the period of 1999 to 2003, according to LandVote data. As we would predict, both states share elements of the New Jersey framework: some type of authority that local governments have to dedicate funds, financial incentives from the state to encourage local participation, and a reliance on the ballot box to enact the measures.

In Colorado, between 1999 and 2003, voters approved fifty-four of sixty-four, or 84 percent, of open space ballot measures across the state, from the fast-growing Denver suburbs to rural southeastern Colorado to fiscally conservative parts of the Western Slope. These measures will raise approximately $1.5 billion. Overall, eighteen of sixty-three counties in Colorado (29 percent) have passed conservation finance measures. This broad participation stems from several factors. Local governments in Colorado have a range of conservation funding mechanisms—the sales tax, property tax, and general obligation bonds—and are eligible to receive grants from the state's Great Outdoors Colorado (GOCO) program for up to 75 percent of the cost of a land conservation project. GOCO's funding has been reliable, with 50 percent of the Colorado Lottery's proceeds directed into the fund. Residents can vote on all bonds and dedicated taxes for open space at the local level; the GOCO program itself has come before the voters twice.

The Florida Communities Trust (FCT) program, part of the larger Florida Forever program, has been instrumental in encouraging local governments to pass local ballot measures. The Florida legislature established Florida Forever as a ten-year authorization of $300 million annually in revenue bonds for a range of land conservation programs. FCT, which provides competitively awarded grants to local governments and nonprofits, receives 22 percent, or $66 million, annually. Because most applicants are required to provide a local match of at least 25 percent of a project's cost (for 2003, the average local match was 40 percent), local governments have been inspired to approve their own conservation finance measures. At present, twenty-seven of Florida's sixty-seven counties (40 percent) have approved conservation finance ballot measures. Most have been general obligation bonds, but counties also have the ability to allocate part of a county infrastructure sales tax for parks and open space. Local general obligation bonds and the infrastructure sales tax are both subject to voter approval.

Barnstable County, Massachusetts, which is on Cape Cod, offers a particularly interesting example. After years of efforts to create a county "land bank" there, modeled on the experience of Nantucket and Martha's Vineyard, the state legislature finally gave voters a chance to approve a real estate transfer tax for land conservation (the type of funding source used in the nearby island communities). Voting took place at a special election in January of 1998. Fierce opposition, backed by some real estate interests, coupled with a low-turnout election, led to a loss. The Trust for Public Land encouraged local supporters to consider the New Jersey model, and they agreed. The state legislature amended the enabling legislation to rely on the property tax, a state matching fund was offered, and the measure was placed on the November 1998 ballot—a general election with high turnout. Just ten months after a devastating loss, every one of fifteen towns in Barnstable County approved the land bank tax, even though it meant a whopping 3 percent increase in property taxes.

At the other extreme is the case of California. Despite its reputation as a liberal state with an electorate that cares deeply about the environment, with considerable wealth, and with widespread concerns about sprawling development, local governments in California rarely dedicate funding for open space protection. Why? A constitutional amendment in 1978—Proposition 13—prohibits local governments from issuing bonds or dedicating taxes for any special purpose without the support of two thirds of the electorate. When it comes to local conservation finance, no other state in the nation faces such a high hurdle.

Conservation Finance Measures Succeed in the Most Unlikely Places

Although conventional wisdom may hold that local conservation finance ballot measures succeed only in resort communities or affluent, suburban, liberal areas, this is not the case. Ballot measures have been approved by voters in conservative areas, such as Colorado Springs, Salt Lake City, and Kendall County, Illinois. Rural voters in Gallatin County, Montana, and Carroll County, Georgia, have approved measures, and voters in heavily nonwhite, lower-income urban areas, such as Hudson County, New Jersey, and Dade County, Florida, have also approved them (see table 4.3).

In November 2002, statewide exit polls showed that Latinos and other communities of color and low-income individuals were among the biggest supporters of California's Proposition 40, the largest resource bond in U.S. history, with $2.6 billion for parks, clean water, and clean air. Proposition 40 passed with the support of 77 percent of African American voters, 74 percent of Latino voters, 60 percent of Asian American/Pacific Islander voters, and 56 percent of white voters. Of voters making less than $20,000 per year, 75 percent supported Proposition 40, and 61 percent with a high school diploma or less supported the measure.[7]

Applying the New Jersey Model to Other States

New Jersey leads the way in funding for local conservation finance ballot measures. How do other states stack up in comparison? How does a state's current local funding compare with the funding that it could have if policies similar to New Jersey's were in place? The Trust for Public Land developed a methodology, using a combination of LandVote data for the period 1999–2003 and Census Bureau data, to answer these questions. Projections were developed for North Carolina and Rhode Island—as examples to show how this methodology can be applied to a state—as well as for the United States overall.

We at the Trust for Public Land chose LandVote as the primary data source for this project because it offered the only comprehensive collection of information on local conservation finance.

Table 4.3.

Conservation Ballot Measures in "Unlikely" Places

Jurisdiction	Date of Vote	Pass/Fail	Fiscal Technique	Total Funds (Million $)	Conservation Funds (Million $)
Dade County, Florida	Nov. 1996	Pass	General obligation bond	200	25
Colorado Springs, Colorado	Apr. 1997	Pass	Sales tax	80	60
Gallatin County, Montana	Nov. 2000	Pass	General obligation bond	10	10
Kendall County, Illinois	Nov. 2002	Pass	General obligation bond	5	5
Colorado Springs, Colorado	Apr. 2003	Pass	Sales tax extension	80	60
Salt Lake City, Utah	Nov. 2003	Pass	General obligation bond	5.4	5.4
Hudson County, New Jersey	Nov. 2003	Pass	Property tax	40	40
Carroll County, Georgia	Nov. 2003	Pass	Sales tax	79.8	19.5

Source

The Trust for Public Land LandVote Database (www.landvote.org).

LandVote does not include local conservation spending that is enacted solely by legislatures, but in our experience, ballot measures raise the vast majority of funding for these initiatives—we estimate 90 percent or more. LandVote tracks funding authorized by voters for land conservation, not actual spending or tax collections by local governments. There is no comprehensive source of information on local government spending or tax collections related to land conservation.

LandVote tracks two major types of conservation funding measures: (1) "pay as you go" measures, such as sales, property, and real estate transfer taxes, and (2) bond measures. With the first type of measure, LandVote counts the estimated revenue generated for the duration of the tax. When the tax is not limited to a specific term, a period of twenty years is used to generate the figure (this is comparable to the average duration of bond repayments). In all cases, the total funds generated throughout the life of the measure are conservatively estimated and do not reflect likely increases in the tax base. When a measure increases an existing tax, LandVote counts only the value of the added increment. For bond measures, LandVote counts only the face value of the bonds authorized, rather than the higher value of total future taxes that will be collected to pay interest in addition to principal.

According to LandVote, between 1999 and 2003, New Jersey voters approved approximately $1.6 billion in new local land conservation funding, or roughly $80 million per year, based on the twenty-year estimate already cited. With a 2001 population of 8.5 million, per capita annual funding in New Jersey on land conservation arising from these measures equals $9.40. Because New Jersey is the nation's most affluent state, the methodology adjusts the per capita funding down for each other state and for the United States overall, based on the ratio of the entity's income relative to New Jersey (see table 4.4, step 1). To get a projection comparable with that of New Jersey, we multiply the adjusted per capita funding by the share of the population located in urban areas (see table 4.4, steps 2 and 3). We make this adjustment because evidence from LandVote suggests that the large majority of local ballot measures occur in urbanized jurisdictions. Finally, we compare the actual funding collected between 1999 and 2003, as reported by Land-Vote, with projections using the New Jersey model (see table 4.4, step 4).

To see how this methodology would apply to an individual state, let's examine Rhode Island. Like New Jersey, Rhode Island has dense urban centers surrounded by sprawling suburbs, yet it also retains a sizable agricultural sector, heavily forested rural areas that protect its drinking water sources, and an unspoiled coastline. Its residents also have a passion for land conservation, approving many statewide open space bond measures by large margins throughout the past few decades. The most recent was a $34 million bond approved in 2000. In addition, voters approved

Table 4.4.

The New Jersey Model Applied to Other States and the Nation

Step 1: Adjust New Jersey annual funding per capita based on income ratio

According to TPL's LandVote database, New Jersey funding equals $80 million per year, or $9.40 per capita; New Jersey median household income: $55,146.

State	Household Income: Median (1999)	Income Ratio: State Income/NJ Income	Income Adjusted: Annual Funding/Capita
Rhode Island	$42,091	76%	$7.17
North Carolina	$39,184	71%	$6.68
United States	$41,994	76%	$7.16

Step 2: Determine share of population in metropolitan areas

(Note: Urban population share is used as a proxy.)

State	Total Population	Urban Population Share: 2000 Census	Metropolitan Population
Rhode Island	1,058,920	90%	953,028
North Carolina	8,186,268	60%	4,911,761
United States	293,000,000	79%	231,470,000

Step 3: Apply funding per capita to metropolitan population to estimate annual funding based on the New Jersey model

State	Income Adjusted: Annual Funding/Capita	Metropolitan Population	Annual Projected Funding with NJ Model
Rhode Island	$7.17	953,028	$6,837,680
North Carolina	$6.68	4,911,761	$32,806,494
United States	$7.16	231,470,000	$1,656,898,072

Step 4: Compare actual funding from 1999 to 2003 with potential under New Jersey model

State	Annual Projected Funding with NJ Model	20-Year Projection with NJ Model	Actual Funding: 1999–2003
Rhode Island	$6,837,680	$136,753,590	$20,300,000
North Carolina	$32,806,494	$656,129,870	$289,330,000
United States	$1,656,898,072	$33,137,961,445	$8,838,015,343

Sources

Funding per capita: TPL LandVote database (http://www.landvote.org); household income: Census 2000 State and County Quick Facts (http://quickfacts.census.gov/qfd/); population estimates: U.S. Census Bureau National and State population estimates (http://www.census.gov/popest/states/NST-EST2003-ann-est.html); urban share: Census 2000 Summary File 3 Urban and Rural Population, Table 5 (http://factfinder.census.gov/servlet/DatasetMainPageServlet?_program=DEC&lang=en).

all seventeen local measures that came to the ballot between 1999 and 2003.

Although Rhode Island has much in common with New Jersey, it would be unreasonable to expect Rhode Island to fund land conservation at the same level as New Jersey, because it has considerably lower household incomes and a slightly lower share of its population in urban areas. Starting with New Jersey's annual funding per capita of $9.40, we adjust this down to $7.17, because Rhode Island's median household income of $42,091 (1999) is 76 percent of New Jersey's. We multiply this income-adjusted figure by the population living in urban areas: 953,028 (in New Jersey, almost 100 percent of the population lives in urban areas). We thus obtain an annual projection of $6.84 million using the New Jersey model. Throughout twenty years, this would multiply to $137 million, more than six times the $20.3 million in actual funding approved during the 1999–2003 period documented by LandVote (see table 4.4). In other words, we believe that, if Rhode Island were to adopt a policy framework identical to New Jersey's, local government spending on land conservation would increase sixfold in Rhode Island in some reasonable period of time.

Based on recent LandVote spending data, North Carolina came closer to the projections yielded by the New Jersey model (see table 4.4). Between 1999 and 2003, North Carolina local governments passed ballot measures totaling $289 million; the New Jersey model reveals a potential of $656 million. Nationwide, $8.8 billion was raised through local ballot measures, compared with $33 billion that would have been raised if every state had a framework comparable to New Jersey's. According to these figures, there are significant opportunities to expand conservation funding in the United States.

Conclusion

Momentum behind conservation finance measures at the local and state levels continues to grow from year to year. LandVote data make it clear that "Americans care deeply about parks and other special places and they will raise their own taxes to protect them."[8] These tax increases have generated billions of dollars for the preservation of open space across the nation throughout the past several years.

New Jersey certainly stands out as a bellwether for states and communities to look to as a model for conservation finance. New Jersey's example provides a clear and robust framework for what policies offer the greatest likelihood for success as other states strive to achieve similar goals of open space preservation. Land-Vote's recent report states that "while laws and practices vary widely in the 50 states, virtually any community can enact a ballot measure to increase local open space funding. Success usually depends on a strong commitment to open space, local leadership, and sustained hard work over a long period of time."[9] Although the full potential for conservation funding has not yet been achieved, innovative policies and creative programs are moving communities and states toward the achievement of that goal.

Notes

[1]New Jersey Department of Environmental Protection, "Green Acres Program: County Open Space Tax Programs," available at http://www.state.nj.us/dep/greenacres/coprograms.htm.

[2]New Jersey Department of Environmental Protection, "Green Acres Program: New Jersey Local Government Open Space Funding Programs," available at www.state.nj.us/dep/greenacres/taxsummary.htm.

[3]New Jersey Permanent Statute, Title 40:12–15.1.

[4]New Jersey Department of Environmental Protection, "Green Acres Program: Planning Incentive Land Acquisition Application," available at www.state.nj.us/dep/greenacres/planincent.doc.

[5]The Mellman Group and American Viewpoint, national poll (sample 800) for The Trust for Public Land, June 1999.

[6]The Trust for Public Land and the Association of New Jersey Environmental Commissions, *A Handbook for Public Financing of Open Space in New Jersey*, Mendham, New Jersey: Association of New Jersey Environmental Commissions, December 2001, 7.

[7]Robert Garcia, Erica S. Flores, and Elizabeth Pine, *Dreams of Fields: Soccer, Community and Equal Justice: Report on Sports in Urban Parks to the California Department of Parks and Recreation*, Santa Monica, California, Center for Law in the Public Interest, December 2002, available at http://www.clipi.org/images/Dreams_of_Fields.pdf.

[8]The Trust for Public Land and Land Trust Alliance, *Americans Invest in Parks & Open Space: LandVote 2003* (February 2004), 2, available at http://www.tpl.org/tier3_cdl.cfm?content_item_id=12030&folder_id=2406.

[9]The Trust for Public Land and Land Trust Alliances, *LandVote 2003*, 2.

Chapter 5

External Revolving Loan Funds
Expanding Interim Financing
for Land Conservation

Mary McBryde, Peter R. Stein, and Story Clark

Located in the Pine Barrens region of New Jersey and comprising approximately 9,400 acres, the "Heart of the Pines" has outstanding natural and ecological values, including pristine streams and wetlands, upland forests, and exceptional wildlife habitat. The property also is surrounded by five existing state-owned protected preserves comprising thousands of acres (see figure 5.1). With such remarkable conservation values, the New Jersey Conservation Foundation was determined to conserve the property when the opportunity arose. In late 2004, with a looming year-end deadline to acquire the Heart of the Pines, the foundation approached the Open Space Institute about providing a short-term loan to secure the property. The Open Space Institute, through its New Jersey Conservation Loan Fund, agreed and awarded a $1.5 million loan. With the loan in hand, the organization had enough time to arrange for the necessary long-term take-out funding. Without such interim financing, this—and many other important land conservation projects across the nation—might not be possible.

Limited financial resources, rising costs of land, and time-sensitive projects that require immediate capital, such as the Heart of the Pines project, have made interim financing (also called bridge financing) an integral component of many land conservation

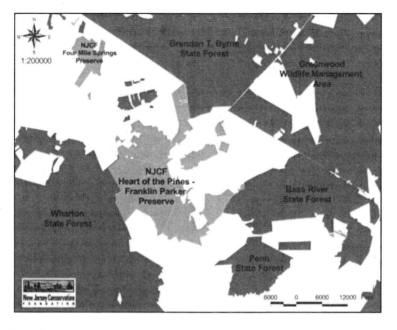

Figure 5.1.

Heart of the Pines–Franklin Parker Preserve: In 2003, the New Jersey Conservation Foundation preserved 9,400 acres of wilderness in New Jersey's Pine Barrens, connecting 250,000 acres of public lands. (Courtesy of New Jersey Conservation Foundation, www.njconservation.org.)

transactions. This type of financing closes the gap between short-term funding needs (e.g., arising when a property is threatened and funds must be acquired in a short period of time) and the availability of permanent (or at least longer-term) funding. Interim financing allows conservation organizations to play on a more even footing with nonconservation-oriented buyers that have access to "ready" capital. Additionally, because interim financing enables a quick response, an organization can pursue its priorities based on conservation significance rather than opportunity and available funding. This encourages a more proactive and strategic approach to land conservation, helping to ensure that limited conservation dollars are allocated to the highest-priority projects.

As interim financing must be repaid, the borrowing organization must be capable of developing and implementing a financial plan. The organization must instill confidence in its interim lenders by showing that it has a good financial track record. And ultimately, it must have the capacity to secure take-out funding (that is, funding that "takes out" the interim lender) and retire the interim debt in a timely manner. These requirements pose significant challenges for some conservation organizations—particularly those with limited or no financial and/or transaction experience. Despite these challenges, interim financing is, at present, of considerable interest to a wide range of conservation organizations and could play a greater role in facilitating land conservation transactions in the future.

A variety of entities and mechanisms provide interim financing, including charitable guarantors, conservation investors, conservation buyers, banks, personal loans, direct program related investments (PRIs), and revolving loan funds. All of these tools are important and are being utilized to varying degrees. This chapter focuses on one increasingly important financial tool: external revolving loan funds. These funds are dedicated pools of capital held by nonprofit organizations specifically to provide short-term (often low-interest) loans for land conservation to multiple organizations with a shared geographic focus or overlapping conservation goals.

Internal and External Funds

Generally, a revolving loan fund is used for a variety of purposes, including the acquisition of land, the acquisition of conservation easements, the purchase of options, or the payment of transactions costs. Traditionally, revolving loan funds have been established *internally*—that is, by a single organization creating a capital reserve to complete its high-priority, time-sensitive projects. Many such internal loan funds exist across the country. One of the most widely known is The Nature Conservancy's (TNC) Land Preservation Fund. The Land Preservation Fund is administered at TNC's national office and lends primarily to TNC chapter offices. The fund is capitalized with $250 million in charitable donations and $300 million in external debt (bonds).[1] A second example of an internal loan fund is the regional loan fund being created by the Vermont Land Trust (VLT) as part of its capital campaign. The loan fund will provide VLT with short-term financing for its own high-priority conservation projects.

An emerging and increasingly important type of revolving loan fund offers loans *externally*, to multiple organizations. These external loan funds provide short-term capital to organizations that have an immediate funding need, often entities that have limited or no internal reserves and that lack access to a national pool of capital or other sources of interim financing. As illustrated in the preceding Heart of the Pines example, external loan funds play an important role for organizations such as the New Jersey Conservation Foundation that have an urgent need for short-term financing. The presence of an external loan fund in a region that has traditionally lacked interim financing can be a catalyst for a variety of conservation organizations to pursue high-priority, time-sensitive projects that may otherwise be lost. Some revolving loan funds serve dual purposes of providing interim financing both internally and externally.

In regions where land conservation organizations have interest and capacity to borrow funds and where take-out financing is available, external loan funds have a much greater probability of success. The availability of ready and inexpensive capital can facilitate many land transactions, including complex transactions with multiple funding sources and multiple partners. Because of their multiorganizational reach, external loan funds increase the likelihood that a greater number of organizations will, individually or collectively, develop or strengthen the skills necessary to become competent borrowers and conduct more sophisticated land transactions. Additionally, the presence of such funds offers the promise of helping conservation organizations to identify and prioritize overlapping goals for a region.

Several external (or internal/external) loan funds are discussed in this chapter, including the Great Lakes Revolving Loan Fund, the Colorado Tax Credit Transaction Cost Loan Program, the Maine Coast Heritage Trust Land Acquisition Revolving Loan Fund, the New Jersey Conservation Loan Fund, the Greater Yellowstone Ecosystem Revolving Loan Fund, the Lowcountry Conservation Loan Fund, and the Greater Yellowstone Loan Fund.[2]

Borrowing Funds: Potential Challenges

As previously noted, although the availability of interim financing from external loan funds offers many benefits, utilizing such funds (as well as other sources of interim financing) can be challenging for some conservation organizations. The reasons are as follows:

- Because interim loans from external sources must typically be repaid, the borrowing organization must secure permanent or longer-term public and/or private take-out funding. This can be a competitive and complex process, particularly given the unpredictability of public funding and limited access to private dollars. It requires specific skills and knowledge, including an understanding of financial planning techniques as well as an ability to make realistic projections about the availability of take-out sources. These skills, although increasing, are not commonplace across the conservation community.
- The process typically requires a borrowing organization to have financial resources to cover the upfront acquisition expenses (title, survey, due diligence, legal), the borrowing costs, and costs associated with activities often necessary to acquire permanent funding (e.g., underwriting participation in meetings or trips with political officials or representatives of other organizations).
- External interim lenders often require collateral (or some other form of guarantee) as security. With secured collateral or a loan guarantee, the lender has greater confidence in the loan and a higher probability of being repaid should the borrowing organization default on the loan. Collateral, however, must be chosen carefully, so as to prevent an important conservation property from being lost in a foreclosure. Among conservation organizations, there is a high degree of variability regarding their ability and willingness to provide collateral or guarantees, whether the source is the conservation property, other real estate, third-party guarantors, or other organizational assets. In some cases an organization may not be able to provide any source of collateral or guarantee, and less traditional forms of security, such as partnering with an organization with greater financial assets, may be possible.
- The greater risks and responsibilities associated with borrowing funds can be a deterrent for those organizations with an aversion to risk.

- Ideally, borrowers should have substantial "field" capacity, including staff, expertise, skills, and technical know-how, that is necessary to conduct land or conservation easement acquisitions or be able to partner with other organizations with such resources. Additionally, lenders are likely to hold conservation organizations to a high standard of due diligence review on every loan application.

Despite these challenges, greater use of external loan funds could occur across a spectrum of conservation organizations, including those that currently borrow only from traditional sources, such as banks; those that have the capability to borrow but are averse to risk; and those that are motivated to borrow but lack the skills or confidence to do so.

Although external revolving loan funds share the same general purpose of providing interim financing to multiple conservation organizations for a range of conservation purposes, they may differ in several key ways, including administrative structure, source of capitalization, and geographic scale.

Administrative Structure

Many types of conservation organizations are administering external revolving loan funds, from statewide land trusts to national conservation organizations to community foundations to conservation intermediary organizations. Notwithstanding their diversity, these entities often have significant financial capacity, as well as staff and board members with extensive financial and/or land transaction expertise. In some situations, such lending organizations are capable of providing technical assistance to borrowers. It allows more experienced organizations to share their skills and knowledge with organizations that are less experienced with complex financial transactions and increases the capacity and competency of its borrowers. When financial knowledge is shared in this manner, complex projects are more likely to be pursued and completed.

Consider, for example, the Maine Coast Heritage Trust (MCHT), one of the oldest and largest land trusts in Maine. MCHT administers a regional revolving loan fund, the Maine Coast Heritage Trust Land Acquisition Revolving Fund, which provides short-term loans both externally to local land trusts, municipalities, and other qualified nonprofits and government entities working to complete time-sensitive deals, and internally to selected projects conducted by MCHT. In making short-term loans to external organizations, MCHT often has an opportunity to share some of its financial knowledge and skill with borrowing organizations. MCHT's initial decision to make short-term loans to external organizations was driven by its critical need to assist smaller organizations with important projects that demand an immediate response. By expanding the program to make loans externally on an ongoing basis, MCHT is building financial capacity within a community of land trusts and other land conservation groups across Maine. The members of this community are increasingly able to deal with reasonably sophisticated financial transactions.[3]

Another example of an external revolving loan fund is the Great Lakes Revolving Loan Fund (GLRLF), administered by The Conservation Fund (TCF), a leading national conservation organization. The GLRLF was created in 2001, when the Charles Stewart Mott Foundation awarded a $3.75 million lead grant to TCF to establish a fund that would provide bridge financing to other land conservation organizations in the Great Lakes basin. At the same time that it provided TCF with the capital to launch the GLRLF, the Charles Stewart Mott Foundation made a second $225,000 grant to TCF to provide technical assistance to local partners in the Great Lakes basin, thereby building capacity among its borrowers. As noted in The Conservation Fund press release: "These two grants bring much needed conservation capital to the nation's most significant freshwater ecosystem, while providing on-the-ground assistance to nonprofit and public partners."[4] In 2002, the Conservation Foundation received an additional grant of $2 million from the Charles Stewart Mott Foundation to support the revolving loan fund. GLRLF funds are available for acquiring property or conservation easements in the U.S. portions of the Great Lakes basin and for two specific types of transactions: direct loans to land trusts and advance purchases of land in partnership with public agencies or nonprofits. The GLRLF provided its first loan in 2001 to a local land trust, the North Woods Conservancy, to help protect Seven Mile Point on Michigan's Keweenaw Peninsula.[5] A second loan was awarded in 2002 to The Nature Conservancy to assist with the protection of more than "6,000 acres of pristine forest and wetlands on Michigan's Keweenaw Peninsula."[6]

There is at least one example of a new approach—a community foundation administering an external revolving loan fund—that is currently being tested in South Carolina. The Lowcountry Conservation Loan Fund is an example of such a fund. It was established in 2002 with grants to The Community Foundation Serving Coastal South Carolina (now the Coastal Community Foundation of South Carolina) made by the Merck Family Fund and the Dorothy and Gaylord Donnelley Foundation. The two donor organizations made matching grants of $500,000 to the community foundation to create a revolving loan fund that would provide interim financing to conservation organizations in the Lowcountry to protect the region's most important lands (see figure 5.2).[7]

External revolving loans funds are also administered by organizations known as conservation intermediaries. Conservation intermediaries comprise a diverse group of third-party finance organizations that are playing an increasingly important role in land conservation. Intermediaries provide a range of services to foundations and individuals supporting land conservation, as well as the conservation organizations conducting land transactions. In addition to the creation and administration of external revolving loan funds, services provided by conservation intermediaries include advising conservation donors, administering grants or PRIs, relending or regranting conservation dollars to local and regional conservation groups, administrating mitigation funds, and providing technical assistance to conservation organizations.

Intermediaries serve a particularly valuable role in helping foundations and other potential funders to launch effective external revolving loan fund programs. The intermediaries have the necessary staff, expertise, and skill to design and implement external revolving loan fund programs focused on specific regions and programmatic objectives. Additionally, these entities are capable of applying the greater level of scrutiny that is required for loan processing but not typically necessary with traditional grantmaking. To varying degrees, the funders and the borrowing organizations rely on the intermediaries to conduct project-specific due diligence, assess risk, evaluate conservation proposals, provide technical assistance, make specific decisions about the distribution of funds, and

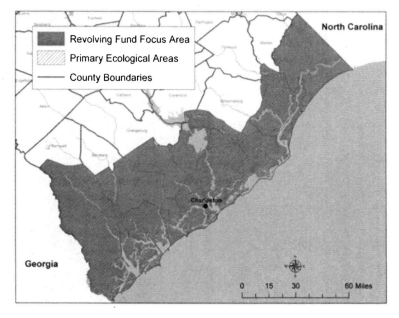

Figure 5.2.

The Lowcountry Conservation Loan Fund provides interim financing to land conservation organizations in the Lowcountry region of South Carolina to conserve the region's most important ecological, wildlife, scenic, and recreational lands. The Primary Ecological Areas shown here were derived from the "Coastal Focus Areas" data set developed by the USFWS S.C. in conjunction with other partners of the Focus Area Task Force. (Map developed by Ben Silberfarb, LTC Conservation Advisory Services.)

secure loan repayments. The results are reduced administrative and technical responsibilities for the funder and the establishment of direct and ongoing relationships between the intermediary and the conservation community.

Several conservation intermediaries currently administering external revolving loan funds are the Colorado Conservation Trust, Conservation Resources, Inc., the Open Space Institute, and Resources Legacy Fund.[8] The Colorado Conservation Trust (CCT) is similar in structure to a general purpose community foundation, except it is solely focused on conserving Colorado's natural resources, including the open spaces, agricultural lands, wildlife habitat, rivers, and scenic corridors. CCT provides a range of services to both funders and conservation partners working in its areas of interest. CCT currently administers two external revolving loan funds, both recently established: the Conservation Easement Tax Credit Transaction Cost Loan Program and the Land Protection Loan Fund. The transaction program provides loans of up to $20,000 to qualified nonprofit land trusts in Colorado to help cover transaction costs incurred when landowners are in the process of donating a conservation easement, in anticipation of receiving a cash payment from the sale of state income tax credits. The Land Protection Loan Fund was created to provide critical interim financing for protection of high-priority open lands. These are the first such funds to operate in Colorado.[9]

The Open Space Institute (OSI) is another type of intermediary that protects scenic, natural, and historic landscapes in several regions, including New Jersey, the Greater Hudson Valley, the northern forest (Maine, New York, Vermont, and New Hampshire), western Massachusetts, and the southern Appalachians. OSI is a different model because it acts directly, through its own land or conservation easement acquisition programs, and indirectly, by administering creative interim financing programs, including loan funds. One such loan fund administered by OSI, as noted earlier in this chapter, is the New Jersey Conservation Loan Fund (NJCLF), which provided a short-term loan to protect the Heart of the Pines property. The NJCLF, as described by OSI, "provides short-term low-interest bridge loans to nonprofit conservation organizations to help with the permanent protection of New Jersey's remaining open space. The fund was launched in January 2003 with a $2.5 million PRI from the Geraldine R. Dodge Foundation; the William Penn Foundation subsequently invested an additional $1 million; and OSI has also committed a portion of its own capital to the fund." As of January 2005, the fund had made six loans totaling $3,935,100, to protect more than ten thousand acres, valued at more than $45 million.[10]

Source of Capitalization

Several methods have been employed for funding the organization, capitalization, and ongoing operations of external revolving loan funds. These include grant funding and PRIs from foundations and private charitable contributions. As described earlier in this chapter, examples of external revolving loan funds capitalized, at least in part, with grants from foundations include the Great Lakes Revolving Loan Fund and the Lowcountry Conservation Loan Fund. A third example of a grant-funded revolving loan fund is the Greater Yellowstone Loan Fund, established by the Doris Duke Charitable Foundation in 2001 as part of a larger effort to support land conservation in the greater Yellowstone ecosystem (see figure 5.3). Unlike many loan funds, the Greater Yellowstone Loan Fund was not intended to revolve permanently, but was created to provide interim financing for a period of four years, after which time the loan funds could be converted into grants. The Greater Yellowstone Loan Fund was capitalized with $1 million as part of a $2 million grant award for the purpose of acquiring land or conservation easements. The fund is administered by The Conservation Fund and makes low- or no-interest loans to its preapproved conservation partners, including the Teton Regional Land Trust, the Jackson Hole Land Trust, and the Idaho chapter of The Nature Conservancy.

There are several examples of PRIs made by foundations to establish revolving loan funds. The Maine Coast Heritage Trust Land Acquisition Loan Fund was initially capitalized with a $900,000 PRI from the MacArthur Foundation. That PRI has since been repaid, and the fund is now capitalized with donations from individuals, foundations, and corporations.[11] As noted already, the New Jersey Conservation Loan Fund was launched in January 2003 with a $2.5 million PRI from the Geraldine R. Dodge Foundation and later a $1 million PRI from the William Penn Foundation. The Greater Yellowstone Ecosystem Revolving Fund, administered by the Resources Legacy Fund (RLF), was funded in 2004 with a $7 million PRI from the David and Lucile Packard Foundation (the RLF-administered fund for the greater Yellowstone ecosystem is described in the next section; it is not to be confused with the previously described Greater Yellowstone Loan Fund funded by a Doris Duke Charitable Foundation grant in 2001).

Although foundations more commonly use grants to support land conservation than other means, PRIs are slowly being employed by a wider group of funders, in part because they offer foundations a particular set of advantages. PRIs are loans or investments made by a foundation to support a charitable purpose

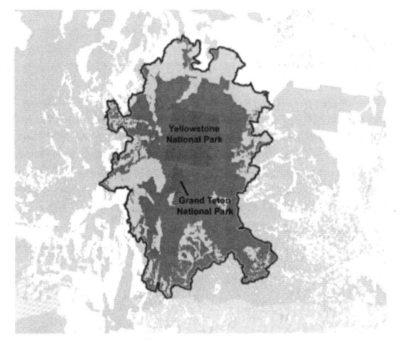

Figure 5.3.

In August 2004, the David and Lucile Packard Foundation awarded a $7 million PRI to the Resources Legacy Fund to create a landscape-scale revolving fund that provides interim financing to designated conservation organizations in the Greater Yellowstone Ecosystem (GYE), shown here in the bold outline. The GYE covers a total of 2.7 million acres; 17.4 million acres are public lands (includes the national parks and other dark gray areas), and 9.6 million acres are privately owned (light gray areas) (Courtesy of GreenInfo Network, www.greeninfo.org.)

identified in the foundation's programmatic goals. Most notably, a foundation can use its corpus, or investment principal, in addition to investment earnings, to fund PRIs. This can enable a foundation to commit far greater resources to land conservation than it might otherwise be able to do and to support land conservation at a much larger scale than possible through traditional grantmaking. Additionally, because PRIs must be repaid, a foundation can recycle conservation dollars and reuse the funds for additional projects, leveraging limited resources and maximizing the impact of foundation support. PRIs typically offer financing at below-market terms, which is likely to be particularly attractive to borrowers, given the competition for and limited availability of conservation dollars.

Because they must be repaid, PRIs impose a higher level of rigor than grants. They demand, of both the lender and borrower, greater accountability, organizational efficiency, and improved accounting and due-diligence practices. In time, greater use of PRIs will result in an increased financial maturity for both lenders and borrowers and may expand the scale of land conservation transactions.

Geographic Scale

It is at the regional or landscape scale that external loan funds may achieve their greatest value. Regional- and landscape-scale revolving loan funds present a new tool for financing, facilitating, and implementing landscape-scale conservation. At this scale, given the diversity and number of conservation projects, lenders seek assurances that conservation dollars are allocated to the most important projects in a landscape. Because an external loan fund is open to multiple organizations there can be a shared interest in making the fund as successful as possible. This creates an opportunity for cross-organizational cooperation and priority setting that, in turn, helps to guarantee the financing of high-priority projects. This potential collaboration between conservation partners can result in a regional- or landscape-scale conservation strategy that is comfortable for lenders, which may mean greater commitments from existing lenders and new funding sources for the region.

One of the most interesting examples of a landscape-scale revolving loan fund is the pioneering effort currently being tested in the Greater Yellowstone Ecosystem. In August 2004, the David and Lucile Packard Foundation awarded a $7 million PRI to the Resources Legacy Fund (RLF) to capitalize the Greater Yellowstone Ecosystem Revolving Loan Fund.[12] This fund was established to provide low-cost bridge financing to multiple conservation organizations in the region for the most critical land transactions. RLF is responsible for the day-to-day implementation as well as the long-term management of the loan fund. RLF has an in-region consultant and they have established a regional advisory committee to assist in the evaluation of potential projects. The first loan was approved in the fall of 2004.

Other Foundation Lending

Some foundations (most notably the Bullitt Foundation, David and Lucile Packard Foundation, Norcross Wildlife Foundation, and MacArthur Foundation) have programs (usually PRIs) that provide direct interim financing for land conservation transactions similar to the revolving loan programs described in this chapter.[13] These programs, however, are technically different from the external loan funds described here, in part because of the different standards that govern such foundation lending. Nevertheless, these programs offer additional and critical sources of interim financing.

For example, the Norcross Wildlife Foundation offers funds to conservation borrowers through the Norcross No-Interest Loan Fund for Land Protection. This fund provides a rare source of financial support: interest-free loans for the acquisition of land (or interests in land) that has priority wildlife habitat.[14] The Norcross program is an example of an effort with a specific ecological focus; some other loan programs have multiple objectives, such as preserving lands that provide clean water, scenic views, and wildlife habitat.

Other foundation-run interim financing efforts include the Packard Foundation's Conserving California Landscapes Initiative, which was launched in 1999 and offers both grants and loans to support land conservation in three high-priority regions of California (the Central Coast, Central Valley, and Sierra Nevada); the Bullitt Foundation's support of loans and grants for land conservation in the Pacific Northwest; and the MacArthur Foundation's ongoing loans to conserve endangered tropical systems.

Looking Forward

Demand for interim financing will continue to grow as land becomes more expensive, the scale of projects increases, market competition intensifies, interest rates rise, organizational sophistication grows, and greater numbers of conservation projects require immediate capital. External revolving loan funds can help to meet the demand for short-term conservation financing. Because they expose a wider segment of the conservation community to a tool that encourages proactive conservation and enables more organizations to pursue time-sensitive projects, external revolving loan funds hold a significant potential to increase the pace and scope of land conservation.

Conservation intermediaries are playing an important role in the creation and administration of many external revolving loan funds and could play an even larger role. A wider acknowledgment and use of these intermediaries may serve as a catalyst for generating additional financial support for land conservation and promoting greater financial sophistication among the land conservation community. It may also be beneficial to create new intermediaries in regions where such third-party lenders do not currently exist but could play a valuable role in facilitating land transactions. The presence of strengthened and expanded intermediaries would likely compel the growth of new regional and landscape loan funds as well as other interim financing tools.

The evolution of land conservation to a landscape scale necessitates a similar evolution in the financial instruments that support land transactions. External revolving loan funds are designed to bring about a more strategic, proactive, and fiscally disciplined approach to conducting land transactions; they are particularly well suited for landscape-scale or regional conservation efforts. In large part, this is also attributable to the potential for external revolving loan funds to stimulate collaboration among conservation organizations and other conservation partners that have a shared interest in the success of a landscape or regional revolving loan fund. This cooperation could be momentous in strengthening existing financial support and attracting new funders to a region— especially for charismatic landscapes, where there is often more funding available than is being tapped. The use of sophisticated financial instruments such as external revolving loan funds, particularly at the landscape and regional scale, holds significant promise for both small and large conservation organizations to grow and evolve. As they engage such financial tools on a greater scale, these organizations will become more dynamic, innovative, risk tolerant, and financially savvy. With such growth and advancement, the conservation community will be increasingly capable of rising to the task of saving the country's most important lands.

Notes

[1]Kevin Schuyler, The Nature Conservancy, personal communication, October 13, 2004.

[2]For more information about these loan funds, see The Conservation Fund, www.conservationfund.org, www.conservationfund.org/?article=2465&back=true; Colorado Conservation Trust, www.colorado conservationtrust.org; Maine Coast Heritage Trust, www.mcht.org; Open Space Institute, www.osiny.org/home.asp; Resources Legacy Fund, www.resourceslegacyfund.org; and Coastal Community Foundation of South Carolina, www.ccfgives.org/. Information regarding the Greater Yellowstone Loan Fund was provided in personal communication, Mark Ellsbree, October 20, 2004.

[3]Maine Coast Heritage Trust, "Revolving Loan Fund Aids Land Conservation," *Land Trust News: The Newsletter of the Maine Land Trust Network*, Summer 2002, available at www.mltn.org/news/ltn_summer_02 .pdf.

[4]The Charles Stewart Mott Foundation, "Revolving Loan Fund to Protect Shorelines of the Great Lakes Basin," January 24, 2002, available at www.mott.org/news/pr-detail.asp?newsid=14. See also The Conservation Fund, "Great Lakes Revolving Loan Fund," available at www .conservationfund.org/?article=2454&back=true.

[5]North Woods Conservancy, "Seven Mile Point," available at www .northwoodsconservancy.org/sevenmile.htm.

[6]The Conservation Fund, "News Release: Revolving Fund Makes Loan, Receives $2 Million Grant," May 31, 2002, available at www .conservationfund.org/?article=2528.

[7]Gaylord and Dorothy Donnelley Foundation, "Conservation Loan Fund a Key Resource for Lowcountry Groups," available at www.gddf.org/ interest/articleDetail.asp?objectID=572. See also www.ccfgives.org/ grantprograms_LCLF.htm.

[8]For more information about these organizations, see the Colorado Conservation Trust, www.coloradoconservationtrust.org; Conservation Resources, Inc., www.conservationresourcesinc.org; Open Space Institute, www.osiny.org/home.asp; and Resources Legacy Fund, www.resources legacyfund.org.

[9]See Colorado Conservation Trust, www.coloradoconservationtrust.org. See also www.coloradoconservationtrust.org/cctprograms/initiatives_

increasefunds.php; and www.coloradoconservationtrust.org/cctprograms/
initiatives_newtools.php.

[10]Open Space Institute, "The New Jersey Conservation Loan Fund: An
Overview," available at www.osiny.org/njclp.asp. Information also provided by personal communication with Peter Howell, January 11, 2005.

[11]See the Land Trust Alliance, "Land Trust Gleanings," www.lta.org/
publications/exchange/exchange_21_02_08.pdf; and the Maine Coast
Heritage Trust Web site, www.mcht.org.

[12]See Resources Legacy Fund Web site, www.resourceslegacyfund.org.

[13]For more information about these foundations, see the Bullitt Foundation, www.bullitt.org; David and Lucile Packard Foundation, www
.packard.org; the Norcross Wildlife Foundation, www.norcrossws.org;
and the MacArthur Foundation, www.macfound.org.

[14]See Norcross Wildlife Foundation Web site at www.norcrossws.org; and
the Land Trust Alliance, "The Norcross Wildlife Foundation Offers a
No-Interest Loan Fund for Land Protection," available at www.lta.org/
resources/norcross.htm.

Chapter 6

Employing Limited Development Strategies to Finance Land Conservation and Community-Based Development Projects

Ned Sullivan and Steve Rosenberg

Entrepreneurial conservationists across the continent, from New York's Hudson Valley to the northern California coast and back to downeast Maine, are saving land for conservation purposes by employing limited development strategies. Such projects often include renewable energy and other "green" design elements. By combining conservation with development and by incorporating environmentally sensitive design and energy systems into landscapes and buildings, unique and creatively financed partnerships are achieving important land preservation and community development goals throughout the nation.

For example, on a contaminated former industrial site on the banks of the Hudson River in the city of Beacon, New York, public–private financing strategies are being employed to create a strikingly beautiful public park and modern hospitality facilities next to a modern art museum. The innovative financial strategies include a ground lease between a land trust and a developer, the use of state grants and brownfield tax credits, and the potential application of federal New Markets Tax Credits and green technology subsidy programs.

Farther up the Hudson, in the town of Hyde Park, property initially targeted for development as a Wal-Mart, across the street from the Franklin Delano Roosevelt Home and Library, is now designated to host a public visitor and transportation center and a linear park linking the region's nationally significant heritage sites. Acquisition of land by a private land trust, the use of federal transportation funds, and the sale of a conservation easement to the National Park Service are being combined in a long-term strategy to protect these former Roosevelt family holdings from sprawling "big box" development.

In a third example, the Santa Lucia Conservancy in California is funding the preservation and stewardship of an exceptional landscape by employing a limited-development strategy. The project is structured so that funds coming from the sale of a limited number of lots in areas deemed suitable for development are being directed to an endowment for the preservation of open space. The fees generated by these house lot sales provide the operating funds for a 501(c)(3) organization that serves as a watchdog for the protected lands.

And in Maine, through the coordinated efforts of a regional land trust and a private conservation-oriented investor/developer, environmentally sensitive land adjacent to Acadia National Park is now protected, providing a link between other existing parcels of national park land. The developer invested in a limited number of clustered house lots, achieving greater conservation outcomes than Maine's land use regulations would have otherwise yielded.

These examples illustrate that land trusts and similar organizations have terrific opportunities to act—as broker, sponsor, or advocate—for conservation initiatives that bring together diverse sets of public and private partners. The risks and challenges associated with such efforts are great, particularly for small organizations working to preserve open space; the conservation benefits, when the appropriate circumstances exist, make the risks well worth taking.

Benefits and Risks of Innovative Conservation Strategies

Initiatives such as those briefly described in the preceding section pose a number of advantages and potential risks to the land trust involved. Advantages include the protection of more land than would otherwise be protected because of funding leveraged through (1) revenues generated by the built elements of the project and (2) innovative partnership and financial mechanisms. The combination of development and preservation may be the best of both worlds, providing, for example, public access to conservation lands, rivers, or lakes in combination with residential, commercial, and recreational development. In addition, this type of arrangement provides opportunities to advance and demonstrate green design technologies and practices. These innovative partnerships and finance techniques also provide mechanisms and incentives that encourage private developers to incorporate open space and green design features into their projects. Without such incentives, traditional commercial and residential development might otherwise pave over many lands with significant wildlife habitat, scenic, and recreational value.

Among the risks posed to a land trust involved in a private partnership are the inherent financial costs associated with investing staff time and money into a project with an uncertain outcome, and potential damage to the organization's reputation if outsiders perceive the organization as deriving inappropriate financial benefits from a project or "selling out" by encouraging development in an area considered "sacred" by local residents. Given the recent critique by the *Washington Post* of projects that blur the lines between development and conservation,[1] it is critical that conservation organizations use these strategies cautiously, with an awareness of the attendant risks.

Many land trusts are not prepared to undertake limited development initiatives for one or more of these reasons: (1) such activities are not clearly within the scope of their mission, (2) they have limited staff expertise with urban design and brownfield conditions, or (3) the financial commitment would be too great. Furthermore, a land trust must be able to demonstrate to its supporters and to the public at large that it is using charitable or public funds prudently to achieve a public benefit, consistent with its mission, in a way that a private developer otherwise would not be likely to provide. In order to succeed, the land trust also must commit to building partnerships with public agencies, citizens and civic groups, local officials, and private-sector participants including lenders and investors. The land trust must seek out competent counsel to ensure compliance with all legal requirements, and it must scrupulously critique its own activities in light of industry standards, such as the Land Trust Alliance Standards and Practices[2] and public perceptions of its activities. Finally, the land trust must ascertain that it has the financial capacity to sustain any unpredicted outcomes.

Rationale for Land Trust Involvement and Public Financing of Projects

The return in conservation value gained through investment in a public–private partnership in many cases should warrant the risks posed by involving one's organization. By sponsoring or participating in certain development projects directly, land trusts can demonstrate strategies to preserve substantial areas of open space; at the same time they can inspire other public, private, and nonprofit organizations to do the same.

The role of the land trust in such a situation is to fill the "public value gap" between a typical development project and one that achieves a broader range of public objectives. These outcomes include the protection of incremental acres of protected public open space; the deployment of cutting-edge, environmentally friendly technology and project design; and better planning than would likely occur through market forces alone. Land trusts can encourage other communities to demand similar outcomes by providing the development community with a how-to model to follow in structuring a master planning and development process that more fully achieves community goals. A land trust may be better suited to act in this role than the community itself because of its ability to mobilize and to advocate for resources, political limitations on local government units that constrain their ability to demand public offsets from developers, and the land trust's ability to pursue mission-related outcomes for an extended period of time.

The use of government grants, tax-advantaged investment techniques, and the involvement and support of government and nonprofit agencies is warranted in such ventures to the extent that the projects achieve measurable conservation goals. Such goals may include the long-term or perpetual protection of land and habitat; the provision of meaningful public access to the properties; the protection of viewsheds for general public enjoyment; and the creation of recreational opportunities—not just for the residents of an adjacent development, but also for the public at large. In addition, in a number of contexts, such projects—with the help of several government incentives and the flexibility provided by partnering with private nonprofits—can serve to advance investment in and deployment of state-of-the-art energy technologies and other green design features.

Case Studies

To illustrate the ideas just discussed, we offer case studies of four projects sponsored by land trusts and public or private partners. Each example is replete with risks and challenges. The individuals and organizations involved assessed these risks and moved forward with their efforts despite the challenges.

Long Dock Beacon, Beacon, New York Consider the following passage, excerpted from the September 12, 2004, *New York Times*:

Signs of a Comeback in Downtrodden Beacon

DURING the waning years of the 20th century, even Beacon's spectacular position between a 1,500-foot-high mountain peak and the eastern shores of the Hudson River in southern Dutchess County failed to lure sightseers or shoppers, much less rouse development interest. One of a number of hard-pressed communities along the river, Beacon had sections along Main Street that "resembled a bombed-out war district," the city's mayor, Clara Lou Gould, recalled recently.

In the late 1960s and early 70s, the city's manufacturers—hat makers, blanket factories and packaging plants, among them—began departing. By the 1970s, a once-thriving inn had become a welfare hotel, and slums were proliferating. To this day, scars remain in the form of boarded-up storefronts in some sections of the downtown.

But especially on the eastern end of Main Street, a mile-long retail strip, and in patches near the river, there is evidence that the city is experiencing a comeback. New cafes and retail establishments have opened, and real estate brokers report that property values are on the upswing.

Although the first stirrings of new economic activity were felt in the late 1990s, the strongest impetus for a rebirth came in the spring of 2003, when Dia:Beacon, a new 300,000-square-foot museum, opened on 31 acres next to the river. The Dia Arts Foundation located its shrine to minimalist and conceptualist art in a skylighted former Nabisco packaging factory, which was built in 1929, began shedding workers in the 1980's and ceased operations in 1991. . . .

There has been more good news for the city, which the folk singer Pete Seeger has called home for 55 years. Developers recently submitted plans for Long Dock Beacon, a 160,000-square-foot mixed-use commercial development with a waterfront park on a 23-acre peninsula near the museum. The $40 million project, a joint effort of the nonprofit Scenic Hudson Land Trust in Poughkeepsie and Foss Group Beacon, a private group, is to include a 140-room hotel, three restaurants, stores and waterfront recreation like kayaking, among other things. It is scheduled to open in the spring of 2007.[3] (Copyright © 2004 by The New York Times Co. Reprinted with permission.)

How did Scenic Hudson, Inc., and its affiliate, the Scenic Hudson Land Trust, Inc. (referred to here collectively as "Scenic Hudson"), become involved in the revival of a place that looked like a "bombed-out war district"? To begin with, it is important to understand that Scenic Hudson has been an active player in the City of Beacon for more than a decade, first acquiring more than 2,000 acres of exceptionally scenic forested ridge near Mt. Beacon, and then saving Mt. Beacon itself and the gateway to the area—the starting point of a historical incline railway that had taken visitors to the top of Mt. Beacon for more than seventy-five years. Scenic Hudson also served as a player in bringing the Dia Arts Foundation to Beacon. In this context, the Long Dock Beacon project on Beacon's Hudson River waterfront is an ideal compliment to these other initiatives.

The Long Dock Beacon project site, a twenty-four-acre postindustrial site on the Hudson River, included three separate parcels acquired throughout a period of five years by Scenic Hudson (see figure 6.1). When Scenic Hudson approached the community to discuss its plans for the property, the group was strongly encouraged to develop the site, not just create a park. Scenic Hudson engaged the public in a thorough multiyear consultative process to create a conceptual use plan for the site. Scenic Hudson then

Figure 6.1.

Aerial view of the Long Dock Beacon site with a schematic of the proposed new development.

(Courtesy of Scenic Hudson and Foss Group Beacon.)

circulated a request for qualifications to developers and reviewed the submissions with a community advisory committee. Aware that the selection of a developer by a nonprofit sponsor is a crucial decision for a project of this type, Scenic Hudson identified the key qualities it sought in its private-sector participant. These included understanding and agreeing to mission-based "core principles," familiarity with and respect for sustainable design issues and brownfield development, an ethically and environmentally responsible reputation, and a track record with regard to community participation and public grant and assistance programs. Scenic Hudson selected Foss Group Beacon, based in Delmar, New York, as the developer. With further advice from the community advisory committee, the developer and Scenic Hudson then selected the architects to prepare the master plan and design the project.[4]

Operative Instruments: Development Agreement and Ground Lease

Scenic Hudson and Foss Group Beacon entered into a development agreement in anticipation of a long-term ground lease that will become effective once the project is fully designed, permitted, and financed. The heavily negotiated agreement defines the unique matrix of rights and responsibilities that arise out of this innovative relationship between a nonprofit conservation organization and a commercial developer. Of paramount importance to Scenic Hudson in the negotiations was not putting its charitable purpose at risk by virtue of the vagaries of the real estate transaction. If the development project fails, Scenic Hudson cannot lose either the property or its ability to continue to advance its public-interest objectives for the project. Equally important, if the developer succeeds, the product will be associated with Scenic Hudson, and, therefore, the development agreement must include mechanisms to ensure that its design and operation are consistent with the organization's environmental mission.

The development agreement included a number of key provisions, ranging from a strict schedule to selection of a design team to an analysis of the project's economic feasibility. The agreement obligates Scenic Hudson to develop the park and other public amenities. The land trust agreed to complete the phase of environmental remediation it had initiated. The schedule included sufficient time for the developer to secure financing and to raise capital financing. See table 6.1 for more agreement details.

The basic structure of the lease is that Scenic Hudson will not subordinate its fee interest to the ground lease, because that could put Scenic Hudson at risk of losing the property and, along with it, its mission-based conservation objectives for the site. As already noted, the ground lease for the eight acres of the parcel on which the commercial structures will be built will not be consummated until the developer has secured all financing to complete the project. The rationale for the project must be considered soberly through the production of full market and financial feasibility analyses by the developer, which will be reviewed by the nonprofit "partner." Requiring that the lease not be subordinated increases the developer's challenge in securing equity and debt financing. However, the developer's feasibility analysis concluded that, with the participation of Scenic Hudson, the mission-based and economic development objectives, and the likely availability of sources of capital to pay for the extra cost of a green design, the project was viable.

The term of the ground lease is 49 years, with the right to extend it for two additional 25-year terms, subject to satisfactory

Table 6.1.

Key Provisions in the Development Agreement Between Scenic Hudson and Foss Group Beacon Regarding Long Dock Beacon Development Site

Schedule	The development agreement commits the developer to a fixed schedule with three major milestones: (1) accepting the master plan, (2) completing land use permitting, and (3) securing project financing. Failure of the developer to meet any of these deadlines may result in termination.	
Programmatic Controls	The development agreement requires the developer to adhere to certain "core principles" reflecting Scenic Hudson's mission-based objectives including (1) cutting-edge environmental technologies; (2) appropriate scale, protection of views, and pedestrian orientation; (3) architectural and historical context; (4) integration of development with water-borne and water-related uses; and (5) linkages between the project and key off-site locations. The agreement also includes a detailed statement of parameters outlining specific programmatic and design objectives. Although Scenic Hudson will monitor the project to ensure that it achieves these objectives, the agreement places all liability relating to design and construction of the project clearly with the developer.	
Design Team Selection	Scenic Hudson has the right to veto the developer's selection of the design team. The contract with the architectural team requires that the project achieve a LEED "Gold" certification: this will make it the first hotel in the United States to achieve this standard.	
Cost Allocation	Land	A key feature embedded in the transaction is Scenic Hudson's ability (and willingness) to assemble and hold the land at its cost, as "patient capital." The zero land cost enhances the developer's ability to carry the project in its early stages and thereby assists in achieving some of the project's more aggressive programmatic goals.
	Site Contamination	Scenic Hudson removed petroleum and PCB contamination and will complete some limited additional remediation during construction of the park. The developer is responsible for all other remediation.
	Public Amenities	Scenic Hudson is responsible for funding and constructing the public amenities on its retained land, and the developer is required to fund and construct all components of the commercial project. The innovative nature of the project has enhanced Scenic Hudson's ability to secure grants to assist with its obligations, including funding from the National Endowment for the Arts, New York's Coastal Zone Program, and other funders.

Table 6.1. Continued		
	Taxes	The developer becomes liable for all taxes on the property on the date of the development agreement; once the project is completed, the developer is required to reimburse Scenic Hudson and commence paying taxes. The public areas retained by Scenic Hudson will be tax exempt.
	Operation and Management	The developer will operate and maintain, at its cost, all of the commercial areas, as well as the public park areas.
Economic Feasibility		The agreement requires the developer to provide analyses of the project's financial feasibility to Scenic Hudson to demonstrate that the project is achievable as planned. Scenic Hudson has the right to have the analyses independently reviewed, and challenge them if appropriate, in which event the developer must provide a satisfactory justification or modify its financial model accordingly.

Source

Scenic Hudson and Foss Group Beacon Development Agreement and Ground Lease.

future green performance and the other terms of the lease. Scenic Hudson and the developer negotiated the rent based on the capitalized value of the leased property. The rental amount is periodically recalculated based on increases in the value of the land. The lease incorporates the conditions relating to environmental sustainability that were included in the development agreement. In addition, the lease requires that the developer price the hotel rooms moderately, so that the project is affordable to local residents and their families.

Scenic Hudson will also receive a variety of other economic benefits from the completed project. These benefits include participation in the gross receipts generated from the project, the right to build a new headquarters building at the site, voluntary daily per-room contributions from hotel patrons, and the availability of a certain number of room nights at the lowest rate. Scenic Hudson is evaluating the potential tax implications, if any, of the proposed project structure. Currently, the project is undergoing permit review, and the developer is assembling the project's capital structure.

Project Financing

The developer's project cost is greater than a traditional hotel project, due to its cutting-edge green design, complex financial structure, and other programmatic requirements. Together with Scenic Hudson's cost to construct the public park amenities, this incremental project development cost is the quantification of the public value gap. Filling the public value gap will require the developer, with assistance from Scenic Hudson and consultants who specialize in this type of development work, to seek various nontraditional public and philanthropic funding sources—sources that are available to the project only *because* of the public benefits it provides.

The developer proposes to fund the project through a combination of conventional sources, including equity investments and conventional debt, but it will require a larger than usual mix of nontraditional sources of funds in order to meet the requirements of the project pro forma. The developer has agreed to provide Scenic Hudson with the names and relevant information about potential equity investors, to ensure that the organization's reputation will not be tainted by a participant whose past development experience or business reputation may be at odds with the agreed-upon environmental standards.

The project's unique environmental profile make it well suited to attract a variety of nontraditional sources of financing. These could include some of the following:

- *New Markets Tax Credits (NMTC)*. The U.S. Treasury awards NMTC to banks or community development organizations that have applied to the IRS to become Certified Development Entities (CDEs) and that apply for NMTC allocations in response to IRS competitive solicitations. CDEs that are awarded an NMTC allocation generate investment resources by the sale of the tax credits to investors utilizing the proceeds to invest in projects in eligible census tracts. Listings of CDEs with tax credit allocations and eligible census tracts can be found at the Internal Revenue Service's Community Development Financial Institutions Web site, www.cdfifund.gov (see chapter 9 for an in-depth discussion of New Markets Tax Credits). There are numerous methods by which CDEs use NMTC proceeds to invest in projects. In this case, we anticipate that Long Dock Beacon will follow the leveraged equity model. The program may generate as much as $10 million in equity for the developer, none of which the developer will need to repay as debt or reward at an equal rate with development investors. The program requires that "substantially all" of the capital stay invested in the project for the seven-year tax credit period, which the financing model easily accommodates.

- *State Brownfield Cleanup Program Tax Credits.* New York State offers a state income tax credit to qualified projects that is equal to a percentage of the total development cost of the project. This could translate into more than $3 million in New York state income tax credits to Long Dock Beacon investors. The tax credit proceeds will be utilized to repay an equivalent amount of mezzanine-financed debt, which will be a capital source for the project. In return for Scenic Hudson's accepting the risk that the developer might not meet the regulatory requirements of the program, the developer will provide Scenic Hudson with environmental impairment liability insurance or compensate Scenic Hudson for the additional risk it will incur.

- *Empire Zone Incentives.* Dutchess County and the city of Beacon included the Long Dock Beacon site in an "Empire Zone," and the developer was certified as a qualified business. Various benefits accrue from this designation, including property tax liabilities being paid to the city of Beacon by the state and sales tax exemption during construction.

- *U.S. Department of Housing and Urban Development–Brownfield Economic Development Initiative (BEDI) Grant and Section 108 Loan.* On behalf of the project, Dutchess County applied for a BEDI and a section 108 loan, which have been approved in the amount of $1.8 million, and will be part of filling the public value gap.

- *New York State Energy Research and Development Authority (NYSERDA).* The project has been approved as a NYSERDA program: it will receive technical assistance and green consulting services and construction financing for approved technologies.

In sum, the Long Dock Beacon project was brought to life by a thoroughly negotiated partnership between a creative non-profit land trust and an enlightened private developer. The resulting built and natural environment will be integral to the rebirth of a remarkable landscape and civic community in the heart of the Hudson Valley.

Franklin D. Roosevelt National Historic Site, Hyde Park, New York
You can see the screen of the twenty-nine-acre Hyde Park Drive-In Theatre from the entrance to the Franklin D. Roosevelt National Historic Site. The projectors first started rolling in 1950, when Roosevelt's brother sold the land to a drive-in operator. In recent years, with drive-in theaters in decline, a series of proposals to build "big box" retail stores at the site generated local controversy and even litigation.

Scenic Hudson became directly involved in the site's development in 1999, when it negotiated an assignment of a contract between the owner and a developer who was hoping to attract a big box user to the site. Following the assignment of the contract, Scenic Hudson purchased the site and another fifteen-acre parcel immediately across the road from the Franklin D. Roosevelt home. Following the sale, Scenic Hudson, along with the National Park Service (NPS), the Franklin and Eleanor Roosevelt Institute, and the town of Hyde Park, met to grapple with the question of how to use these lands.

The group, whose meetings were facilitated by John Nolon of the Pace University Land Use Law Center, agreed that its purpose would be to determine "how to best utilize the lands in the vicinity of the Roosevelt home to preserve and enhance the historic character of the sites, while creating a vibrant local economy." After more than a year of meetings, the group coalesced around a concept plan that identified certain areas for preservation and other areas that would be suitable for appropriate, complementary development. The plan identified as a key feature for protection the 1.5-mile historic Roosevelt carriage trail that FDR used to travel between his family home and the Valkill retreat used by Eleanor Roosevelt and her family. With that plan in hand, Scenic Hudson then purchased the 336-acre property, which included the carriage trail.

The National Park Service, Scenic Hudson, the town, and the Hudson River Valley National Heritage Area also secured federal transportation enhancement funds to plan and develop a regional visitor center and transportation hub that will include public and private components. The private components may include a redeveloped drive-in theater, a year-round farmer's market, facilities for recreational activity vendors, and a restaurant. As of late 2004, Congress had appropriated $2.8 million for planning and design toward an estimated total cost of the project of $9.5 million.

Based on its cooperative agreement with the National Park Service, Scenic Hudson plans to sell fee title or a conservation easement (or both) to the National Park Service for the historic carriage road and associated lands required for the proper functioning of the project. This sale will allow Scenic Hudson to cover a portion of its acquisition costs. The project may redevelop the drive-in as part of the transportation hub. Scenic Hudson may allocate the remainder of its property at the site for other public or private uses envisioned by the plan. This may result in a one-time payment or a stream of income (or both) to Scenic Hudson, which it can utilize for other conservation projects.

San Carlos Ranch, Carmel, California   The creation of the Santa Lucia Conservancy in Carmel, California, is yet another model of combined conservation and development. In a reversal of the roles played by the conservation institution in the previous case histories, the developer in this case, under pressure from the local community, created a new nonprofit. The conservation organization was created specifically to protect a portion of the land in question.

Just inland from Carmel by the Sea, along the central California coast, there are 20,000 contiguous acres of ecologically valuable land, originally known as Rancho San Carlos. In the 1980s, a developer proposed a new planned community of 2,800 house lots for the land. This proposal met with strong opposition, both at the local and the statewide levels, and the initial development project eventually failed. A group of investors that included Union Pacific Real Estate then purchased the land for $70 million.

The new owners developed a plan that evolved over time. Ultimately, the project structure provided for three interrelated objectives: (1) resource protection, including the long-term conservation of the area's scenic beauty, habitat values, and biodiversity; (2) the creation of a community within a preserve, where a human settlement would be created as part of a healthy rural and wild land ecosystem; and (3) sustainability, in that the residential community would provide the financial and cultural support necessary for the preservation of the open land. The plan involved a limited development community restricted to a small number of carefully selected sites, just large enough to sustain the preservation of these lands in perpetuity. Residents would be responsible for assuring the landscape's long-term preservation at no incremental cost to the public.[5]

The Monterey County Board of Supervisors required the creation of the Santa Lucia Conservancy as a condition for issuing of the necessary permits allowing the developers, known as the Rancho San Carlos Partnership, to proceed with building plans for 300 homesteads. The enabling resolution (number 93-115) passed by the county commissioners required the establishment of "a legal and entitlement framework to guide the Rancho San Carlos Partnership in its planning to develop a community within a preserve."[6] Accordingly, the conservancy was incorporated in 1995 "to ensure the presence of a strong, stable, independent resource protection organization in perpetuity."[7]

The conservancy owns in fee 12,000 acres of land that are designated as wildlands, in accordance with California regulations. These lands are intended to remain in pristine condition in perpetuity. The conservancy also holds easements, again in perpetuity, on an additional 6,000 acres, designated as open lands. Three hundred individual landowners hold title to this open lands portion of the preserve. These landowners also hold title to additional homestead lots on another 2,000 acres of the property. The developers have sold many of the homesteads and have built substantial amenities, including a golf course and an equestrian center.

The nonprofit Santa Lucia Conservancy has an executive director who answers to a board of governors and who maintains a "supporting organization" relationship with the Sonoran Institute of Tucson, Arizona. The conservancy, in conjunction with the University of California Santa Cruz and the Sonoran Institute, has plans to develop conservation-related educational programs (e.g., a workshop on community stewardship organizations) that will serve both local residents and nonresidents.

Financial Structure

To date, the Santa Lucia Conservancy's financial support has been from one single source, the Rancho San Carlos Partnership, which has subsidized the conservancy with quarterly contributions. The Rancho San Carlos Partnership began contributing to an endowment fund at the end of 2004, with the expectation that this fund would reach its target amount of $25 million by 2008, when the subsidies will cease.

The endowment (as amended) is structured to build up a $25 million fund by collecting $85,000 per lot from the intended sale of 294 planned lots. The partnership pays installments throughout time until they reach the full amount of the endowment. A letter of credit backs the obligation to provide the subsidies.

The conservancy's tax-exempt status as a 501(c)(3) organization depends on both the federal tax code definition of *supported/ supporting organizations* and the state of California tax exemption for parcels held by the conservancy and described as wildlands. One of the elements of the structure that is beneficial to the conservancy is that—until the endowment is funded—the partnership bears responsibility for any property taxes or assessments that might become due. The partnership also provides for the general liability insurance and for the directors and officers' insurance for the conservancy.

Acadia Woods, Bar Harbor, Maine Limited development strategies have proven useful in creating new conservation areas and in buffering existing parkland. For example, in 1991, the Maine Coast Heritage Trust (MCHT), a pioneering land conservation nonprofit, joined forces with The Lyme Timber Company, a private real estate/timberland investment partnership, to devise a plan for the purchase of 380 acres of land adjacent to Acadia National Park in the town of Bar Harbor on Mt. Desert Island, Maine. The property had been identified by the National Park Service (NPS) as a keystone linking other NPS-owned properties, but at the time, the NPS lacked the authority or the funds to make the acquisition itself.

Lyme Timber bought the property out of foreclosure after a prior plan for development of the site failed. Lyme Timber then created a conservation and development plan for the site in consultation with MCHT, the NPS, neighbors, and local officials.

The development plan clustered residential housing, resulting in reduced road construction and land clearing costs. The clustered development plan was able to move through an expedited approval process involving both the Maine Department of Environmental Protection and the town of Bar Harbor. Reduced development and approval process costs allowed Lyme Timber to make an acceptable return on its investment, even though the total number of housing units constructed on the property was fewer than half of the number permitted under existing land use zoning regulations.

The project yielded several conservation benefits: MCHT now holds conservation easements on 265 acres of the 380-acre parcel, as well as protective covenants on an additional 25 acres that previous development separates from the parcel. This new arrangement protects all the lands directly adjacent to the NPS properties, including an important riparian corridor. A new recreational trail was established on the protected land, and the new residential construction was realized on land that was less environmentally sensitive.

Conclusion

Proactive limited development efforts spearheaded by conservation nonprofits, private developers, and local governmental officials can be highly effective in achieving important conservation and environmental benefits, as well as generating significant economic returns.

By embracing carefully negotiated, well-conceived limited development strategies, municipalities can achieve several aims at once: stimulating economic development in once abandoned areas, guiding additional development dollars toward designated growth areas, protecting areas appropriate for conservation, and providing local residents as well as visitors with valuable civic and recreational amenities. Similarly, conservation organizations and private developers can achieve substantial conservation outcomes and market-based economic returns by thinking creatively and acting flexibly with regard to limited development opportunities. Certainly, achieving such results through complex political processes can be a difficult task, but as the case studies demonstrate, the resulting conservation and community development results may be well worth the effort.

Often the difference between success and failure in such efforts is the ability to finance such projects with an appropriate (and sometimes unique) mix of public and private financing mechanisms. The Long Dock Beacon project, for example, has required a complex mix of private, nonprofit, and public financial expertise to negotiate a win-win-win ground lease that keeps a developer and a land trust working together toward a common goal. It is likely that, as more projects like those in Beacon, Hyde Park, Carmel, and Bar Harbor are realized, the state of the art of limited development finance will continue to advance.

Acknowledgments

Assistance in preparing this chapter was provided by Ned Foss and Matthew Rudikoff of Foss Group Beacon LLC. Max Friedman, Esq. of Pillsbury Winthrop Shaw Pittman LLP; Margery Groten of Scenic Hudson; David MacDonald of Maine Coast Heritage Trust; Marcus Mello of Foss Group Beacon LLC; Cyndi L. Nelson of Santa Lucia Conservancy; and Peter Stein of The Lyme Timber Company graciously provided information included in this chapter.

Notes

[1]David B. Ottaway and Joe Stephens, "Nonprofit Land Bank Amasses Billions," *Washington Post*, May 4, 2003.

[2]Land Trust Alliance, *Land Trust Standards and Practices* (rev. ed. 2004), Washington, D.C.: Land Trust Alliance, 2004.

[3]Elsa Brenner, "Signs of a Comeback in Downtrodden Beacon," in Real Estate Desk, SQUARE FEET/Duchess County, *New York Times*, September 12, 2004, late edition final, section 11, page 13.

[4]For details of the master plan and conceptual design, visit the Long Dock Beacon Web site at www.longdockbeacon.com.

[5]Alfred J. Lima, "Open Space Through Limited Development," talk presented at American Planning Association meeting, San Diego, California, 1997.

[6]From Santa Lucia Conservancy fact sheet provided by Cynthia Nelson of Santa Lucia Conservancy (personal communication), 2004.

[7]Ibid.

Chapter 7

Expanding the Frontiers of Conservation Finance

Kevin W. Schuyler

The conservation community can be proud of its growth and its ability to make an impact. Total philanthropic giving in the United States to environmental organizations is now about $7 billion per year.[1] Together, seven of the largest conservation organizations in the world have combined assets of about $5 billion.[2] This is a significant level of resources, yet it pales in comparison with the resources controlled by the capital markets. Consider that General Electric alone—the world's largest corporation—has annual revenue of $134 billion and assets of $648 billion.[3]

Now, imagine what the conservation community could accomplish if given access to the capital markets that have allowed General Electric and thousands of other companies to grow to their current size and reach. The Nature Conservancy (TNC) believes that this is possible and is realizing the possibility through focused efforts to engage Wall Street, and the capital markets it controls, to further TNC's conservation mission. TNC is expanding the scope of conservation finance beyond traditional philanthropic and government sources. Its mission and values keep it firmly rooted in the inspiration of such places as Walden Pond. At the same time, its drive to make more progress toward preserving biodiversity on Earth has encouraged TNC to push the frontiers of conservation finance and embrace many of the financial tools—many created in lower Manhattan, around Wall Street—that have been so effectively leveraged by the private sector.

The Nature Conservancy's Mission

The mission of The Nature Conservancy is to preserve the plants, animals, and natural communities that represent the diversity of life on earth by protecting the lands and waters they need to survive. To achieve this mission, TNC has three significant strategies:

1. Increase the amount of traditional philanthropic or government resources dedicated to conservation.
2. Better leverage philanthropic and government resources with other sources of capital, including that from the capital markets, to accomplish more conservation.
3. Better direct all sources of capital to the highest conservation priorities globally.

Increasing the amount of traditional philanthropic and government resources is important, but these sources are limited both in their magnitude today and in growth prospects for the future. These resources are not sufficient to meet the goals of TNC or the broader conservation community. Meeting these goals will require additional pools of capital.

But before addressing the quest for capital, note that the third strategy of TNC is to ensure that it utilizes the capital available, whatever the amount, to protect the highest-priority conservation sites around the world. The conservation community's current geographic presence and the stated wishes of our donors limit our ability, in some cases, to move capital freely across the globe.[4] Organizations such as Conservation International and the World Wildlife Fund are joining TNC in a joint effort to better identify global priorities and, where possible, direct resources toward these priorities.

Conservation Finance and Traditional Conservation Resources

Most conservation organizations spend considerable time and energy identifying and pursuing philanthropic or government resources for conservation. These efforts have historically defined the limits of conservation finance. Recent data suggest that the environment's share of the philanthropic and government resource pie has stabilized after a thirty-year period of rapid growth.[5] These sources, in total, grow modestly throughout time, largely associated with changes in Gross Domestic Product (GDP); long-term GDP growth has averaged about 3.5 percent annually.[6] Growing the resources available to fund conservation objectives at this rate is unlikely to result in the outcomes sought by the conservation community.

Achieving the conservation goals shared by TNC and others requires that we move beyond these traditional sources of conservation capital and adopt an expanded view of conservation finance. Although we will continue to draw our inspiration from the "last great places on Earth," achieving our global conservation goals demands that we engage the vast pool of investment capital managed by investment professionals. To do so TNC is pushing the frontiers of conservation finance.

The Capital Frontier

One of TNC's financial goals is to expand the pool of capital available to support conservation priorities around the world. It seeks to accomplish this by gaining access to four additional sources of capital beyond its traditional philanthropic and government efforts. These four sources are (1) debt, (2) emerging tax benefits, (3) private equity investments, and (4) project financing. Each of these sources of leverage enlarges the pool of capital available for conservation and, as this capital is invested, expands the portfolio of assets conserved.

Pushing the capital frontier is not an easy task. It requires visionary boards and leadership, skilled staff, and a willingness to take appropriate risks. TNC has embraced the challenge and charted a path to move forward (see figure 7.1). Today, TNC is proud of the accomplishments that mark its progress toward the outer limits of the capital frontier; it also realizes that most of the voyage lies ahead.

Debt Capital   Between December 2002 and June 2003, TNC issued $325 million in bond debt. Today, this debt competes for investor attention with bonds offered by the world's major corporations and governments. The experience of the past eighteen months has proven that not only do investors want to own TNC bonds, but

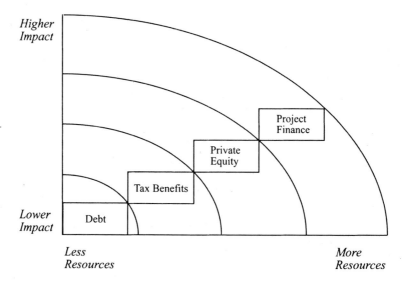

Figure 7.1.

The Nature Conservancy (TNC) is seeking to expand the resources available to fund conservation and thus increase its impact and its progress toward its mission. This graphic shows how TNC expects to move increasingly toward higher-impact strategies that yield more financial resources. TNC already uses debt capital and tax benefits; in the future, it expects to use private equity and project financing. This process is called expanding the capital frontier.

they are willing to pay a premium to do so. As evidence of this fact, TNC bonds trade as if they were rated AAA, even though Standard & Poors rates TNC as AA– and Moody's rates TNC as Aa3.[7] TNC attributes this premium to two factors. First, buyers prefer to support conservation and are willing to pay slightly more to do so. Second, most tax-exempt bonds are issued by hospitals, universities, and municipalities. Investment managers who seek to build a diversified portfolio may prefer to buy a TNC bond instead of buying additional bonds offered by the more traditional issuers. This premium has reduced TNC's annual interest expense by about $300,000. Several recognizable investors, including the Vanguard Group of mutual funds, own TNC bonds.

Debt's Contribution Quantified

Debt is an important component of the strategy to push the capital frontier. TNC estimates that the debt issuance described in the preceding section will enable an additional $750 million in conservation investments throughout the next ten years and an additional $2.25 billion over the life of the bonds.[8]

Others in the conservation community should also consider debt, including large conservation organizations and land trusts. In financial terms, debt that is secured by balance sheet assets reduces the overall cost of capital and creates a more efficient capital structure. TNC estimates that if the conservation community collectively embraced more efficient capital structures, it could, together, expand its conservation assets by an additional $9.4 billion through 2013 (see table 7.1).

TNC made the following assumptions to determine the impact throughout the ten-year period:

- The beginning revenue base is $7 billion.
- The beginning asset base is $10 billion.
- The beginning aggregate level of debt outstanding across the conservation community is $1 billion. Further, TNC has targeted a debt-to-asset ratio of 20 percent as a general guideline. Should the conservation community adopt a similar guideline, we could collectively secure $2 billion in total debt, versus $1 billion estimated today. Throughout time, the debt would grow as the conservation community's assets

Table 7.1.
Additional Assets Acquired Through Debt Optimization (2004–2013)

	Beginning Assets (Million $)	Increase in Assets (Million $)	Ending Assets (Million $)	Ending Debt (Million $)
Status Quo Scenario	10,000	51,677	61,677	1,000
Debt Scenario	10,000	61,032	71,032	12,655
Difference Between Scenarios	0	9,355	9,355	11,655

Source

The Nature Conservancy.

grew. Higher asset levels allow for higher debt levels without compromising the 20 percent debt-to-asset ratio target.

- Revenues grow at 3.5 percent per year; this is in line with long-term GDP growth.
- Revenues convert into assets at a rate of 50 percent; this is consistent with the conversion experienced by TNC in recent years. Note that TNC invests the other 50 percent of revenues in programmatic activities that enable or support asset building, public and private partnerships, scientific research and planning, and education.
- Assets on the balance sheet appreciate in value at a rate of 3.5 percent annually; this rate is a blend of appreciation in conservation assets and in financial assets. Organizations with a higher ratio of financial assets will experience a higher appreciation rate, because long-term returns on financial assets, such as endowments, average 8 percent or more.
- The long-term average cost of debt is 5.5 percent annually; historically, short-term interest rates (that is, London Interbank Offered Rates, or LIBOR) have averaged about 5.5 percent.
- The annual interest expense reduces the amount of revenue converted to assets. By doing so, the added interest burden of increased debt would not displace other necessary expenditures.
- Although TNC has successfully cycled debt in order to conserve more assets per dollar borrowed, it assumes that not all organizations will be able to do so. Therefore, the positive impact of debt cycling is not included, and it assumes the holding of acquired assets indefinitely.

Considering that TNC estimates the total assets of conservation organizations today at $10 billion, an extra $9.4 billion would mark significant additional progress in building the financial capacity to do essential conservation work!

Emerging Tax Benefits   TNC has been a leader in gaining access to new pools of capital for conservation. Between 1994 and 2004, for example, TNC completed more carbon sequestration projects than any other organization in the world.[9] Today, TNC continues to forge ahead in the area of emerging tax benefits. Two are highlighted here: the New Markets Tax Credits and convertible tax-exempt financing.

The New Markets Tax Credits

The New Markets Tax Credits (NMTC) is a federal program created by the U.S. Congress and administered by the U.S. Department of the Treasury. Like its predecessor, the Low Income Housing Tax Credit, the Treasury designed the NMTC to spur investment where it otherwise would not occur. Congress has allocated about $2.5 billion per year toward this program.

The NMTC is an economic development initiative. Because of its awareness of and commitment to human needs, TNC has found opportunities to facilitate economic development that supports its conservation efforts. For example, TNC participated in the inaugural round of NMTC applications and received a $30 million award to support a struggling paper mill in northern Maine. By including this tax credit in an attractive refinancing package for the mill, TNC enabled the mill to become more competitive, saved 5,000 jobs, and ensured the protection forever of approximately 200,000 acres of threatened forestland habitat. For an in-depth discussion of this exciting tool and its application in Maine, see chapter 9, authored by Steve Weems of Coastal Enterprises, Inc. (CEI). Note that the success of NMTC-related conservation finance is illustrated not only by this trailblazing project, but also by the fact that, based on its promising experience in the first round of NMTC funding, CEI applied for and received an additional $60 million in awards in the second round of NMTC funding awarded by the Department of the Treasury.

Convertible Tax-Exempt Financing

In 2003, TNC received "Bond Deal of the Year" honorable mention for a first-of-its-kind transaction that involved the issuance of taxable bonds with two unique provisions.[10] The first unusual provision was that bonds could be converted to tax-exempt status upon thirty days' notice to existing bond holders. The second creative provision was that all bonds were issued through a single public bonding authority while the ability to use the proceeds anywhere in the United States was preserved.

This ground-breaking transaction demonstrated that tax-exempt bond proceeds could be used to finance fast-moving conservation transactions using very low cost, high-leverage capital.

Historically, high transaction costs have been a barrier to the use of tax-exempt financing. To overcome this barrier, TNC substantially reduced the transaction costs by using a single bonding authority—the Colorado Educational and Cultural Facilities Authority—and is using the proceeds where needed. Colorado's visionary legislation enables issuance of tax-exempt debt through the Colorado authority, but allows the proceeds to be used anywhere in the United States.[11]

Quantifying Emerging Tax Benefits

TNC estimates that the benefits to the conservation community associated with the NMTC and tax-exempt financing will expand the base of conservation investments by $2.3 billion through 2013. This estimate is based on the expectation that the conservation community can secure about $500 million in NMTC awards throughout ten years. In addition, it estimates that converting taxable debt to tax-exempt debt will fund an increase in assets of $1.8 billion. Tax-exempt interest rates are assumed at a 2 percent discount to taxable rates. Lower rates allow for higher levels of borrowing when all other factors stay the same. It is reasonable to conclude that most, if not all, of the assets acquired to further conservation will qualify for tax exemption.

Private Equity   The use of private equity to fund sustainable, cash-generating activities on important landscapes provides a tremendous opportunity for leverage. Traditional conservation approaches often have the conservation community buying an entire land asset. Alternatively, financial investors might buy the entire asset and resell portions of it—often an easement—to conservationists at a retail price, including a mark-up from the wholesale price.

TNC seeks a better approach. The following key principles guide its efforts:

• Conservation determines the outcomes blueprint (i.e., shapes the deal).
• Conservation participates in wholesale pricing (not retail).

- Conservation pays for impaired future cash flows using a discounted cash flow model at a fair market rate of return.
- Conservation buys only what it needs to ensure the desired outcome, and no more.

TNC has worked hard throughout the years to realize these principles within the context of the current market. Unfortunately, it has been difficult to find partners who are willing to participate under all of the guiding principles. Financiers have demanded retail pricing in even the largest transactions. These same financiers discount their own cash flows at 6.5 percent while demanding a return on sales to TNC that yields as much as 12 percent. Financiers have even demanded that conservation pay for the impairment of an easement twice, both at purchase and in the terminal value used in the discounted cash flow calculations. The conservation community is an important source of capital and has the opportunity to assert itself more strongly to achieve its collective mission.

TNC is taking this opportunity. It has engaged many of the existing financiers in a discussion involving the creation of a new class of sustainable timber investment funds. Such funds would seek a fair market rate of return for investors while adhering to TNC's principles. In addition, although these discussions have been fruitful, TNC is actively encouraging the start-up of new timber investment funds that adopt sustainable forestry as a strategy that leads to better risk-adjusted returns for investors—and better outcomes for conservation.

In the summer of 2004, after three years of hard work, TNC achieved its goal. A group of experienced timber and private equity investors founded Conservation Forestry LLC (CF). CF's funds will invest in sustainable forestry projects in partnership with the conservation community. CF has agreed to third-party certification and other important measures to ensure the convergence of conservation and investor objectives. The fund will start out with $150 million in capital.

Sizing the Opportunity for Private Capital

TNC estimates that the use of private equity to leverage philanthropic, debt, or tax-benefited capital will contribute from $10.2 to $12.6 billion toward the asset base of the conservation community by the end of 2013. This estimate is based on the following assumptions:

- The conservation community will invest between $51 and $63 billion in conservation assets through 2013.
- Approximately half of these investments will be made in forested landscapes.
- Of these forest investments, approximately one-third will be acceptable to private equity investors.
- Private equity investors will fund 50 percent of the project value on average. Conservation will fund the other 50 percent of project value on average.

The Power of Compounding

Each of the sources already profiled (debt, tax benefits, and private equity) greatly expands the base of capital available to acquire conservation assets. In addition, these sources are complementary, and together they enlarge the total resource pie through a compounding effect. For example, the accumulation of assets using the New Markets Tax Credits increases the debt capacity and therefore increases the level of assets accumulated using debt. Table 7.2 shows the contribution of each source and the combined compounding effect.

TNC projects that the sources of funding already detailed will enable the accumulation of $89 billion in conservation assets through 2013. This represents a 53 percent increase over the base case in the expected accumulation during the same period due to the pursuit of innovative capital market opportunities.[12] At the same time, the total level of debt will have increased to $15.7 billion from an estimated $1 billion today. Due to the compounding effect and the sources of leverage discussed here, asset accumulation will increase at nearly twice the rate of debt accumulation.

In addition to these opportunities, TNC is pursuing what may be the single largest opportunity of all—project financing. Project financing represents the very edge of the conservation finance frontier.

Project Financing   Some of the most successful asset-based corporations in the world have grown considerably through project financing. Project financing is feasible when the cash flows generated

118

Table 7.2. Sources of Conservation Capital Through 2013	
Source	**Million $**
Current asset base (estimate)	*10,000*
Growth in current base and new assets acquired through revenues and asset appreciation	51,677
Debt optimization	9,355
NMTC	500
Tax-exempt debt	1,832
Private equity	10,247
Compounding effect	5,516
Total, all sources	89,127

Source

The Nature Conservancy.

through the investment opportunity are sufficient to sustain high debt-to-equity ratios. In other words, the strength of the project generates its financing, not the strength of the sponsoring organization's balance sheet or cash flow. Companies in energy, real estate, and other industries have used project financing to become multi-billion-dollar corporations in a matter of years.

AES, an energy company, serves as an interesting example of the power of project financing. AES built an asset-based business using project financing to achieve spectacular growth. Founded in the early 1980s with eight people and $1.5 million in capital, AES had grown by the end of that decade to be the largest independent power producer in the United States, with about four hundred people and a public stock valued at $90 million. By 1998, AES had more than ten thousand people and had joined the S&P 500. In 2000, one year shy of its twentieth birthday, AES had grown to $6.7 billion in revenue and a staff of thirty-six thousand. AES's growth was limited only by its capacity to find good deals. The growth of AES is symbolic of the growth in development on Earth, as measured by the demand for energy. Development forces often linked to the destruction of habitat are fueled by the principles of finance and the creativity of Wall Street. Perhaps the conservation community should consider using the same tools for its own purposes.

Moving toward project financing is important, especially as the other sources of capital already identified come into common use. Even the strongest balance sheets cannot sustain unlimited debt. In theory, project financing does allow for as much debt as individual project cash flows can service. Note that using tax-exempt debt could reduce project debt service obligations. In effect, this could facilite the use of project financing and higher debt-to-asset ratios. This added benefit would be included when sizing the opportunity for project financing.

Project financing is more of a vision than a reality today. Use of debt, tax benefits, and private equity are prerequisites to a robust project financing strategy. However, TNC sees the potential and is working diligently to make project financing a reality that vastly increases the capital invested in conservation.

Sizing the Opportunity for Project Financing

Institutional capacity and deal flow limit the size of the opportunity for project financing more than financial factors. Essentially, every deal where the cash flow can pay the debt obligations is achievable, provided such deals are available and conservation organizations have the capacity to complete the transactions.

TNC estimates that as much as $40 billion in projects could be funded using project financing through 2013 if the use of this tool became widespread.[13]

Conclusion

Pushing the frontier of conservation finance is essential to expanding the ability of the conservation community to achieve its collective mission; and although the task ahead may seem daunting, the power of leverage, tax advantage, and compounding can lessen the burden.

TNC estimates that the total investment in conservation assets can grow more than tenfold if the conservation community embraces all of these financing opportunities. Figure 7.2 shows the cumulative impact of debt, tax benefits, private equity, the com-

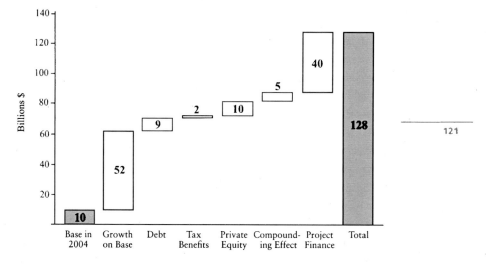

Figure 7.2.

This chart depicts the projected growth of the conservation community's assets from the current base of $10 billion to the estimated potential of $128 billion during the period of 2004 to 2013. Each of the bars shows the estimated incremental impact projected as a result of each of the strategies discussed in this chapter. It is expected that the 2004 base will grow by $52 billion without the use of these innovative strategies. The strategies are expected to add an additional $66 billion during the period. Of this amount, $5 billion is due to the compounding effect associated with the use of more than one strategy.

pounding effect, and project financing benefits, as measured through 2013.

TNC is optimistic about the future of conservation. Its task is enormous, yet the world's leading corporations and entrepreneurs have successfully used in other sectors the financial tools that TNC seeks to employ in conservation. As TNC gains more leverage with every philanthropic dollar, it believes that this advantage will encourage traditional providers of capital, including philanthropists and governments, to be even more generous in their own contributions to conservation goals.

Notes

[1]American Association of Fundraising Council, *Giving USA 2003: The Annual Report on Philanthropy* (Indianapolis: The Center on Philanthropy at Indiana University, 2003).

[2]The combined assets of The Nature Conservancy (TNC), Trust for Public Land, Ducks Unlimited, World Wildlife Fund, National Audubon Society, National Wildlife Federation, and Conservation International. Sources for this information include internal financial reports from TNC and annual reports issued by the other six organizations.

[3]General Electric, *Growing in an Uncertain World: General Electric 2003 Annual Report* (February 13, 2004), available at http://www.ge.com/ar2003/tools_download.jsp.

[4]Interestingly, this is a challenge shared with those seeking capital in the private sector. Investors, too, do not always have the best information when they make their investment decisions.

[5]American Association of Fundraising Council, *Giving USA 2003*.

[6]United States Department of Commerce, Bureau of Economic Analysis, "Historical Gross Domestic Product Estimates," available at www.bea.gov/bea/A-Z/A-ZIndex_h.htm.

[7]Bonds are rated by one or more of the independent bond rating agencies. These agencies research the financial strength of bond issuers, such as The Nature Conservancy, and assign a rating. Ratings, like academic grades, follow a letter system. A-rated bonds are deemed more secure than B-rated bonds, and, as a result, A-rated bonds pay lower rates of interest than B-rated bonds. The highest-rated bonds are given a rating of AAA by Standard & Poors (S&P) and Aaa by Moody's, two of the most well regarded ratings agencies. TNC bonds receive a slightly lower rating : AA– and Aa3 by S&P and Moody's, respectively. Despite the slightly lower rating from these two major research firms, the interest rates on TNC bonds that investors require are the equivalent of those required of higher-quality AAA and Aaa bonds. This is evidence that investors are showing a preference for TNC bonds that is based on more than their credit quality.

[8]TNC expects to cycle $300 million of its debt 2.5 times throughout the next ten years and 7.5 times throughout thirty years for an average cycle time of four years; it expects that $25 million of current debt will not cycle during these periods.

[9]Carbon sequestration projects are ones in which industrial corporations buy carbon credits to offset carbon reduction requirements under regulations such as the Kyoto Protocol. The corporation invests the money with TNC into a project that generates such credits and also achieves a significant conservation goal. To date, TNC has secured more than $35 million in carbon investments.

[10]The Bond Buyer, "The Bond Buyer's 2nd Annual Deal of the Year Awards," *A Bond Buyer Supplement* (January 2004): 24.

[11]The Colorado legislation does require a clear demonstration of the benefit of an issuance to the people of the state of Colorado. The Nature Conservancy has several offices in Colorado with nearly one hundred staff across the state; following the issuance of the bonds, TNC invested in several very large projects within Colorado, including the creation of the new Great Sand Dunes National Park in September 2004.

[12]Without these tools, TNC expects that conservation organization assets will grow to $61.7 billion by 2013, an increase of $51.7 billion. Using all the sources discussed would yield an increase of $79.1 billion, which is $27.4 billion more than the base case. The increase of $79.1 billion is 53 percent higher than $51.7 billion.

[13]Based on an estimate that the conservation community could increase its transaction volume by as much as 50 percent, project financing should become prevalent.

Chapter 8

Transferable State Tax Credits as a Land Conservation Incentive

Philip M. Hocker

Our options are expiring. . . . The land that is still to be saved will have to be saved in the next few years. We have no luxury of choice. We must make our commitments now and look to this landscape as the last one. For us, it will be.

—William H. Whyte,
The Last Landscape

On April 1, 2002, the governor of Virginia signed legislation that my colleague Charles Davenport and I had written and promoted. The new law makes the state's income tax credit for land conservation donations transferable. This new tool has led to a startling acceleration in voluntary donations of conservation easements to protect open space, farmland, and natural sites across the commonwealth of Virginia. In Colorado, a parallel independent history is also creating impressive conservation success.

On New Year's Eve 2003, I drove to Warrenton and delivered several hundred thousand dollars in cashier's checks to the accountant for H.L., a classic Virginia Hunt Country estate whose owners had sold tax credit in the 2003 market. A family limited liability company (an "LLC") with a score of members owned H.L. For years, the family had discussed putting a conservation easement on the land, but had been unable to decide on action. When the proconservation members of the family learned that donating an easement would earn the LLC state income tax credit that they could sell for cash, they were able to convince the rest to make the conservation commitment for perpetuity.

A few days earlier, I had e-mailed a bundle of PDF electronic file attachments to M., another Virginia landowner. These were my firm's standard "Agreement to Transfer Virginia Land Preservation Tax Credit" contracts and state reporting forms. M. printed them out and faxed signed copies to our office. Then I sent a stack of cashier's checks to his farm. The conservation restrictions he had imposed on his land in 2002 had just reaped more than $100,000 in cash benefit.

But these are weighty transactions, and a few of the stories are less silvered: O. and his wife, P., donated a conservation easement for their 160-acre Virginia farm during 2002. Relying on an appraisal report that they had obtained, O. and P. expected to be able to sell more than $100,000 worth of tax credit. Early in 2004, O. and P. started the process of putting the tax credit on the market. As usual, my firm requested that they send us documents to verify that the credit met basic regulatory tests. Unfortunately, when we reviewed the appraisal report, we found that the writer had based his valuation on a "percentage reduction" due to the easement, rather than any of the three recognized formal approaches to value. O. and P.'s land is now restricted by the perpetual easement they donated in 2002, but they cannot sell the tax credit.

Conservation Tax Credit Overview

In the past, the principal U.S. tax incentives for land conservation have been via income tax *deductions* for charitable gifts, and via property tax reductions to assess land at its current, rather than its "highest and best," use. Reduction of the taxable value of property in an estate has also been an incentive.[1]

Providing *credits* against income taxes due, which are more valuable than *deductions* from taxable income, has been a more frequent goal in historic preservation campaigns than in land conservation efforts. The argument made by historic preservation advocates has been that a tax credit to a real estate investor who buys and renovates a dilapidated structure with historic value stimulates secondary construction spending, generates sales and payroll taxes on that spending, and increases the taxable value of the real property. All these effects are posited to justify the greater public expenditure of a tax credit program. Other public purposes have been promoted with tax credits, but usually these purposes entail a presumably discretionary cost or expenditure (tragically, W. C. Fields never had the opportunity to file IRS Form 2441, to claim a tax credit for "Child and Dependent Care Expenses").

But today's public anxiety regarding urban sprawl and the loss of open spaces, combined with a relentless ideological campaign to discredit government as a competent means to provide public benefits such as open space protection, has driven strange bedfellows to search for something, beyond the incentive that tax deductions offer, that might assist land conservation. In several states, enacting a state income tax credit for land preservation has been one result. Transferable tax credits are that result taken to the next logical level.

In 1983, North Carolina established the first state income tax credit for owners who donated conservation restrictions on their land. The credit allowed in North Carolina is 25 percent of the Fair Market Value (FMV) of the donation. The state sets a ceiling on the amount of credit any donation can obtain; throughout the years this has risen from a starting level of $5,000 in credit to the present maximum credit per donation of $250,000 for individuals or $500,000 for corporations. The program requires state certification of the conservation value of the gift, but the state has not made the certification process a troubling hurdle.[2]

The Proliferation of State Tax Credit Incentives

In the years after North Carolina's 1983 legislation, several other states attempted to create tax credit programs. None succeeded. Finally, in 1999, the booming economy, widespread public concern about sprawl, and creative work by many dedicated conservationists led to enactment of a flurry of new state income tax credit programs. Virginia came first, followed quickly by Colorado, Connecticut, and Delaware. In 2000, California and South Carolina enacted credit incentives. Maryland followed in 2001, and in 2003, New Mexico joined the roster. Several of these state laws are the fruit of diligent work by The Nature Conservancy's incentive program, led by Philip Tabas. Tabas has drafted a model state tax-credit statute that TNC has promoted effectively. Nonetheless, several of the state laws have totally independent intellectual roots.

Most of the laws grant credit for any conservation donation that would qualify for Internal Revenue Service (IRS) deductibility under Internal Revenue Code section 170(h).[3] Some, though, are much more restrictive (Delaware, California, and Maryland). The credit value is usually computed as a percentage of the FMV of the donation value, pursuant to IRS procedures. The allowed tax credit percentage of FMV ranges from 25 percent (North Carolina and South Carolina) to 100 percent (Colorado and Maryland). Most programs allow unused credit to be carried forward into succeeding tax years—the number of carry-forward years ranges from five (North Carolina, Virginia, and Delaware) to twenty (Colorado) to South Carolina's allowance of unlimited carry-forward until consumed.

The different laws contain a variety of "caps" to constrain their tax cost to the respective state treasuries. Some limit the amount of credit allowed per conservation donation (North Carolina, Colorado, and Delaware). Others restrict the amount of credit any taxpayer may use in a year to pay tax, such as Virginia's requirement that any taxpayer may use credit only up to a maximum of $100,000 (or taxes due if lower) in any tax year, though the total credit a donation can earn is not limited. I favor this approach because it allows large conservation acquisition projects to employ the tax credit as leverage, rather than limiting the credit program's stimulus to small parcels and low-cost regions.

Moving On to Transferability

Land conservationists were justifiably delighted in 1999 to have passed four new state income tax credit programs. But almost before the ink was dry, conservationists began to assess how much incentive these programs would really give a land-rich/cash-poor landowner. State income tax rates are typically low compared with federal rates. Virginia's top income tax rate is 5.75 percent. To use the maximum $100,000 of credit per tax year in Virginia requires taxable income of $1,743,609—not a common problem for Virginia farmers.

In both Colorado and Virginia, independent efforts arose to make the tax credit more meaningful as a financial incentive for landowners. In Colorado, state Representative Lola Spradley—who had sponsored the state's original 1999 credit legislation—convened a colloquy among ranching and land trust interests regarding means to make the value of the credit accessible to low-tax landowners. In Virginia, several of us who had experience in tax-leveraged historic preservation projects involving multiple investors studied options. We looked for ways to make the large pool of tax credit that a conservation donation might create available to cash-burdened taxpayers.

Allowing a tax credit incentive to be "transferable," that is, allowing one entity entitled to the credit to sell it freely to another entity with a tax obligation, has been a standard technique of the tax-incentive world for years. In Colorado, the folks who wanted to make the state tax credit a stronger conservation incentive suggested that the credit be made "transferable" and that it also be made "refundable"—that is, that unused credit could be submitted to the state treasury for a direct cash refund, even if the credit exceeded the holder's taxes owed. In 2000, Colorado enacted both these provisions, subject to a $100,000-per-donation cap and other limits. The state allows refundability only in years it has a fiscal surplus, but credit holders can carry unused and unrefunded credit forward as long as twenty years, until an "open" year occurs.

In Virginia, we initially searched for a viable way to use "pass-through" business structures (which were allowed by the 1999 statute) to move the tax credit from land-rich/cash-poor landowners to parties with high tax bills. Limited-liability partnerships have long been a standard business form to convert tax credits for historic preservation and other tax-preferred actions into cash. I had organized and managed an LLP in the 1980s for a San Francisco historic rehabilitation venture. Tax professor and scholar Charles Davenport[4] worked with me to see if pass-through entities would work for land conservation under Virginia's credit law. However, IRS rules require that partnership activities be undertaken for business purposes, not just to reduce taxes. Although owning a limited share of ownership in a rehabilitated historic building gets through the eye of this needle, we were dubious that owning land and giving away a substantial part of its value for conservation would pass. So Davenport concluded, "I think we can solve this problem more directly." We went to William J. Howell, a creative and thoughtful leader in the Virginia House of Delegates, and proposed an amendment to the Virginia law to make conservation tax credits directly transferable. Howell agreed. His bill HB1322 passed in Virginia's House and Senate without opposition and was signed in April 2002, making the state's conservation tax credit transferable.

Federal Tax Issues

First in law, the Colorado transferable credit community was also "first to market." They quickly learned that people who buy state income tax credit tend to pay a lot of federal income tax—and, that those folks' tax advisers are hypersensitized to IRS treatment of any financial action that affects tax items. Because state income taxes are an important federal tax deduction, the fair pricing of conservation credits depended on whether the IRS would allow a full deduction for state taxes paid with a purchased state tax credit. The federal tax treatment of any difference between the "credit value" to pay taxes and the actual cash paid by a credit purchaser was also important.

This article is not tax advice, but it is my opinion that after several years we now have a fairly good impression of the Internal Revenue Service's likely position on the relevant issues: State income taxes paid with a purchased transferable tax credit may be deducted at full value from federal taxable income. When a purchaser acquires state income tax credit at a discount from full value, the difference between the purchase price and the tax obligation discharged is taxable as income for federal purposes. Sellers of credit should report any income from the sale of a state income tax credit received for a conservation charitable contribution as ordinary income for federal purposes. There are other opinions on many of these questions, however, so do not rely on this article for tax guidance. State income taxation of transferable credit sales varies; for example, Virginia's statute specifically excludes gain on conservation credit sales from state taxable income.

Contrasting Market Dynamics: Colorado Versus Virginia

Though the transferable conservation credits in Colorado and Virginia were created for the same purpose, and although "a buck is a buck" in both, the markets for credit evolved along very different paths in the two states.

The initial market for trades in Colorado conservation tax credit was organized by Michael Strugar, an attorney, and the Conservation Resource Center (CRC), a Colorado 501(c)(3) corporation that he leads. Strugar did a pioneering job in locating buyers and sellers of tax credit, and in closing trades. CRC took the position that the "right" price for tax credit trades would be a cost of $0.90 to the buyer, with a payment of $0.80 to the seller and the difference staying with CRC for its programs. The market began to function in May 2001, when federal tax questions were resolved. By the end of 2001, CRC had closed trades of about $700,000 in Colorado tax credit, and everyone was modestly pleased.

This Colorado traded credit volume has grown steadily, as buyer confidence has risen and since the Legislature raised the cap on credit per donation from $100,000 to the current ceiling of $240,000. In 2003, brokers estimated they marketed about $30,000,000 of credit in Colorado.

Despite the growth in volume, the credit market pricing in Colorado has remained static, based on the original "right" price of $0.80 paid to the seller/landowner. Margins for brokers have ranged from $0.10 to $0.05, and the buyer's price thus has varied from $0.90 to $0.85. Private trades can obviate brokerage, but the general opinion is that these are not a significant volume.

Virginia's market has been dramatically different. Conservation organizations did a quick and effective job of publicizing both the initial 1999 tax credit incentive and the 2002 enhancement of transferability. Because the value of credit per conservation donation was not limited, a sizable supply of credit was available almost immediately. The transferability legislation signed on April 1, 2002, was effective retroactive to January 1 of that year. However, the Department of Taxation ruled in March 2003 that any credit used on 2002 tax returns had to have been purchased before the end of that calendar year (a surprise position). Subsequently, the Department of Taxation did not issue reporting forms for credit transfers (a requirement for using the credit) until October 2003, delaying the creation of a market.

Virginia landowners had heard about the "right" $0.80/ $0.90 credit pricing from Colorado, and initially both the landowners and brokers were proposing to buyers that they should pay $0.90 per dollar of credit value. The buyers were unpersuaded. After many months of stalemate, my firm, Virginia Conservation Credit Pool, LLC (VCCP), abandoned the idea that there was a "right" price and strove to gather "ask" and "bid" terms from sellers and buyers with no preconceptions.

There is no general disclosure or reporting system, and only sparse rumor, from which to gather market information. We are told that a sale of $200,000 of Virginia credit closed at $0.45 per dollar in mid-2003. Trades that VCCP handled in 2003 opened at a price to buyer of $0.60, with a net to seller of $0.50. Buyers' prices on our trades moved up as the end of the year approached, and final trading was at a buyer price of $0.80. Sales we did not facilitate covered a wider price range.

In credit trades at the end of 2004, the Colorado market remained very stable at a price paid of $0.80 per dollar to the conservation donor/credit seller. Brokerage fees in Colorado were competitively negotiated, between $0.05 and $0.10, so total cost to credit buyers ranged from $0.85 to $0.90. In Virginia, growing buyer confidence and improvements in market outreach during 2004 created enough growth in demand to overmatch the growth in supply. Early Virginia trades that my firm handled were at an overall price to buyers of $0.70, and that price level held steady for almost all trades we did in the year. There were trades handled by other brokers at other prices, and a growing number of sophisticated landowners arranged the sale of their credits directly, without using a broker.

Supply and Demand Tomorrow

Since these two markets were born, a question has simmered: Will taxpayer demand for discounted credit keep up with the volume of supply that landowners, spurred on by conservation groups, can provide?

Given fair pricing, this would be a silly question. The state budgets of Virginia and Colorado run in the tens of billions of dollars, of which a large portion is income tax revenue. If even 1 percent of state income tax collections were paid in tax credit instead of cash, several hundreds of millions of dollars could be paid to landowners for conservation. No state tax credit program comes close to that volume today.

However, persuading taxpayers to part with cold cash for a putative tax credit is a more complicated process than the arithmetic alone suggests. Some other tax credit incentives require precertification by the taxing authority and, in some cases, prior documentation of actual expenditures and of accomplishment of the objective (e.g., rehabilitation of historic structures). By contrast, conservation tax credit, like the section 170(h) deduction, is based merely on the appraised value of a donation that is averred to provide public conservation benefit. The U.S. Senate Finance Committee and the IRS have recently pilloried The Nature Conservancy about both the valuation of, and the question whether public benefit is truly conveyed by, similar transactions. Nonetheless, the state tax credit market has been remarkably unshaken by either the Senate's investigation or by recent *Washington Post* articles on the subject, although many buyers are aware of both.

After two years of active credit trading, the Virginia tax credit market appears to be maturing. An increasing number of buyers and financial advisers are comfortable that buying conservation tax credit provides a very attractive return on investment at recent prices. Although the dramatic increase in conservation easement donations has created, in theory, a large overhanging supply of available tax credit, that supply has not forced prices down to my knowledge. Some observers think that, because the unsold supply is, by statute, viable for only five carry-forward years after the original easement donation, this supply will be "dumped" as it nears its expiration year. But my guess, based on the climate of discussions I hear from buyers and sellers, is that prices will hold and continue a modest climb as the buyers gain confidence in the process. The whole psychology and level of understanding is still evolving rapidly. Only time will tell.

The Credit Market Process

Closing trades in conservation tax credit is an exercise in both personalities and legalities. Although tax deductions as a conservation incentive require the participation of only the landowner and the taxing authority (with acquiescence by a qualified donee), the marketing of transferable credits involves hard cash passing hands. Things are different. There are more liabilities. A good contract for transfer of conservation tax credit must address indemnification of the buyer in the event of a state or IRS audit later overturning the appraisal, or the conservation benefit, of the donation. Some agricultural landowners are not facile with tax issues or legal liability problems. Because Virginia has ruled that all credit transfers must close before the end of the tax year for which the credit will apply, there is an extreme rush in late December to move paperwork and funds quickly and accurately.

Protecting Natural Lands

> **incentive** . . . *something that incites . . . to determination or action*
> —Merriam-Webster's Collegiate Dictionary, 11th ed.

The conservation incentive effectiveness of state income tax credits has been spectacular. Measurement is easiest in Virginia, because a state-chartered land trust, the Virginia Outdoors Foundation (VOF), is donee or participant in most easement gifts. During the 1990s, donations to VOF averaged 10,000 acres per year. A recent tally illustrates the effect of tax credit:

- 1998: 13,523 acres donated
- 1999: 11,419 acres (tax credit passed but not effective until January 1, 2000)
- 2000: 28,725 acres (bump due to tax credit)
- 2001: 22,701 acres (great increase from 1990s average)
- 2002: 36,486 acres (first year with credit transferability)
- 2003: 44,000 acres approved by VOF Board: only 22,502 acres recorded

Markets are clever. Because Virginia law allows a five-year carry-forward of unused tax credit, and because the Department of Taxation holds that to be used for a tax period, credit must be acquired during the same time span, landowners have learned to hold the recordation of their year-end gifts until the succeeding year, when they plan to sell the credit. Whether VOF should condition its board approval of a donation on recordation within a limited time is one fresh question of many.

These conservation donations earned Virginia landowners about $45 million in tax credit in 2002; in 2003, the total rose to $64 million. Preliminary statistics suggest that the credit claimed for 2004 donations will be 60 percent above the 2003 level.

However, the amount of credit *actually applied to pay taxes* on Virginia tax returns for 2002 was only $5 million. For 2003, the near-complete figure for credit *applied* was about $30 million. The large amount of credit that is being created by easement donations has raised some concerns at the Department of Taxation. However, how much of that theoretically created credit will ultimately cause a reduction of the Commonwealth's cash income tax collections remains a mystery. It is indisputable that the transferable tax credit has led to a dramatic increase in land conservation. So far, it seems reasonable to speculate that much of that tax credit incentive may not, in fact, be charged against the state's treasury. The situation may be like a mail-in rebate for cereal: the marketer calculates that only some of the eligible coupon holders will, in fact, collect. However, a few large and professionally marketed easement projects could generate large volumes of *applied* credit and shift the ratios in a hurry.

For North Carolina, the state with the most mature tax credit program, the cumulative effect of the conservation credit incentive since its inception in 1983 is evangelic: More than 108,000 acres have been placed under conservation, with a total value of more than $300 million. All this was done with a theoretical cost in tax expenditure of $54 million, offset by a *known* savings, through bargain-sale acquisitions by public agencies below fair market value, of $48 million. But don't be fooled by this focus on figures. It wasn't just arithmetic. Caring people worked diligently, quietly, and patiently to make these gains happen. Appreciate.

Quid Pro Query

In July 2002, Pat Noonan convened a meeting at The Conservation Fund to discuss the then-new Virginia transferable tax credit law. At its close, he turned to me and said, "Now that you've got this in place for Virginia, aren't you going to move on and get transferable conservation tax credits established in a lot of other states?" I scratched my head dully and replied, "That's probably a great idea, Pat, but I think I'm going to stick with just trying to make this market really work in Virginia, for a start."

It's been enough to keep me busy. This policy field is accelerating beyond warp speed right now. I could write pages on myriad unresolved issues, but I will merely list a few. I invite your reactions or suggestions.

Should states certify conservation tax credits before allowing trades? Should brokers preferably be 501(c)(3) organizations or for-profit entities? Should trades be managed through state-administered exchanges? What is the optimum "percentage" for credit relative to the FMV of conservation donation? Should there be a cap on total state tax expenditures via credit? If so, how should it be imposed without artificially constraining conservation enterprise? Should the "conservation purpose" be tested more stringently to earn a state *credit* than the standards of IRC section 170(h) for *deductions*? Shouldn't donations of *cash* for land conservation receive credit similar to that for donations of *land or interests in land*? Should state taxation staff be required to report on the costs and benefits of tax credit incentives?

How much tax credit that is earned by conservation donations will never actually be used? Are land trusts using tax credits affirmatively as a financial lever to protect coherent conservation units, rather than merely relying on owners' volition? Are nonprofit recipients of *credit-earning* conservation gifts obliged to scrutinize those donations more severely than they would view gifts mobilized merely by *deductions*?

Don't Look Back

Lastly, as S. Behrman in *The Octopus* by Frank Norris would *not* have asked audibly, "How much will the traffic bear?" How much tax expenditure will states leave at the mercy of landowners' donations, and taxpaying credit purchasers' avarice, without requiring more stringent control than compliance with IRC section 170(h)? The land conservation community worries about that issue now, but to the outside world the dollar amounts at issue are merely "dust on the monitor screen" of state budgeting, as one friend put it.

State tax credit for voluntary land conservation choices by landowners has an immense, diverse, and powerful political constituency. Once these incentives are enacted, the land conservation community can defend them with the combined support of all the proenvironment, antisprawl, antitax, and prolandowner constituencies in every state. If the mining industry can defend the federal 1872 Mining Law from repeal for 132 years, we in the land conservation community ought to keep transferable state conservation tax credits on the law books into the fourth millennium.

And we can and should expand the use of state tax credits, and transferability, into new regions and levels. North Carolina tried to enact three new provisions to improve its tax credit program in its 2004 legislative session. Virginia successfully defended the Commonwealth's credit against a proposal to cripple it in 2004. In several other states, activists are poised to enact new conservation tax credit programs as soon as the economy improves. The tendency now is for these state programs to grow incrementally, and along idiosyncratic paths. Conservationists in one state seek to add credit transferability, in another they target refundability. In yet another, the dollar caps on allowed credit are raised. There is no normative tendency yet, except the general reliance on section 170(h) criteria for qualification (clarifying reliance on section 170(h) was a recent incremental improvement made in Colorado).

The growth of state tax credit programs, and the introduction of free-market principles (and hazards) through transferability, is an exciting event in U.S. land conservation. Yes, the power of the credit incentive brings a call for responsibility by donees and appraisers. But foremost we need more conservation incentives and more protected land.

Acknowledgments

Many people have worked tirelessly to create these beginnings of the United States of America's growing transferable state income tax credit movement, and I have benefited from their guidance and suggestions, both in forming the Virginia credit program and in compiling this chapter. Colleagues and friends, thanks. I particularly thank my colleague Charles Davenport; Bill Flournoy of the North Carolina Department of Environment and Natural Resources; Michael Strugar of Conservation Resource Center in Boulder, Colorado; and Larry Kueter of Isaacson, Rosenbaum, Woods & Levy in Denver: Thank you for your generous assistance with data and reflection. Notwithstanding my debt to them, any errors of fact or opinion in this chapter are entirely my responsibility. Persevere.

Note: The epigraph to this chapter is drawn from William H. Whyte, *The Last Landscape* (New York: Doubleday & Co., 1968). The bible.

Notes

[1]For further background and history regarding state and federal tax credit programs that have been employed for land conservation initiatives, see the following:

- C. Timothy Lindstrom, Attorney, "State Tax Incentives for Conservation Easements Can Benefit Everyone," *Journal of MultiState Taxation and Incentives*, November/December 2002, pp. 20ff.
- Steven J. Small, *The Federal Tax Law of Conservation Easements* (Washington, D.C.: Land Trust Alliance, 1989). This publication includes a history of tax incentives for conservation gifts.
- Virginia Conservation Credit Pool, LLC, "Tax Credit Sellers Information Memorandum" and "Credit Buyers Information Memorandum," available on request from the author at 703-683-4990, or at phil@hockers.com.

[2]For a chart comparing various state programs and statutes, see ConServCo/Conservation Service Company, LLC, *State Conservation Income Tax Credits Side-by-Side*, available on request from the author at 703-683-4990, or at phil@hockers.com.

[3]To view the language in Internal Revenue Code section 170(h), go to http://assembler.law.cornell.edu/uscode/html/uscode26/usc_sec_26_00000 170----000-.html. Note that the U.S. Treasury regulations are important to understanding the rules in many cases. To find them, go to http://www.gpoaccess.gov/cfr/.

[4]For an intense examination of current thinking on federal tax issues related to state incentives, see Charles Davenport, Attorney, "Federal Taxes and Transferable State Tax Credits," *Tax Notes*, Vol. 110, No. 10 (December 8, 2003), pp. 1213–1231.

Chapter 9

Payrolls Versus Pickerels Redux
A Story of Economic Revitalization and Timberland Conservation Using New Markets Tax Credits

Steve Weems

"Do you want payrolls *or* pickerels?" This venerable question is how the debate in Maine about economic development versus environmental protection used to be posed, although it has been superseded by more modern phraseology. Stated in many different ways, the same debate still rages all around the world. In whatever terms this apparent choice is postulated, the question is too simplistic, not reflective of actual trade-offs. The inescapable reality is that the only viable long-term approach is sustainable development, which is shorthand for a future of both payrolls *and* pickerels.

Coastal Enterprises, Inc. (CEI), a nonprofit community development entity based in Maine, and The Nature Conservancy (TNC), the renowned worldwide conservation organization dedicated to "saving the last great places on Earth," have collaborated to use their respective strengths and the federal New Markets Tax Credits (NMTC) program to synthesize the goals of *e*conomic progress, *e*cological sustainability, and social *e*quity (the 3Es) in Maine's northern forest. This is what people are calling 3E or triple bottom-line underwriting: measuring the success of an investment not just in terms of financial return, but also by the degree to which it creates human (social) and environmental capital.

Triple bottom-line underwriting is the heart of this approach to community development. It is the wellspring of CEI's commitment to financing sustainable development through the NMTC program and other CEI initiatives (see box 9.1 for more information about the NMTC financing program). CEI undertook the Katahdin project in northern Maine within the context of its overall investment strategy and leadership role in the creative use of NMTC financing.

The Katahdin Story

The Great Northern Paper Company (GNP) has a long history in Maine. It was created in 1898 in Millinocket in the heart of the north woods. During the twentieth century it *was* the economy of north central Maine. GNP operated two massive pulp and paper mills (with seventeen paper machines in its heyday), owned and managed more than a million acres of forestland, and employed more than 1,500 people harvesting wood and making paper. GNP was a key asset that propelled Maine into the lead as the number one papermaking state in the country. See figure 9.1 for a map of the Katahdin region.

By the 1990s, as an older mill complex in a region of the country where trees grow slowly, the GNP mills were struggling to remain competitive. It became clear that these mills needed to specialize and required major capital investments to modernize. As a result, the mills began to focus on recycled-content directory, groundwood specialty, and high-quality coated and uncoated (super-calendered) specialty papers, and invested $150 million to $250 million of capital in paper machines and plant improvements. In the ensuing years, this proved to be an extraordinarily difficult strategy to implement due to depressed worldwide paper prices. Another key phenomenon was the economic pressure on "industrial forest" landowners to divest themselves of their land assets due to both low current financial returns associated with owning trees and the need to raise capital for mill improvements. Selling timberlands exposed this critical natural resource to liquidation harvesting practices and conversion to other uses.

Against this backdrop, TNC, recognizing a major conservation opportunity coexisting with a compelling economic need,

Location of Katahdin Project Forestlands

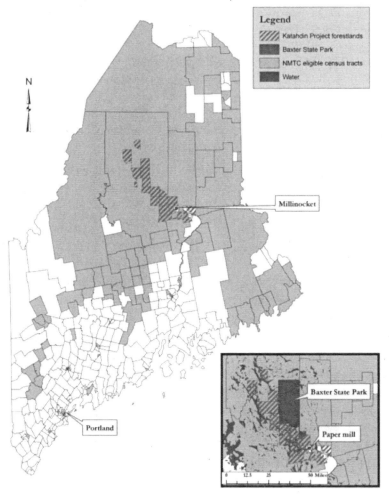

Figure 9.1.

The Katahdin project forestlands are located within the north central region of Maine, south and west of Baxter State Park, where Mount Katahdin is located, at the northern terminus of the Appalachian Trail. (Map developed by Hannah Thomas, Coastal Enterprises, Inc., working with Katahdin Forest Management LLC, and The Nature Conservancy, Maine chapter.)

approached CEI with the idea of being its working partner in a major 3E deal. Working with GNP, the company's lenders, and Maine's political leadership, CEI and TNC came up with an economic revitalization plan, contingent on NMTC financing, with the following features:

- CEI would apply for an NMTC allocation and, if successful, use the tax credits to alter the economics of owning the forestlands (via lower-cost debt financing), allowing the continued use of a large tract of forestland to supply mill needs. A consistent fiber supply was essential to the viability of the GNP mills and other area lumber and paper mills.
- GNP would make major upgrade investments in its paper machinery and related mill infrastructure (such as pulping facilities) to modernize the entire operation and position it to compete effectively in worldwide paper markets.
- Of the total 341,000-acre land base still owned by GNP, TNC would purchase in fee simple 41,000 acres of especially critical lands in the Debsconeag watershed and place a perpetual conservation easement on 200,000 of the remaining 300,000 acres to be retained by GNP.
- All parties would agree to forest use and harvesting practices that (1) provided for long-term availability of the wood for industrial uses by harvesting wood consistent with sustainable forestry management practices; (2) encouraged other compatible economic development activity, such as eco-tourism and recreational uses; and (3) protected critical areas, such as lakes or important watersheds. These provisions would be written into the permanent conservation easement on the 200,000 acres; similar provisions also would be included in the documents for the long-term NMTC financing covering all 300,000 acres to be retained by GNP.

With this plan in place, TNC moved ahead by providing approximately $50 million of short-term financing to pay off GNP's existing mortgage note (held by John Hancock Life Insurance) on the forestlands and infused several million dollars of working capital into the mills. To pay for the land and easement purchases, TNC agreed to a $14 million write-down in its mortgage with GNP, leaving GNP with a $36 million note to TNC at a favorable 4 percent interest rate. GNP invested more than $100 million in a new super-calendered paper machine and made other paper machine and mill upgrades.

With implementation of the plan under way, a "slight problem" arose: the paper company encountered even tougher times and ran out of money. In the winter of 2002–2003, both mills were shuttered and placed in bankruptcy. Nearly all of the 1,000 remaining mill workers lost their jobs. This was the end of the line for GNP. It was a bleak winter in the Millinocket area, with unemployment rising to 30 percent.

The CEI/TNC partnership held its ground, however, and Maine's political leadership put its collective shoulder to the wheel to craft a viable revitalization plan. The basic assets—the forestlands, the mills (including the new investments already made), and the skilled workforce—were valuable and served as the building blocks of the revitalization strategy. Specifically, Maine's political leaders—Governor-elect John Baldacci, U.S. Senators Olympia Snowe and Susan Collins, and newly elected U.S. House Second District Representative Michael Michaud, a former forklift driver at one of the GNP mills—spearheaded a public initiative to find a new, substantial corporate owner and secure the necessary financing, including the NMTC component.

Just a few months later, Brascan Corporation, a large, diversified publicly traded company headquartered in Toronto, Canada, purchased both the forestlands and the two mills. It reopened first one mill and then the other, re-employing 500 to 600 workers. It made additional capital improvements in both mills to improve their long-term viability. Experienced timberland and paper mill operational support came from Nexfor/Fraser, Inc., another publicly traded, established paper and building products company in which Brascan held a 44 percent interest.

Thus the revitalization plan eventually came to fruition. General Electric Commercial and Industrial Finance (GECIF) emerged from among several potential investors to make an "equity investment" in a special-purpose community development entity, or CDE (see box 9.1 for more information), named CCM Working Forests I LLC (WFI), which, in turn, allocated tax credits to GECIF as an incentive to provide its equity capital. WFI then provided $31.5 million to Katahdin Forest Management LLC (KFM), a

---

Box 9.1
NMTC Basics

The NMTC program is a recent federal initiative to mobilize private investment capital to fund businesses in low-income areas. The incentive comes in the form of a 39 percent federal income tax credit spread throughout seven years and is available to U.S. federal income tax payers who provide funds for projects in distressed areas. Community development corporations, such as CEI and other entities with a primary mission of serving low-income people, can become certified community development entities (CDEs) and apply to the Community Development Financial Institutions Fund (CDFI Fund), a unit within the U.S. Treasury Department, for an investment allocation under the NMTC program. These CDEs, in turn, can convey the tax credits to capital sources that provide funds for eligible projects. The eligible projects (businesses) benefit by gaining access to capital with special terms and conditions, such as below-market interest rates and longer loan amortization schedules.

NMTC investment capacity is awarded to CDEs through a highly competitive application process. Initial NMTC program awards were made in spring 2003 and the first deals were closed that fall. The pace of closing NMTC financings is accelerating. In the first two competitive rounds, $6 billion of NMTC investment capacity was awarded to more than 129 CDEs, with another $2 billion awarded in May 2005 to 41 CDEs. Applications totaling more than $80 billion have been filed for the $8 billion awarded, from CDEs that are affiliated with a variety of community development organizations, from banks and unregulated corporate financial institutions, and even from public entities, such as cities. CDEs who obtain NMTC allocations then have the responsibility to convey suballocations on worthy projects in low-income areas serving the objectives of the program and consistent with the investment plans presented in their applications. These investment plans specify the CDE's geographic service area, investment themes, types of "investment products" (e.g., equity investments and below-market-rate loans), and potential projects.

---

forestland subsidiary of Brascan, in the form of a long-term loan. KFM used the loan, and the proceeds of other new debt, to pay off its remaining $36 million note with TNC. Now, KFM has a loan with WFI with favorable terms, providing below-market-rate financing on the forestlands, which effectively provides additional working capital for two large pulp and paper mills trying to survive in an extraordinarily challenging competitive business climate worldwide.

On February 27, 2004, the collaboration among CEI (WFI), TNC, Brascan (KFM), and GECIF paid off with the successful closing of the NMTC financing. As a result, WFI holds a $31.5 million note from KFM (a Brascan subsidiary), the manager of CEI (WFI) receives fees from using a portion of its NMTC investment capacity for this deal, TNC owns 41,000 acres of critically important watershed land and a permanent easement on 200,000 acres of working forestland, Brascan owns two operational paper mills and 300,000 acres of forestlands important for mill supply purposes, north central Maine improves its economy, and GECIF receives income tax credits and dividends on its equity investment. This deal is a synergistic marriage of resource conservation and economic development.

Investment Strategy Considerations

As noted, the process of obtaining NMTC investment capacity is highly competitive. Conventional wisdom holds that it is difficult to utilize the program in rural areas, where CEI has historically concentrated its efforts, due to high transaction costs and NMTC program restrictions that drive the program toward large real estate financings in urban areas. In these early days of NMTC program implementation, many urban real estate projects are being financed. Furthermore, there is nothing in the NMTC statute or regulations about conservation or environmental protection, although clearly the program is oriented toward economic development and social equity, because it can be used only for businesses and projects in low-income areas. Thus two of the three "bottom lines" in the triple bottom-line underwriting equation are part of the NMTC program.

CEI has made a strategic decision to introduce the third bottom line—conservation or environmental protection—into the equation to enhance the value of the program. This is consistent with CEI's overall mission "to help create economically and environmentally healthy communities in which all people, especially those with low incomes, can reach their full potential." This defines what CEI means by "sustainable development" and determines its triple bottom-line (3E) approach to all its activities. CEI has authority under the NMTC program to finance deals throughout the country, and it aspires to a national leadership role in demonstrating the power of the triple-bottom line approach in serving the needs of low-income people.

CEI was a substantial award winner during the first two rounds of the NMTC program, obtaining a total NMTC investment allocation of $129 million. It hopes to build a portfolio of several hundred million dollars of NMTC capital under its management. Integral to this is its 3E investment strategy, which it sees as a prototype for other CDEs. This permeates all of CEI's work, and it explicitly defines two of its four investment themes under the NMTC program.

The Katahdin project was a leading project under CEI's natural resource–based development investment theme. Natural resources are the most important economic assets of most rural economies, whether for industrial or recreational tourism purposes. Within this investment theme, CEI's primary focus is on sustainable working forests, with a secondary emphasis on working waterfronts and small working farms. The purposes of choosing this investment theme are to (1) guarantee the availability of large blocks of forestland for industrial use, (2) protect the long-term economic value of these assets by implementing sustainable forestry practices, and (3) promote compatible recreational tourism, value-added wood processing, and other economic activities. To achieve these objectives, CEI partners with large-tract forestland buyers; major mill owners; large investors, such as GECIF; socially motivated investors, such as the Calvert Social Investment Foundation; and conservation organizations, such as TNC. CEI has a goal of encouraging more commercial bank participation in this specialized area of financing.

The natural resource–based development investment theme grew from a regional initiative in CEI's first-round NMTC application to become a national initiative in the second round, building on CEI's success in north central Maine with the Katahdin deal, and a pipeline of highly desirable projects with similar characteristics throughout the country. The unique coalition of interests that made the Katahdin deal a success demonstrates that it is possible to achieve development, multiple-use, and environmental protection objectives simultaneously. CEI is working on a number of other projects consistent with this theme. The Katahdin project set a standard and introduced this concept into the national consciousness. An increasing number of organizations are considering triple bottom-line initiatives under the NMTC program, some based on sustainable natural resources development.

A related way to employ the "sustainable working forest" strategy is to work with sustainable timber harvesting operations looking to develop eco-tourism or recreational activities as a compatible second major business activity on the same land. Businesses using this approach often see the financial value in formal conservation easements that are consistent with their business purposes. Another method is to use the negotiating process to achieve internal and external project-related objectives. For instance, with forestland deals, CEI could require third-party certified sustainable forestry practices or preservation of certain high conservation value lands. At the same time, some of the value of the tax credits could be used to capitalize other projects, such as an eco-tourism revolving loan fund or a conservation fund to acquire conservation easements in the region. CEI is working on projects in the northeastern United States and elsewhere that embody these ideas.

The triple bottom-line approach is not limited to natural resource–based projects. CEI is extending the same principles to projects under its "major business and real estate investments" theme. Investments in substantial operating businesses and large real estate projects are a bread-and-butter element of the NMTC program for CEI and others using this development incentive. This investment theme encompasses industrial and commercial real estate development projects undertaken by both for-profit developers and nonprofit entities, community facilities (e.g., business incubators, child-care facilities), operating business investments (e.g., manufacturing start-ups or expansions), mixed-use projects (e.g., commercial development combined with rental housing in the same project), and even for-sale housing with benefits to low-income communities and people. Typically, these are projects financed on a one-off basis requiring NMTC investment capacity of $2 million to $40 million.

CEI is unique in its ability to combine triple bottom-line underwriting into its major business and real estate investments area, distinguishing CEI from virtually all other NMTC applicants and award winners. CEI looks for projects that have strong resource conservation (e.g., energy conservation, clean energy use/production, or use of recycled materials), environmental protection features (e.g., buildings ranking high on the Leadership in Energy and Environmental Design (LEED)[1] rating system), and distinctly positive impacts on low-income communities and people.

The NMTC program makes this kind of 3E investing possible. CEI is committed to projects in especially economically distressed communities, as defined by the Community Development Financial Institutions (CDFI) Fund, to reinforce the value of the NMTC program to low-income areas and people (see box 9.2 for

Box 9.2

NMTC Requirements and Legislation

The NMTC program is a major new federal financing initiative with great potential to finance worthy projects serving multiple objectives. Passed in the waning days of the 2000 Congress, the NMTC program is a seven-year initiative with a statutory authorization of $15 billion of investment capacity. Based on the 39 percent federal income tax credit that is the economic engine of the program, the NMTC program is a $6 billion cash equivalent economic development program, perhaps the most significant contemporary program of its type. It has strong bipartisan support in Congress.

NMTC is, by statute, an economic development program directed at the needs of low-income communities and low-income people. The enabling legislation limited its use to businesses and projects in defined low-income areas, as delineated by U.S. Bureau of the Census tracts and economic data. Capital mobilized under the NMTC program must flow to qualified active low-income community businesses (QALICBs). Eligible businesses include for-profit and nonprofit entities engaged in a wide range of activities, including most operating businesses, real estate projects, and community facilities (e.g., food cooperatives, child-care centers, and charter schools). Financial businesses (e.g., banks and insurance companies), large-scale agricultural entities, gambling, rental housing, and some recreational enterprises are not eligible. Under the initial legislation, the businesses must be in census tracts with either a poverty rate of at least 20 percent or a median family income of less than 80 percent of the statewide or metropolitan average, whichever is higher. These census tracts are typically in distressed sections of older cities or in poor rural areas.

In an important action, the corporate tax bill of 2004 contained a provision that would broaden the applicability of the program. This provision directs the Community Development Financial Institutions Fund (CDFI Fund)—the organizational unit of the U.S. Treasury Department that administers the NMTC program—and the Internal Revenue Service—another unit of the Treasury that issues the regulations governing the NMTC program—to collaborate in issuing new regulations that would make projects or businesses serving low-income people eligible, wherever these projects or businesses are located. This development is promising. Regulations implementing this change are expected during 2005.

more information about the CDFI Fund). Especially economically distressed communities are defined as areas with economic problems even more dire than those that qualify a census tract for NMTC financing. Finding the best projects under this investment theme involves working directly with project and economic developers, banks and nonregulated sources of capital, and operating businesses; it also means working extensively with CEI's local and regional community development partners.

Issues Related to a Broader Application of the 3E Concept

The Katahdin project is a compelling success story for the paper industry, for Maine—and for the NMTC program. This project is playing an integral part in the overall revitalization of northern Maine. But the Katahdin project appears to be just the first of what will be many equally worthwhile and powerful successes. In the case of the Katahdin project, delivering below-market-rate financing on the forestlands was essential to keep them intact and achieve the objectives described earlier.

The NMTC program provides investors in qualified, selected projects in low-income areas with a 39 percent federal income tax credit, calculated on the amount of the gross investment capital provided and spread throughout seven years. NMTC-generated investment capital can flow to an operating business as either debt or equity. When the capital reaches the operating business in the form of a loan, typically it is on terms and conditions substantially better than market, fundamentally changing the viability of projects and the debt service or capital return characteristics of the deal. Loan rates to the operating company borrower typically are 200 to 300 basis points below market and are usually fixed for the seven-year period of the tax credits. Moreover, as discussed in more detail in the explanation of the mechanics of NMTC (see box 9.3), sometimes the leveraged model can be used to provide permanent equity in projects of value to low-income communities and with prospects that can be underwritten financially.

Although there are many clear benefits to using NMTC tax credits, there are also several challenges to using this program more widely for worthy projects. Some of these challenges are:

- *Getting sufficient NMTC allocations.* The NMTC program is a $15 billion federal initiative with a seven-year Congressional authorization (2001–2007). The U.S. Treasury Department awards NMTC investment capacity to CDFI Fund–approved community development entities (CDEs) with a primary mission of serving low-income areas, both rural and urban, in a highly competitive process. Dollar requests outnumber awards ten to one. CEI's natural resource–based development investment strategy is only one of many investment strategies advanced by NMTC applicants. Financing good projects and getting recognition and political support for this initiative will be critical to obtaining substantial future investment allocations for CEI and others who see the value in

Box 9.3
NMTC Financing Mechanics

The mechanics of NMTC financing are interesting and sometimes complicated. After all, the program is designed to finance difficult projects in locations that are underserved by traditional capital sources. Individual NMTC transactions are being structured in many creative ways, but all are variations on the following two basic investment models.

Direct Investment Model

In its simplest form, a single source of capital finances a stand-alone project through a CDFI Fund–approved, special-purpose community development entity (CDE) set up by a sponsoring CDE with an NMTC allocation. This is the direct investment model. The special-purpose CDE receives a suballocation of tax credit capacity from the sponsoring CDE, which serves as its managing member. The capital source provides capital in an agreed-upon amount and becomes the investor member of the special-purpose CDE. The capital must be a cash qualified equity investment (QEI) in the special-purpose CDE, which entitles the investor member to a federal income tax credit of 39 percent of its QEI, spread throughout seven years (5 percent per year for three years and then 6 percent per year for four years). The investor member also may receive cash flow from the project (similar to interest payments) and a return of all or a portion of its capital at the end of seven years, depending on the intricacies of the deal. The sponsoring CDE receives fees for using its NMTC capacity to convey the suballocation to the project. The business receiving the funds gets financing for all or a portion of its project, typically on favorable terms and conditions. Structured properly and in balance, it is a win-win-win situation for all three of the major participants (the sponsoring CDE with an NMTC allocation, the investor member, and the business), and low-income people benefit from the project financed in their community. Figure 9.2 is a schematic of how direct investment works.   *(continues)*

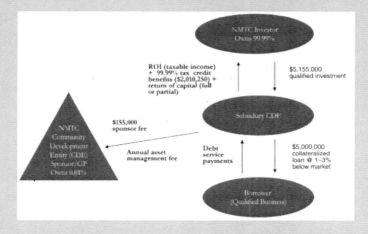

Figure 9.2.

An illustration of the direct investment model of NMTC program investing. The capital source makes a direct equity investment in the subsidiary CDE set up by a sponsoring master CDE with NMTC investment capacity. (Diagram developed by Steve Weems, CEI Capital Management LLC.)

One obvious requirement of the direct investment model is that the investor must have a use for the tax credits. As a general business tax credit, the utility of the credit is limited for individual investors, so the direct investment model is most applicable when the investor is a corporate U.S. taxpayer. Many other capital sources, such as individual investors, pension funds, and foundations, would like to participate in the program and finance worthy projects, but cannot use the tax credits, so can only participate as lenders under the "leveraged investment model."

Leveraged Investment Model

Another NMTC financing technique, the leveraged investment model, can be employed to source investors who, by themselves, would not be eligible to participate in the program. This model can be highly complex; in essence, a second, investment-level entity is set up to make the QEI in the special-purpose CDE. This investment-level entity is a pass-through limited liability corporation (known as an investment LLC), which is treated as a partnership for federal income tax purposes. Its purpose is to pool capital from various sources to make the QEI on which the tax credits are calculated. It thereby obtains capital in the form of both loans and equity investments, depending on the capital source, and makes one or more lump-sum investments into the special-purpose CDE, which, in turn, finances the NMTC-eligible business or project. This is similar to the direct investment approach, except that in this scenario, the lender to the investment LLC receives interest and return of principal, while all the credits are allocated to the equity investor.

If the ratio of equity to debt at the investment LLC level is balanced properly, the equity investor may not need to get any cash flow from the project or any significant return of capital to earn an acceptable rate of return. For example, say the equity investor provides 30 percent (say $30) of the capital to the investment LLC, with the other 70 percent ($70) coming in the form of loans. All the capital ($100) is invested in a special-purpose CDE, which triggers $39 (i.e., 39 percent of $100) in tax credits. If all the credits are allocated to the investor providing the $30, these credits may generate an acceptable rate of return for the equity investor without providing any cash flow or return of capital from the business or project. The equity investor is satisfied based solely on the tax credit value. At the end, the lenders get an acceptable interest rate and principal repayment. Depending on how the deal is structured, the business gets a below-market-rate loan on a blended cost of capital basis: 30 percent of the capital with no cost or 30 percent of the financing does not have to be paid back—or both. It all depends on the allocation of the benefits among the parties to the transaction and the rate paid by the project borrower. This is a highly creative way to bring capital into distressed areas, which is the fundamental purpose of the NMTC program. Figure 9.3 is a schematic of the leveraged investment model.

this investment strategy to serve the needs of low-income people in their service areas.

- *Securing investment capital.* Investing in an NMTC deal may not be appropriate for all investors, for a number of reasons. The NMTC program is relatively new and investing in forestlands, for example, is a specialized financial activity. Furthermore, the NMTC credit is a general business tax credit in the federal tax code. Although the credit is available

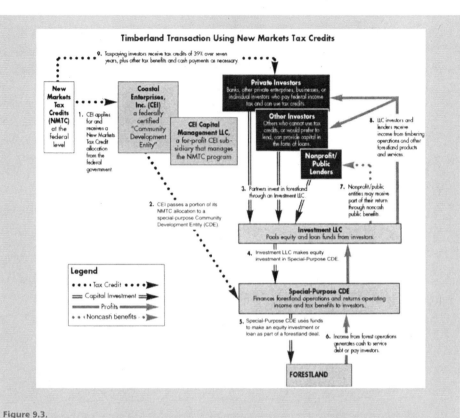

Figure 9.3.

A flowchart of how the leveraged investment model can be used, utilizing a timberlands financial transaction as an example. Several debt and equity sources provide capital in different forms to an investment LLC, which functions as a "pooling of capital" entity that, in turn, makes an equity investment in the subsidiary CDE. (Diagram developed by Steve Weems, CEI Capital Management LLC, working with Ann Ingerson, The Wilderness Society, and Bill Ginn, The Nature Conservancy.)

to both corporate and individual taxpayers, there are limitations on its attractiveness to individuals (e.g., alternative minimum tax considerations, passive investor limitations, and section 183 provisions), and all taxpayers (corporate and individual) have other tax credit opportunities and a finite appetite for tax credit deals. Moreover, there are, of course, special aspects of any federal financing program that affect its applicability and attractiveness.

On the plus side, the viability of NMTC program tax credits does not hinge on the continuing success of the business that is financed. On the negative side, investors cannot get any *return of capital* for the seven-year period of the tax credits (except through the tax credits themselves and other tax benefits potentially available via the leveraged investment model), although they can get cash distributions in the form of *return on capital*. These add up to a set of circumstances where it is a significant challenge to find the required investment capital for an NMTC deal, particularly in a specialized, industrial category such as timberlands. Fundamentally, though, the potential returns often are sufficiently attractive to meet this challenge.

- *Finding good projects.* There is no shortage of forest-based projects with worthy conservation elements, and the economies of many rural, forested areas are in dire straits. The NMTC program is a mission-oriented economic development program. Although many people want to embrace 3E thinking, it has not yet made it into the federal statute book. It is imperative to find projects that have strong, legitimate economic development impacts and have sufficient scale to make 3E financing viable. To date, TNC and CEI have found more than a dozen projects nationwide that meet these criteria; given the relative scarcity of NMTC investment capacity, it appears that sufficient projects can be found.

- *Eligibility issues.* Currently, the eligibility of projects is keyed to census tracts and income criteria on each tract (i.e., projects must be in defined low-income census tracts). In rural areas, census tracts sometimes cover vast areas of land, with limited population. What happens in one part of a tract can be magnified and affect the eligibility of other parts of the tract, even though the areas are not related in any meaningful way. There was an established process to qualify *portions* of whole census tracts in otherwise ineligible areas, but such approvals were difficult to obtain because the applicant had to prove that there is a "lack of access to investment capital" in the specific area under consideration. Given the propensity of capital to flow to good projects and specific data limitations, this was a difficult burden, particularly in urban areas, where a project might just be on the wrong side of a street. Fortunately, Congress has acted positively by including a "targeted population" provision in the 2004 corporate tax bill, which, if implemented thoughtfully by the CDFI Fund, will extend the benefits of this program to low-income people through projects not located in eligible census tracts but providing direct benefits to low-income citizens.

- *NMTC program uncertainties.* There remain many uncertainties (specific issues on which there are no definitive rulings or guidance) about the NMTC program. Investors in general are averse to risk, and uncertainty equals risk. In addition, some of the most compelling uncertainties relate to the attractiveness of the credit for individual investors. In particular, there appears to be merit in getting regulatory or statutory clarifications or changes to allow the tax credits to be stripped out in an NMTC deal and sold to equity investors, without a requirement for the investors to have a "profit motive" or be dependent on the performance of the project for part of the investment return (the doctrine of "economic substance"). In time, these uncertainties probably will be resolved, which will enhance the viability of the program if the resolutions are consistent with the "mission character" of the NMTC program. Further federal statutory changes may be justified to bring in additional capital from socially motivated individual investors and to enhance the value of the NMTC program for small businesses.
- *NMTC program reauthorization.* In 2006 and 2007, the U.S. Congress will decide whether to reauthorize the NMTC program and extend its effectiveness and reach. The program has strong bipartisan support, but it must be effective to warrant reauthorization. The prospects for reauthorization hinge on what the program accomplishes. This will be a matter of *substance and form*: substance as defined by the nature of the projects financed and the resulting benefits to low-income people, form in the way these successes are made a part of the public and popular record. The program is designed to give tax credits to corporations (and, it is hoped, individuals) that do not really need them, as an incentive to provide capital to low-income areas, so there

always will be opportunities for enterprising reporters to write the titillating story. It will be incumbent on the NMTC "industry" to finance strong projects, with mission-related benefits, and get the full story out.

One way or another, how and when the foregoing issues are resolved will affect the breadth and depth of the applicability of the NMTC financing program to projects similar to those described already. Triple bottom-line thinking is blossoming, and the NMTC program offers an opportunity to be at the front of this movement. Being able to marry economic development and conservation objectives in a synergistic way, one that truly stimulates the economies of rural areas in a sustainable fashion, presents an opportunity for the U.S. Treasury Department and progressive community development entities to be visionary leaders via the NMTC program. It has been a long time coming, but now we can have both payrolls *and* pickerels.

Note

[1]The Leadership in Energy and Environmental Design (LEED) green building rating system is a voluntary, consensus-based national standard for developing high-performance, sustainable buildings. Members of the U.S. Green Building Council, representing all segments of the building industry, developed LEED and continue to contribute to its evolution.

Chapter 10

Mainstreaming Environmental Markets

Adam Davis

Imagine a marketplace where each unit of improvement in environmental quality was worth real money and competition managed cost so that the greatest amount of improvement per dollar could be purchased. In fact, this kind of market activity is already under way. In June 2004, the government of Collier County, Florida, issued a request for proposals (RFP) for the purchase of wetlands mitigation credits. State and federal laws governing wetlands impacts put many areas completely "off-limits," and they clearly state that damage to wetlands is to be avoided when possible. However, these laws also allow an "offset," or mitigating action, when impact cannot be fully avoided. This means that a county road, park, or sewer line project, or a private development project, could get a permit even if it had an impact on the wetlands, if it paid a third party for an interest in a qualified wetlands recovery project within the same watershed and the net impact to those wetlands was positive.

The county was already a reasonably sophisticated buyer of these credits and had arranged to buy credits at a rate of $35,000 each under a 2001 contract with a qualified group known as the Panther Island Mitigation Bank (each credit represents about 1.25 acres of restored wetland). By 2004, a competitive source of wetlands mitigation credits had come on the scene, and the county wanted to see whether it could drive a better bargain and buy more environmental offset for the same cost. It issued an RFP for a new round of wetlands mitigation credits, hoping that market forces would yield a lower price per credit. The market answered yes.

The new competitor, Big Cypress Mitigation Bank, responded to the RFP with a price of $26,667 per individual credit, while Panther Island made an offer of $24,000 per individual credit. On September 28, 2004, the Collier County commissioners voted to award a new "purchase as needed" mitigation credit contract to Panther Island, designating Big Cypress as a secondary source for such credits.

In effect, the commissioners provided a case in point for a concept of growing importance: it is possible to effectively buy and sell ecosystem services (in this case, the provision of biodiversity habitat and enhanced hydrology) produced by well-managed property in a competitive marketplace. By engaging market forces, the county managed, throughout the course of several years, to reduce the cost to the public for wetland mitigation credits by about one third.[1]

Valuing Our Ecosystems

There is an increasing worldwide recognition of the value of ecosystems. So-called ecosystem services used to be, in financial terms, free, because they were enormously abundant in comparison with human uses and human needs. With the world population on the way from 6 billion to 8 billion or more, and with consumption per person on the rise, these services are increasingly scarce and, therefore, increasingly valuable in the marketplace.

So what are ecosystem services? Essentially, they are the things that ecosystems *do*, rather than what they *are*. Ecosystems clean water and store it, they help to regulate climate and weather, and they provide habitat for creatures we depend on for our food. Without sufficient provision of ecosystem services, humans are infinitely worse off: our water supply is threatened, we are subject to increasingly severe and unpredictable weather, our apple trees are not pollinated, and our fishing boats come home empty.

In the United States, environmental law has limited or prevented some impacts to ecosystems through major legislation, such as the Clean Air Act, the Clean Water Act, the Endangered Species

Act, and the Resource Conservation and Recovery Act. The rules and regulations within these acts aim to protect ecosystems or, at a minimum, to increase the cost of affecting them. However, this type of traditional "command and control" regulation has its limits: there is typically conflict between the scientific process and the need for expediency in setting compliance targets, and such regulation imposes costs on the polluter in a way that limits the incentive for improvement in environmental performance. Even if the compliance target were a reasonable compromise, why would a rational actor invest in environmental improvement beyond the objective of compliance?

Mitigation banking is one answer to this fundamental question. Allowing private investment on private land to create public benefit generates a set of incentives that send the message that conservation and restoration of ecosystems is valuable. It also provides a more effective, less expensive way to achieve conservation and environmental objectives.

How Mitigation Banking Works

The U.S. government definition of wetland mitigation banks is straightforward:

> Wetland restoration, creation, enhancement, and in exceptional circumstances, preservation undertaken expressly for the purpose of compensating for unavoidable wetland losses in advance of development actions, when such compensation cannot be achieved at the development site or would not be as environmentally beneficial. It typically involves the consolidation of small, fragmented wetland mitigation projects into one large contiguous site. Units of restored, created, enhanced or preserved wetlands are expressed as "credits" which may subsequently be withdrawn to offset "debits" incurred at a project development site.[2]

Essentially, private landowners and investors who work with them are fulfilling regulatory goals and are rewarded for doing so. These are private dollars on private land for public benefit. Of course, there is potential private benefit as well, and the key to understanding the power of this approach is that it aligns the interest of the private landowner with the interest of the public.

Once all parties involved approve the plans and the bank meets its ecological success criteria (defined by the government, not the landowner), the mitigation banker earns credits that regulatory agencies will recognize. The landowner can then sell these mitigation credits to permitees and others who must compensate for adversely affected wetlands or other natural areas. The sale of wetland credits legally transfers the liability for wetland mitigation from the permitee to the wetland banker.

The Benefits of a Market Approach   Although mitigation banking[3] is a new application of market-based or incentive-based regulation for environmental improvement, it is a logical extension of previous steps taken to protect and restore public goods. In a sense, all environmental regulation internalizes the cost of pollution, "take," or other impact by imposing a related cost on the economic actor producing the impact. We know this purely regulatory approach is imperfect, however. For example, if emitting 11 parts per million of a substance makes one a criminal, then emitting 10 parts per million of the same substance cannot be "just fine," even though it is not against the law. By providing incentives for private actors to achieve high levels of performance, mitigation banking complements and enhances the regulatory approach.

In the area of land management, the benefits of a market approach are as follows:

- An incentive is provided for private landowners to invest in protection, enhancement, restoration, and creation of environmental features on their property.
- The ability to complete project design, approval, and success criteria becomes a competitive advantage for suppliers of environmental services.
- The presence of competing service providers provides cost-effective procurement of environmental offsets for public and private-sector projects that affect environmental features.
- A regulated industry of environmental service providers improves financial assurance, monitoring, and enforcement, thus resulting in a higher likelihood of ecological success.

Although these benefits present compelling arguments for the establishment of mitigation banking schemes, a number of structural requirements are needed for these benefits to be realized. Required structural elements can be divided into the following general categories:

- *Predictable enforcement of environmental laws.* No one will mitigate the impact of a project on species habitat or water resources unless they must. To do otherwise confers a competitive disadvantage, as it adds project cost without adding commercial value to the project.

- *An incentive to achieve and surpass specific environmental objectives.* Landowners and investors in mitigation projects must be able to get a rate of return on the actions required (e.g., placing a conservation easement on their property, engineering stream restoration, or removing invasive species from endangered species habitat), or they will not voluntarily take these actions.

If you want the benefits of a market for environmental performance improvements, then you have to let the market provide real benefits for participants as well.

Lessons from Waste and Energy Policy

The most obvious relationship between the United States of America's solid waste and its wetlands is that many wetlands were used as dumpsites because they were seen as low-value land that could not be developed. Fortunately, these two parts of the environmental puzzle also fit together in other, more positive ways.

Consolidation of small, fragmented wetland mitigation projects into one large, contiguous site has a number of benefits. From an ecological perspective, contiguous wetlands generally provide greater benefits in hydrologic function (water purification, flood storage, aquifer recharge, and related functions) and habitat. From a regulatory perspective, it is easier to monitor and enforce success criteria at these larger sites as well.

From this "economy of scale" point of view, there are some similarities between the environmental benefits and the economic benefits of large-scale mitigation projects and another class of large-scale environmental activity: regional landfills. The volume of material that regional landfills can handle means higher revenue, which, in turn, means that these facilities can afford a higher level of environmental protection investment. Regional landfills also reduce the cost and difficulty of monitoring and enforcement, as they reduce the number of small and substandard facilities requiring site visits. In 1972, there were 25,000 landfills in the United States, many no more than glorified town dumps and unlined quarries. Following the passage of the Resource Conservation and Recovery Act, Subtitle D, which greatly improved the environmental performance standards required to site a landfill, the number has shrunk to less than 2,000.[4]

At the same time, improved environmental standards conferred a competitive advantage on those firms that had both the will and the means to invest in high-quality environmental protection. In fact, environmental groups found themselves lobbying for these higher standards alongside the larger national companies, not exactly a commonplace occurrence.

Another lesson that is relevant to mitigation banks comes from the recycling industry. Since World War II, contracted solid waste service providers had financial incentives to collect and landfill (or incinerate) discarded materials, but not to recycle them. In the late 1980s, some contract structures were changed to allow a return on investment from the provision of curbside recycling services. As a direct result, recycling has gone from being a marginal activity provided by hippies at drop-off centers, to a mainstream service provided to the vast majority of U.S. homes.

Although we continue to generate 230 million tons of discarded material each year, nearly 30 percent (68 million tons) is now recycled, up from 6.4 percent in 1960.[5] The cost increases in environmental protection that led to investment in recycling services also resulted in waste prevention. In 2000, design, process, and management changes prevented more than 55 million tons of material from entering the waste stream.[6] By 2001, there were nearly ten thousand residential curbside recycling programs in place across the United States, and private waste companies had invested between $7 billion and $10 billion in recycling infrastructure over the preceding two decades.[7]

By aligning the profit motive with environmental outcomes, it became more expensive to waste material and more lucrative to recycle or recover it. In just this sense, providing a price signal for the value of wetlands and species habitat will make it more expensive to have an impact on ecosystems and more lucrative to protect and restore them. The solid waste sector provides us with examples of environmentally significant self-interested investment resulting from an alignment of incentives and clear policy goals.

Not long ago, utilities were in the same position that solid waste companies were before the provision of recycling incentives. They were paid by the kilowatt produced, just as solid waste companies were paid by the ton disposed. As a result, it was in their fundamental self-interest for customers to use as much energy as possible. This began to change when public utilities commissions provided contract incentive structures and companies could earn a return on investment by providing energy-efficient solutions for customers as well.[8, 9] Specific actions in which utilities invested included rebates on energy-efficient appliances, home improvements such as insulation and double-glazed windows, and even consulting on process design for energy-intensive businesses.

These actions are clearly justified by their cost effectiveness. U.S. utilities and their customers spend approximately $5 billion per year on investment in energy efficiency, with an average cost of 2 cents per kilowatt-hour (kWh). In contrast, each kWh delivered by a power plant costs an average of 5 cents.[10] The key lesson here is that it is usually cheaper to prevent a problem than to create one and clean up afterward. Just as the price signal for energy cost stimulates energy efficiency programs, sending a cost signal to those that affect natural features on the land will result in more careful site selection and design to avoid such impacts.

Although some have argued that recycling and energy efficiency advances "enable" continued consumption of materials and energy, many environmental organizations are highly supportive of these activities, citing them as positive contributions toward a sustainable society.[11] Similarly, although mitigation banking clearly does enables development, the environmental ethics question hinges on whether the total production of ecosystem services was increased or decreased through the combined results of the development and the associated mitigation.

More broadly, if we accept that the production of goods and services will, in fact, affect the environment and that we will, in fact, continue to produce goods and services, the fundamental question is, How can we produce goods and services in a manner fundamentally aligned with natural systems? This question is the heart of the challenge posed by the word *sustainability*, and it provides guidance for thinking about what types of mitigation are ultimately acceptable.

Case Studies in Mitigation Banking Best Practices

Although mitigation banking is a tool that has been utilized in the United States for more than two decades, the latest generation of programs increasingly demonstrates the principle of reliable compensation for verifiable conservation action. The following are examples of specific variations in the approach to providing incentives.

North Carolina Ecosystem Enhancement Program: Government as Wholesale Buyer   The North Carolina Ecosystem Enhancement Program (EEP) is an example of government acting as a consolidated purchaser of environmental improvement results through a competitive procurement process. A collaborative effort between the North Carolina Department of Environment and Natural Resources, U.S. Army Corps of Engineers, and North Carolina Department of Transportation (NCDOT), the program intends to provide programmatic mitigation and develop watershed level protection and enhancement to replace *functions* prior to these impacts occurring.[12]

As NCDOT identifies impacts, it contracts with private firms to facilitate wetland or stream mitigation projects that are planned, designed, constructed, and monitored on property acquired by the firm. This process includes the following steps:

- Solicit proposals from interested contractors.
- Review qualifications and prequalify contractors (currently thirty listed).
- Identify mitigation needs by location, habitat type, and amount.
- Issue a Request for Proposals to qualified contractors.
- Review proposals.
- Conduct site visits with NCDOT staff.
- Evaluate and select appropriate sites based on price and potential.
- Negotiate and enter into contracts with selected firms.

NCDOT's environmental staff evaluate contractors' proposals based on two criteria: technical quality and cost. After NCDOT makes a selection, the contractor's proposal is integrated into permit applications. Through 2003, this program had executed thirteen contracts that involved 1,975 acres, 848 wetland credits, and 31,025 feet of stream restoration, at a total cost of $31.5 million. The most recent awards for "full delivery mitigation" took place in October 2004 and provided for restoration of 143,000 feet of stream, 625 acres of wetland, and 75 acres of buffer for a total contract value of $39.6 million.[13]

Application of the EEP projects benefit communities around the state. In Greensboro, North Carolina, South Buffalo Creek was actively eroding its banks and threatening to undermine a local road. Local residents brought this potential hazard to EEP's attention, and the agency supplied funds to restore the creek to flow in its natural floodplain while alleviating erosion of Southside Boulevard.[14] In another effort in Chatham County, monies from EEP helped to purchase a 1,022-acre section of land along lower Haw Creek, creating a new natural area for the state to enjoy.[15] Other benefits include reduced delays in major transportation projects, such as the Raleigh Outer Loop, which had been continually plagued by slowdowns due to mitigation needs.[16]

A number of key defects remain in this "market" for environmental services that continue to prevent efficient and effective performance. One defect is the continued presence of in-lieu-of-fee mitigation options for those that affect wetlands, streams, and habitat. Even more problematic is regulatory agency acceptance of ad hoc mitigation of impacts.[17] Neither of these options results in a predictable, measurable offset of impacts.[18] History shows that in-lieu-of-fee programs typically achieve only modest mitigation, which occurs well after the harm is done. The history of ad hoc approaches is that the work is done without regard to meaningful success criteria and long-term monitoring and maintenance, and that a collection of small projects provides limited ecosystem benefits.

Another major issue is the lack of ongoing analysis comparing ecological impact with ecological restoration resulting from projects. Ecological success criteria are implicit in the EEP goals, described as "watershed-need-based ecosystem enhancement," and the program is clearly moving in the direction of more explicit replacement of ecological functions lost through the utilization of functional assessments.[19]

Florida Water Management Districts: Government-Enabled Retail Market[20]　The Florida Legislature passed rules for development of private mitigation banking in 1993.[21] In 1996, the legislature passed SB 1986, directing the state Department of Transportation (DOT) and the state Department of Environmental Protection (DEP) to address effects of transportation infrastructure development on a regional, rather than project-by-project, basis. Water management districts are given the responsibility to develop regional mitigation plans and to establish the technical, legal, and financial criteria for evaluating mitigation bank proposals. The law clearly states that private parties can establish banks if all of the following are true: the bank site meets ecological criteria, the banker has sufficient legal interest to operate the bank, and the banker can meet financial responsibility requirements.

As a result of this basic framework, the state has facilitated the establishment of a $20 million per year market, with an average sales price of $34,000 per credit, and approximately 50,000 acres of wetlands protected and restored.[22]

Little Pine Island Mitigation Bank in southwest Florida is "one of the first and most successful, large-scale public–private partnerships in mitigation banking."[23] Located within the Charlotte Harbor Estuary and the Matlacha Pass Aquatic Preserve, the 4,700-acre Little Pine Island was drained and dredged in the 1960s to facilitate the construction of canals in that region. Initiated in 1997 as a joint effort between Mariner Properties Development, Inc., and Florida DEP, the restoration project has three phases. In the first phase, thirty to forty tons of exotic biomass were removed from the site. The second phase, which is ongoing, will see a complete reconstruction of the natural hydrology of the system, including replanting of native species (see figure 10.1). Phase three constitutes a monitoring program that will continue in perpetuity through the establishment of an endowed trust. Managers of the project anticipate it will take an additional ten or twelve years before the bank credits sell out.[24, 25]

The Florida program incorporates rigorous enforcement of both wetland and associated upland buffer mitigation requirements, resulting in consistent demand for conservation and restoration measures on private property. The program also provides an ongoing analysis of impact versus mitigation benefit, as well as ex-

Figure 10.1.

White vine is native to Little Pine Island and is being restored to the property by Mariner Properties Development, Inc., following the removal of invasive species. (Photo by Richard B. Kelly, provided courtesy of Mariner Properties Development, Inc.)

plicit scientific success criteria through the Uniform Mitigation Assessment Rule.[26] This assessment rule reviews wildlife utilization, overstory/shrub canopy of desirable species, wetland vegetative ground cover of desirable species, adjacent upland/wetland buffer, field indicators of wetland hydrology, and water quality input and treatment.

Finally, under the Florida program, the private mitigation banking industry provides mitigation of impacts resulting from government-sponsored infrastructure build-out. The state DOT and county public works departments are required to obtain their mitigation needs from the water management districts, which, in turn, are required to obtain the mitigation credits from the ecosystem service providers whenever suitable credits are available. This combination of rigorous and uniform enforcement of environmental regulations and the avoidance of competing government mitigation projects or price restrictions has resulted in an efficient mitigation marketplace that values ecosystem functions fairly.

Conservation Banking for Endangered Species Habitat   Although conservation banking to mitigate harm done under the Endangered Species Act (ESA) is a recent practice compared with wetlands mitigation, new clarity in the regulatory framework is opening markets for private investment in habitat conservation.

In May 2003, after the establishment of species and habitat conservation banks across the country under a variety of implementation approaches, the U.S. Fish and Wildlife Service released conservation-banking guidance at the federal level.[27] This guidance outlines specific requirements for conservation banking agreements,[28] including the following:

- Meet the conservation needs of one or more covered species.
- Determine the service areas where credits may be used.
- Award credits for conservation outcomes, rather than management actions.
- Make conservation commitments on a permanent basis.
- Provide a management plan that ensures long-term funding and terms for remedial action.

The general practice of species credit trading has occurred under a number of different types of agreements; all of these can be understood as conservation banks, and participants in these agreements self-identified their projects as such. The amount of activity in this new market is documented in table 10.1.

The case of Hickory Pass Conservation Bank in Texas provides a key example of a conservation bank that is working to meet the needs of a private landowner, public and private developers, and government restrictions imposed under the ESA. The 3,000-acre Hickory Pass ranch is prime habitat for the endangered golden-cheeked warbler—a migratory songbird that nests only in mature Ashe juniper forests of central Texas (see figure 10.2). Being unwilling to sell their property outright, ranch owners negotiated a deal with the U.S. Fish and Wildlife Service (FWS) to manage 500 acres of their land as a conservation bank, with each acre acting as one "credit" they can sell to parties required to compen-

Table 10.1.

U.S. Conservation Banks as of November 2004

Type of Agreement	Number of Confirmed Agreements
Conservation Banking Agreements	35
Wetland Banking Agreements	18
Habitat Conservation Plans	5
Memorandums of Agreement	6
Safe Harbor Agreements	6

Source

Jessica Fox and A. Anamaria Nino-Murcia, "Status of Species Conservation Banking in the United States," *Conservation Biology* August 2005, vol. 19, no. 4, pp. 996–1007.

Figure 10.2.

The U.S. Fish and Wildlife Service is utilizing conservation banks to preserve essential habitat for the golden-cheeked warbler, an endangered bird endemic to central Texas. (Photo by Steve Maslowski.)

sate for lost warbler habitat elsewhere. The owners hold the option to convert the remaining 2,500 acres to a conservation bank
in the future.[29] The outcome of this case clearly reveals the benefits of conservation banking for all parties involved: (1) the
landowners have transformed their property from a potential liability into an asset, (2) the FWS secured contiguous, high-quality
habitat to meet its needs under the ESA, (3) developers in the area
have a mitigation bank from which they can purchase credits and
facilitate their projects going forward, and (4) of great importance,
the golden-cheeked warbler is assured a high-quality habitat over
the long term.[30]

Conclusion

As understanding and acceptance of sustainability as an organizing
principle for environmental policy increase, it will be essential to
use markets to align the production of goods and services with natural systems. For wetland, stream, and endangered species, mitigation banking is an essential component of this larger picture. In order for mitigation banking to become an accepted feature of U.S.
life and an accepted price signal guiding economic and development
activities, it must evolve further. Essential elements include the
following:

- *Clear and predictable enforcement of laws regulating impacts.*
  Projects that have an impact on environmental features must
  be required to plan and budget for internalizing the current
  externality of those impacts. Enforcement provides the demand for conservation actions, without which there will be
  no supply.
- *Leak-proof pricing.* No one will pay to buy credits from banks if
  he or she can make a deal with the regulator on an ad hoc
  basis. If ad hoc arrangements are needed, they must incorporate the same monitoring and enforcement of meaningful
  long-term success criteria and financial assurance mechanisms that are required of banks.
- *Sound science.* Criteria for success can incorporate real flexibility
  for permittees through the intelligent use of "credit ratios,"
  "currency types," and "service territory" variations, as long
  as ecological functionality is truly replaced.

When we look back twenty years from now, the most significant aspect of mitigation market development will not be the cost-effective procurement of offsets for environmental impacts, as important as this is. The real object lesson here will be the creation of a clear price signal that shows the economic value of conservation actions on private property. Each step in establishing markets for such conservation actions provides impetus to *avoid and minimize* environmental impact in order to reduce the now-clear cost of mitigation. Each step concurrently provides impetus to invest in conservation actions on private property.

Just as price signals for emission reductions, energy efficiency, and waste reduction have resulted in environmental infrastructure at landfills, recycling investment, and energy efficiency innovation, mechanisms that enable a price signal for conservation of ecosystem services will foster investment in such services.

Notes

[1]Eric Staats, "Collier's Manager Looks to Trim Costs of Environmental Mitigation," *Naples Daily News*, Naples, Florida, September 27, 2004. Follow-up information provided by phone by Collier County Purchasing Department, October 19, 2004.

[2]Office of the Federal Register, *Federal Guidance for the Establishment, Use and Operation of Mitigation Banks* (Washington, D.C.: Office of the Federal Register, November 28, 1995), volume 60, number 228, pages 58605–58614.

[3]*Mitigation banking* is defined broadly, for the purposes of this chapter, to include "conservation banking" as well as more conventional water resource–based "mitigation banking." So mitigation banking could be used for government-certified preservation, enhancement, restoration, or creation of environmental features on private property, including both wetland and stream features, as well as habitat for endangered species.

[4]U.S. Environmental Protection Agency (USEPA), *Municipal Solid Waste in the United States: 2000 Facts and Figures*, Figure ES-5, available at http://www.epa.gov/epaoswer/non-hw/muncpl/pubs/report-00.pdf.

[5]U.S. Environmental Protection Agency (USEPA), "Municipal Waste in the United States," available at http://www.epa.gov/epaoswer/non-hw/muncpl/pubs/msw-sum01.pdf.

[6]USEPA, "Municipal Waste."

[7]Private communication with Waste Management, Inc., government affairs office, April 21, 2004.

[8]For an excellent description of the process by which E2 investment became allowable by one utilities commission, see *Dynamos and Virgins* (New York: Random House, 1984) by David Roe, who happens to be the grandson of the founder of Pacific Gas & Electric.

[9]For a complete rundown on U.S. energy efficiency data, see "Measuring Energy Efficiency in the U.S. Economy: A Beginning," published by the U.S. Department of Energy, available at http://www.eia.doe.gov/emeu/efficiency/contents.html.

[10]Rocky Mountain Institute, "Electric Efficiency," available at http://www.rmi.org/sitepages/pid321.php.

[11]See, for example, Environmental Defense, "Global Warming: Undo It," available at http://www.environmentaldefense.org/home.cfm. This Web site encourages consumers to undertake a number of energy conservation practices to reduce each household's global warming impact.

[12]North Carolina Ecosystem Enhancement Program, "About EEP," available at http://www.nceep.net/pages/abouteep.html.

[13]"Progress Report to the EEP Liaison Council, 11/16/04," available at www.nceep.net.

[14]Taft Wireback, "Workers Restoring Stream's Old Flow," *News Record*, Greensboro, North Carolina, June 26, 2004.

[15]Joe Miller, "Lower Haw Reveals Treasures," *The News and Observer*, Raleigh-Durham, North Carolina, April 2, 2004.

[16]Suzy Barile, "State's Environmental Mitigation Takes a Proactive Turn," *Triangle Business Journal*, Raleigh, North Carolina, February 20, 2004.

[17]For comprehensive information on both ad hoc and in lieu arrangements, please see General Accounting Office report number GAO-01-325, "Wetlands Protection: Assessments Needed to Determine Effectiveness of In-Lieu Fee Mitigation," May 2001, available at http://www.gao.gov/new.items/d01325.pdf.

[18]GAO, "Wetlands Protection."

[19]"North Carolina's Ecosystem Enhancement Program: A New Approach to Mitigation"; presentation by Bill Gilmore of the North Carolina De-

partment of Environment and Natural Resources at National Mitigation Banking Conference, New Orleans, March 2004.

[20]For general information on Florida's mitigation banking programs, see *Florida Trend*, June 9, 2000, issue "Swamp Repair," available at www.floridatrend.com.

[21]Environmental Reorganization Act of 1993 (section 373.4135).

[22]For a complete list of permitted banks in Florida, see http://www.dep .state.fl.us/water/wetlands/mitigation/mitbanks.htm.

[23]NMBA News, "The Best of Mitigation Banking: Little Pine Island Mitigation Bank, A Public–Private Partnership," Spring 2004, publication of the National Mitigation Banking Association, available at http://www.mitigationbanking.org/PDFs/NMBA_Spring04.pdf.

[24]NMBA News, "The Best of Mitigation Banking."

[25]National Mitigation Banking Association, "The Little Pine Island Wetland Restoration and Mitigation Bank, Lee County, Florida," available at http://www.mitigationbanking.org/PDFs/FL-MarinerLITTLEPINE ISLAND.pdf.

[26]State of Florida, Department of Environmental Protection, "Development of the State-wide Uniform Wetland Mitigation Assessment Method," http://www.dep.state.fl.us/water/wetlands/mitigation/ uwmam2.htm.

[27]For full details of the federal guidance, see http://endangered.fws.gov/ policies/conservation-banking.pdf.

[28]Marybeth Bauer, Jessica Fox, and Michael Bean, "Landowners Bank on Conservation," *Environmental Law Review*, 34 (August 2004): 10720–10721.

[29]Bauer, Fox, and Bean, "Landowners Bank on Conservation," 10718–10719.

[30]Ibid., 10719.

Chapter 11

The Gray and the Green
The Built Infrastructure
and Conservation Investment

Jeffery T. More

The lion's share of federal investment in conservation in the next decade will come through our nation's largest infrastructure, agriculture, and energy development programs. The funding of conservation through the federal programs most noted for erecting massive "gray" infrastructures and for disrupting the natural environment reflects a confluence of budget realities, societal interests, and political pressures that will ultimately lead to billions of "new" dollars for conservation initiatives. This chapter considers the genesis of this new conservation paradigm and attempts to chart a course for those seeking to pursue conservation funding through transportation, water, and wastewater infrastructure, agriculture, and energy development programs.

Our nation's infrastructure, agriculture, and energy development programs contain by far the largest pots of money within the federal budget, outside of defense and "third rail"[1] social programs. So it seems logical in the current budgetary climate for people and organizations concerned with "green" land and biodiversity conservation to turn to these robust federal programs for funding. Since the days of John Muir, John Burroughs, and Theodore Roosevelt, however, the proponents of conservation have often been in a bitter struggle with those who viewed progress in miles of roads, acres in tillage, numbers of dams, and barrels of oil.

The unlikely marriage of conservation, infrastructure, agriculture, and energy interests in recent years reflects not only budgetary realities, but also changing societal views on the relative importance of natural and developed landscapes and the growing prominence of conservation issues in national politics.

Consider the following federal investments in conservation and environmental protection. Programs under the Department of Transportation contribute more than $3 billion annually to conservation and environmental protection. The U.S. Army Corps of Engineers is currently spending 20 percent of its $4.2 billion budget on habitat restoration and environmental projects. And, according to the Congressional Budget Office, the 2002 Farm Bill will provide $20.8 billion for conservation programs over six years. These conservation and environmental investments appear even more remarkable when juxtaposed with the recent annual budgets of the U.S. Fish and Wildlife Service ($1.2 billion) and the Environmental Protection Agency ($7.6 billion).

The budgetary, societal, and political pressures that have led to this new conservation-funding paradigm are growing. In the coming decade, we can expect infrastructure, agriculture, and energy programs to contribute far more to conservation than traditional conservation programs, both in percentage of dollars and in absolute dollars invested.

The Paving and Saving of the United States of America's Landscape

The Intermodal Surface Transportation Efficiency Act of 1991, known commonly as ISTEA, set in motion a new approach for meeting our nation's transportation and conservation imperatives. For the first time in history, significant dollars in highway legislation were designated for conservation and environmental objectives. The statement of the Federal Highway Administration (FHWA) prepared prior to the passage of ISTEA perhaps best illustrates this new approach to transportation policy: "The FHWA in partnership with the states is committed to working vigorously to preserve, and where practicable, enhance our environment." In signing ISTEA, President George H. W. Bush noted that we are now committed to "the design and building of transportation facilities that fit harmoniously into communities and the natural environment."

Specifically, ISTEA called for 10 percent of all surface transportation program (STP) dollars to be set aside for transportation enhancement activities, including the mitigation of damage to ecosystems and habitat, wetland banking, the acquisition of scenic easements, and the preservation of lands identified as critical habitat by states and metropolitan planning organizations. That 10 percent of STP funding equaled an investment of $2.4 billion over six years. The successor to ISTEA, called the Transportation Equity Act for the 21st Century (TEA-21), retained the provisions that set aside 10 percent of STP dollars for transportation enhancements, providing approximately $3.3 billion for enhancement projects between 1998 and 2003.

Also as part of ISTEA, Congress created the National Recreational Trails Trust Fund (now the Recreational Trails Program) with revenue from federal taxes on nonhighway recreational fuel. A national program to provide and maintain recreational trails, with a $30 million annual obligation ceiling, was in place for the first time. The Recreational Trails Program has flourished. Transportation reauthorization legislation pending in 2005 calls for substantially increased investment in recreation trails throughout the next six years. Since 1991, the year ISTEA was signed into law, thousands of miles of bike and hiking trails have been developed and enhanced using transportation dollars.

There has been a similar evolution regarding the use of gas taxes collected on boat fuel purchases. The Aquatic Resources Trust Fund was established with boat fuel tax receipts. In recent years, that program has generated more than $300 million annually for sport fish restoration, wetland restoration, and boating safety. Pending transportation reauthorization legislation continues this use of boat fuel taxes devoting substantial resources to the Aquatic Resources Trust Fund. Today, this fund represents one of the largest and most important sources of federal conservation dollars for freshwater and marine conservation.

In addition to continuing and enhancing conservation programs established in ISTEA and TEA-21, pending congressional efforts to reauthorize our nation's transportation programs include several new environmental financing measures that have garnered broad bipartisan and bicameral support. For example, pending surface transportation legislation includes a new stormwater-discharge mitigation program. Such a measure would require states to utilize 2 percent of their STP dollars on projects designed to improve water quality through the control of stormwater from highways. This legislation also includes $15 million annually to improve fish passages where forest roads and streams intersect. Throughout much of the western United States, bridge and culvert systems have for many years threatened anadromous fish populations (e.g., several species of salmon and steelhead that spend part of their life cycle at sea) by inhibiting upstream fish migration. For the first time, Congress is considering the use of substantial highway funds to address this long-standing fisheries problem.

Furthermore, highway legislation under consideration by Congress calls upon the secretary of transportation to study methods to reduce collisions between motor vehicles and wildlife. Once such a study is completed, the secretary would be required to develop a manual of best management practices for reducing wildlife mortality on our nation's highways and provide training courses for state transportation officials on the implementation of these measures.

The growth in conservation and environment funding in transportation legislation contrasts distinctly with recent declines in federal investment in traditional conservation and environmental programs. For example, Congress cut the Clean Water State Revolving Fund budget by $250 million for fiscal year 2005, while advancing new clean water funding initiatives in the context of legislation reauthorizing transportation programs.

Policy makers' awareness and appreciation of the impact of our nation's highways on water quality and wildlife continue to grow, as reflected in both the House and Senate versions of the Highway Bill advanced in the 109th Congress. Conservation organizations have worked successfully with members of the House and Senate to secure billions of dollars in funding for fish and wildlife habitat, recreational trails, and programs to reduce wildlife mortality on the nation's highways.

A Less Structured Corps of Engineers

Perhaps no entity within the federal government has had a greater impact on the natural environment than the U.S. Army Corps of Engineers (USACE). Large-scale navigation and flood control projects have been the hallmark of the USACE for more than a century. However, starting with the Water Resources Development Act of 1986 (WRDA 1986), we have witnessed a gradual greening of the Corps of Engineers.

For example, section 1135 of WRDA 1986, titled "Project Modification for the Improvement of the Environment," provides the USACE with the authority to investigate, study, modify, and construct projects for the restoration of fish and wildlife habitat where degradation is attributable to water resource projects previously constructed by the USACE. In each subsequent WRDA bill, acceptance and interest in expanding the USACE green mission have grown. WRDA 2000, for instance, included a $4 billion authorization for the restoration of the Florida Everglades; in a similar vein, WRDA 2005 proposes $1.58 billion for ecosystem restoration on the Upper Mississippi River–Illinois waterway system.

Moving beyond the correction of past environmental engineering impacts, USACE and Congress have also initiated programs to promote nonstructural solutions to flooding and habitat degradation. A prime example of this new thinking is seen in section 567 of WRDA 1996, which provides for the restoration of the upper Susquehanna River basin. This measure authorizes $10 million for "wetland restoration, soil and water conservation practices, and nonstructural measures to reduce flood damage, improve water quality, and create wildlife habitat." Largely with this funding, the USACE, working with Ducks Unlimited and a host of other nonfederal sponsors, has in the past decade completed extensive wetlands restoration projects in the upper Susquehanna River basin.

Similar initiatives can be found in WRDA 2005. For example, WRDA 2005 contains a new $20 million upper Connecticut River basin ecosystem restoration program modeled after the upper Susquehanna River basin program. Habitat restoration projects, involving partners such as Ducks Unlimited, are likely to become increasingly prominent features of USACE work around the nation. In another conservation-related initiative, on July 2, 2004, the USACE submitted to the Environmental Protection Agency a $2 billion Louisiana coastal restoration plan. Acting on this USACE conservation initiative, Congress is now poised to include $1.3 billion for Louisiana coastal restoration in WRDA 2005.

At present, 20 percent of the USACE's $4.2 billion budget goes to conservation and environmental projects. The USACE has embraced its green mission and appears committed to using its substantial engineering and hydrology expertise to improve the natural environment.

As WRDA 2005 works its way through Congress, there is an expectation that the percentage of USACE funds spent on protecting and improving habitat will expand, building on existing USACE programs that finance nonstructural, natural flood control; water quality enhancement; soil conservation; and habitat restoration throughout the nation.

Upstream Investment

For more than a decade, there have been discussions at all levels of government about the wisdom of addressing water quality issues on a watershed basis. Central to this discussion is the assertion that it often makes more sense to invest limited resources in controlling upstream sources of pollution than to clean up the problem with massive downstream infrastructure. Perhaps no example better illustrates this point than the New York City watershed, which provides drinking water to 9 million New Yorkers.

The city of New York was faced with a straightforward choice: invest $6 billion to $8 billion in a drinking water filtration infrastructure, or go upstream and invest a few hundred million dollars in protecting drinking water at the source. The city opted to embark on an aggressive plan to protect riparian areas and upgrade small wastewater treatment facilities in the 2,000-square-mile upstate New York watersheds that provide the city with its drinking water. The wisdom and effectiveness of this approach have been recognized both in Congress and by the Environmental Protection Agency. In the 1996 reauthorization of the Safe Drinking Water Act, Congress authorized $105 million to upgrade small wastewater treatment plants and purchase riparian lands in the New York City watershed. To facilitate this watershed experiment, New York City was provided with a temporary drinking water filtration avoidance waiver by the EPA.

New York City's investments in watershed protection have paid tremendous dividends. Thousands of acres of critical riparian lands have been permanently protected from development, trout fisheries have been enhanced, and, most important, the quality of drinking water for 9 million U.S. citizens has been safeguarded. The success of this upstream investment was recognized most recently by President George W. Bush. On October 5, 2004, President Bush signed into law legislation amending the Safe Drinking Water Act to reauthorize the New York City watershed protection program through 2010.

The future of water quality protection will undoubtedly feature the movement of funds once targeted for downstream infrastructure into investments in the management and preservation of critical upstream watersheds and associated streamside habitat.

Conservation and the Future of Farming

The future of conservation investment in the United States and the fate of the nation's agriculture appear to be inextricably tied. As production and trade-distorting agriculture subsidies come under greater scrutiny by the international community, conservation incentives may become the single most effective method of providing federal assistance to the U.S. farmer. This thesis is gaining acceptance within the farm community, at the Department of Agriculture, and on Capitol Hill.

However, assisting the U.S. farmer through conservation payments is not a new development. In fact, the 2002 Farm Bill increased mandatory spending on conservation programs to $20.8 billion throughout six years, up $9.2 billion from the conservation funding provided in the 1996 Farm Bill. Agriculture programs such as the Wetlands Reserve Program (WRP), the Conservation Reserve Program (CRP), the Wildlife Habitat Incentives Program (WHIP), and the Farmland Protection Program (FPP) have been responsible for protecting millions of acres of critical habitat across the United States over the past several decades. These programs, administered by the U.S. Department of Agriculture's Natural Resource Conservation Service (NRCS), build upon the heritage of the NRCS's predecessor, the Soil Conservation Service (SCS). Indeed, the SCS has been working with U.S. farmers and other landowners on soil and other natural resource conservation efforts since its creation in 1935.

The scope and promise of agricultural programs to serve critical conservation interests is perhaps best illustrated by CRP, the largest federal program for the retirement of private lands. Under the 2002 Farm Bill, the cap on CRP acreage was increased from 36.4 million acres to 39.2 million acres. The 2002 Farm Bill for the first time made wildlife habitat enhancement an explicit purpose of the program. Building on growing enthusiasm for wildlife conservation at the U.S. Department of Agriculture (USDA), in August 2004, the department announced two new CRP initiatives designed to protect critical habitat. The first called for the enrollment of 250,000 acres of bobwhite quail habitat; the second called for enrollment of 250,000 acres of nonfloodplain wetlands.

In the face of growing urban and suburban development pressures, conservation efforts at the USDA are gaining the support of both agricultural and conservation interests, who with increasing regularity see the commonality of their interests. Both groups acknowledge that protecting agricultural lands from development is a high-priority issue. Working together, conservationists and farmers may well enjoy considerable success in land and biodiversity protection efforts in coming years.

When Oil and Water Mix

The concept of using royalty payments from offshore oil and gas production to fund conservation initiatives has a long history. Since enabling legislation was signed by President Lyndon Johnson in 1964, the Land and Water Conservation Fund (LWCF), largely funded from offshore oil and gas royalties paid to the U.S. government, has supported the acquisition of millions of acres of recreational landscapes and critical wildlife habitat.

But only a fraction of total oil and gas royalty revenues paid into the U.S. Treasury have actually been appropriated for land and water conservation. Since the fund's creation in 1964, $27.2 billion in oil and gas royalty revenues has been credited to the LWCF; of that, only $13.8 billion has been appropriated over the period for the purposes of the LWCF.

In recent years, there has been a significant bipartisan effort in Congress to establish a permanent conservation trust fund that would receive a predictable annual flow of funds from Outer

Continental Shelf (OCS) oil and gas royalties and lease payments. For example, a recent proposal would have directed the secretary of the treasury to annually deposit $3.125 billion of OCS-deposited revenues (out of a total of about $5 billion) to a new conservation trust fund, which would, in turn, finance the LWCF, wildlife habitat initiatives to assist in the recovery of threatened and endangered species, and the enhancement of coastal wetlands and fisheries.

The establishment of a permanent conservation trust fund is viewed by many as the most reliable means of ensuring long-term, sustainable funding for our nation's traditional conservation programs. The federal budget and appropriations process has proven extremely volatile in recent years, with dramatic swings in conservation funding being one of the few constants. The push for a conservation trust fund is one of the most important battles that will be waged in the conservation arena throughout the next four years.

On March 31, 2004, Representative George Miller (D-CA) and Representative Don Young (R-AK) introduced legislation to advance the concept of a permanent conservation trust. This legislation, the "Get Outdoors Act" (HR 4100), generated the enthusiastic support of conservation organizations representing millions of hunters, fishermen, hikers, and bikers. A similar measure, the "Americans Outdoors Act" (S 2590), was introduced in June 2004 by Senator Lamar Alexander (R-TN) and Senator Mary Landrieu (D-LA). Both proposals garnered significant interest and are likely to be reintroduced in 2005.

For many in Congress and in the conservation community, the time has come to fulfill the promise of the LWCF and fully fund the programs authorized in 1964. As conservation funding decreases and revenues from OCS energy development increase, pressure is building to apply energy royalties to the conservation programs they were collected to support.

A Road Map to Conservation Investment Opportunities

Federal infrastructure, agriculture, and energy programs represent by far the best opportunities for increased conservation investment throughout the next decade. Informed and assertive conservation advocates may have considerable success by focusing their efforts on these programs.

In navigating this new world of conservation finance, there are three critical elements to success. First, learn the legal and legislative landscape. As highlighted earlier in this chapter, there are exceptional conservation opportunities within existing programs—programs that are in many cases undersubscribed—at the Departments of Transportation, Agriculture, Defense, and Energy. Conservationists who gain a working knowledge of these nontraditional conservation-funding sources will be better armed to gain access to current funding programs and to think creatively regarding the development of new conservation financing mechanisms.

Second, learn to identify and work with well-informed proponents of various conservation initiatives within the federal superstructure. The approaches to conservation taken by transportation officials are fundamentally different from those taken by agriculture advocates, which are, in turn, different from the approaches taken by engineers at the USACE. By developing working relationships with key conservation players within the federal bureaucracy and Congress, conservation proponents will gain insight on short-term funding practices and priorities, as well as the process of developing long-term conservation policies and practices.

Finally, learn to build large and diverse coalitions. Success in pursuing conservation funding often lies in building coalitions among seemingly disparate groups. Broadening public and political support for infrastructure, agriculture, and energy programs is a central motivation of many recent conservation converts. Providing policy makers with a significant and supportive constituency will usually pay big dividends.

As noted in chapter 1 of this book, the U.S. tradition of investing in landscape conservation goes back to the establishment of the Boston Common in 1634 and has been developing ever since. The political effort to protect and preserve nature received a huge boost when Theodore Roosevelt elevated conservation in the national consciousness. In the past century, organizations such as Ducks Unlimited, Trout Unlimited, The Nature Conservancy, and the Trust for Public Land have had remarkable success in advancing our capability to finance land and wildlife conservation. In a remarkable twist of budget realities, societal norms, and political imperatives, however, conservation in the new millennium may well be financed largely in conjunction with federal infrastructure, agriculture, and energy programs.

Note

[1]*The American Heritage Dictionary of the English Language*, Fourth Edition (Boston: Houghton Mifflin Company, 2000), defines "third rail" as (1) the rail that supplies high voltage to power a train on an electric railway, and (2) a subject that tends to be avoided because of its offensive or controversial nature ("Social Security: the 'third rail' of American politics" (Charles Stein)).

Chapter 12

Financing Private Lands
Conservation and Management Through Conservation Incentives in the Farm Bill

Robert Bonnie

John Markham[1] and his family own a ranch in a county in central Utah, where 96 percent of the land is government-owned. The Markham ranch is potential habitat for the threatened Utah prairie dog (see figure 12.1), a species numbering just a few thousand, thanks to decades of persecution. In what many in the region consider a cruel irony, private lands host three quarters of the world's Utah prairie dogs. In fact, most U.S. endangered species rely on private lands to a significant degree for their recovery.

The region's semi-arid grassland ecosystem, its prairie dogs, and, notably, the Markhams' cows, could all benefit from the reestablishment of native grasses and the control of invasive shrubs. But, as Aldo Leopold writes, restoration is not free: "We must first examine briefly the time-honored supposition that conservation is profitable and that the profit motive is sufficient to motivate its practice."[2] Moreover, no law, not even the Endangered Species Act (ESA), compels the Markhams to manage their lands for the benefit of an endangered species or the restoration of an ecosystem. The ESA only requires that landowners avoid take, or destruction, of occupied habitat, not that they help restore endangered populations to healthy levels. If they are to eventually recover and be removed from the endangered species list, however, most endangered species

Figure 12.1.

Threatened Utah prairie dogs rely on landowners to protect and restore the grassland ecosystem they depend on in order to recover and eventually be removed from the endangered species list. (Photo by Edward Snow.)

populations are dependent on the willingness of landowners to restore and manage suitable habitat. Although necessary, the regulatory controls of the ESA and other laws are, by themselves, insufficient to accomplish the task of conserving crucial habitat found on U.S. farms, ranches, and private forests.

So why not buy the Markham ranch and allow the government to manage the land? Well, the Markham land isn't for sale. Indeed, 73 percent of the United States (excluding Alaska) is in private ownership, and most of it will stay that way. The government has neither the resources nor the will to purchase all the land necessary to protect every endangered species or to ensure that we will continue to benefit from all of the other important natural resource–related services provided by private lands.

Though purchasing land will remain a critical conservation strategy, financing conservation on private lands is not just about real estate transactions. Conservation finance is also about providing incentives (financial and otherwise) to private landowners and managers that encourage them to protect and manage their lands in ways that maintain and enhance the environment.

The Farm Bill

The central importance of private lands to conservation is already reflected in U.S. conservation policy. Indeed, the U.S. government spends billions of dollars annually on the conservation and management of private lands. In particular, as a result of the Farm Security and Investment Act of 2002 (a.k.a. the 2002 Farm Bill), the U.S. Department of Agriculture (USDA) devotes about $3.5 billion annually to a number of private land conservation programs, which provide funding for land management, restoration, conservation easements, water quality protection, and other activities. Those programs provide, or at least should provide, the resources necessary to assist the Markhams and other landowners in producing both income and environmental benefits from their lands. Yet, in practice, the USDA must significantly improve both the design and implementation of its conservation programs to maximize their conservation benefits.

Targeting Resources   Increasing the conservation benefits of the USDA's programs will require at least three things. First, those programs must do a better job of targeting resources to landowners and regions where the benefits of restoration and environmental management are the greatest. Conservation programs should also bolster projects that work across property lines by involving many landowners in protecting important natural resources. With respect to biodiversity protection, targeting resources toward endangered, threatened, and rare species will require efforts to address landowners' reluctance to manage their lands in ways that might invite federal regulation under the ESA. The U.S. Fish and Wildlife Service has developed mechanisms for providing landowners with assurances that their regulatory burden will not increase as a result of stewardship activities. Until the USDA can provide similar assurances for its conservation programs, as it could by seeking authority from the Fish and Wildlife Service to do so under the ESA, landowner trepidation about restoring habitat for rare species will remain a barrier to expanding the conservation benefits from USDA programs.[3]

Rewarding Higher Levels of Performance   In addition, USDA programs must spur higher levels of performance by rewarding landowners who have a greater commitment to stewardship. The Markham family, for example, are rare ranchers to be considering aiding threatened prairie dogs, a competitor for forage that many ranchers prefer to do without. Conservation incentive programs should seek out and reward such landowners, whether they commit to protecting an endangered species or to implementing a superior manure management program that protects water quality from nutrient runoff. USDA programs have not done enough to encourage higher levels of stewardship.

Increasing Capacity for Outreach and Technical Assistance   Finally, the USDA must increase its capacity to provide outreach, technical expertise, and other forms of assistance to landowners. Part of the solution to this problem is, of course, having the staff resources necessary to implement Farm Bill conservation programs—programs that have grown dramatically in size, scope, and complexity throughout the past two decades. In addition, the USDA must do a better job of partnering with land management consultants and conservation groups who can help bring private landowners into USDA programs and provide the expertise to implement conservation activities on private lands.

To better understand the multifaceted challenges facing the USDA, consider the following discussion of three of the most important Farm Bill conservation programs: the Environmental Quality Incentive Program, the Conservation Reserve Program, and the Conservation Security Program.

The Environmental Quality Incentive Program: Improving Management on Working Lands   In the case of the Utah prairie dog and other rare species, the USDA's Environmental Quality Incentive Program (EQIP) has the potential to provide significant financial incentives to assist landowners meshing livestock operations with wildlife conservation. At approximately $1 billion annually, the program is the USDA's second largest to deal with conservation, and it offers landowners up to 75 percent of the costs of carrying out specific conservation practices on cropland, pastureland, rangeland, and forestland. Of its funding, 60 percent is set aside for livestock operations. Furthermore, the Natural Resources Conservation Service (NRCS), the USDA agency overseeing the program, has established conservation of rare and declining wildlife as one of the four national priorities for the program. Nevertheless, EQIP has yet to provide much promise for the Markham ranch.

EQIP allocates funds to the states through a complex national formula based on agricultural and conservation needs. NRCS state offices work with State Technical Committees (that is, a stakeholders' advisory committee within each state) to develop ranking systems that prioritize statewide resource concerns and project types. Using these ranking systems, NRCS chooses among landowner applications and allocates EQIP dollars within each state accordingly. In short, the development of these state ranking systems is key to the allocation of funding and selection of projects.

Unfortunately, many state EQIP ranking systems are severely lacking. They often simply award more points for larger projects without weighing cost effectiveness, thereby overlooking well-designed small projects. Ranking systems have also failed to reward higher levels of performance or the use of innovative environmental management systems. Most state ranking systems lump together different project types (e.g., mixing a manure management project together with habitat restoration efforts) when, in fact, such comparisons are difficult at best.

Some states are taking steps to address this latter problem. For example, in 2003, North Carolina's EQIP program set aside $200,000 for special projects to protect the habitat of at-risk species—especially those associated with aquatic ecosystems and Piedmont prairies (an ecosystem type containing several endangered plants). In 2004, EQIP funded several projects for at-risk species. The state is now looking at improving delivery of the program to rare ecosystems and increasing the funds available for this purpose.

Although the USDA has established national priorities for EQIP, far too many states are not implementing them: North Carolina's experience is more the exception than the rule. In the Markham case, the NRCS at the local level does not yet award extra ranking points for range improvement projects that also benefit rare or endangered species, even though endangered species conservation as part of a livestock operation would seem to fit the program perfectly. To its credit, the NRCS leadership has taken steps to encourage its field offices to improve EQIP implementation, recently issuing a national directive emphasizing that ranking criteria must address levels of performance, innovation, and cost effectiveness. This may be having an impact even with regard to the Utah prairie dog, as the NRCS in Utah is now showing increased interest in addressing wildlife conservation through the program.

Further improvement in EQIP's implementation will depend in large part on ensuring that state and local decisions reflect the program's national priorities. Indeed, this is a tension within many Farm Bill programs. Many in the NRCS praise Farm Bill programs for being responsive to local landowner concerns and correspondingly taking a bottom-up approach to funding decisions. However, local decision making dilutes the potential of conservation programs to have a large-scale influence across watersheds and regions. Furthermore, local decision making can result in funding allocation choices driven more by trying to appease landowner demands than by trying to solve environmental problems. Given that there is far more landowner demand for EQIP and other Farm Bill program funding than there are available funds, NRCS has the ability to require measurable environmental benefits in return for funding.

The use of local decision making by the NRCS is motivated at least in part by the large (and growing) amount of EQIP funding available relative to limited staff resources in an agency already stretched thin in implementing a series of conservation programs. A bottom-up approach makes it easier for the NRCS to move funding out the door quickly. More highly coordinated efforts would likely take more staff time. It is fair to ask those who support increased funding for Farm Bill programs whether the NRCS (and, more broadly, the USDA) has adequate staff to implement the programs, even at current funding levels, in a way that maximizes the conservation benefits per dollar spent. Incentive programs do not run themselves.

One option already in practice is to privatize a portion of the program's implementation by funding private consultants and conservation groups to help landowners design conservation projects and enroll in Farm Bill programs. For example, Ducks Unlimited, Pheasants Forever, and other organizations are heavily involved in Farm Bill program implementation and landowner outreach in many states. In addition, technical service provider provisions of the Farm Bill have been used to fund outreach and program implementation by consultants and conservation groups. Besides increasing staff for program implementation, technical service providers may be able to offer specific expertise that the NRCS lacks (e.g., information about certain manure management technologies or the restoration of habitat for a specific rare species). However, barriers to the technical service provider's success include low reimbursement rates for some conservation work and excessive paperwork. Nonetheless, the creative use of the technical service providers program could go a long way toward satisfying gaps in program implementation.

The Conservation Reserve Program: Retiring Cropland to Restore Ecosystems   The EQIP is a working lands program, meaning it targets working farmlands, ranchlands, and forestlands. The Conservation Reserve Program (CRP), on the other hand, pays landowners to take environmentally sensitive cropland and marginal pastureland temporarily out of production and restore grasses and trees. The CRP is the federal government's largest private lands conservation program, with an annual budget of about $2 billion and a current enrollment of approximately 34.7 million acres out of a Congressionally authorized 39 million acres (about 10 percent of the nation's croplands). Participating landowners receive both cost-share payments for undertaking specific conservation practices and annual land rental payments for a ten-year to fifteen-year contract period.

Originally, the CRP's primary purpose was to reduce soil erosion. Throughout time, the USDA and Congress have broadened the purposes of the program to include improving water quality and quantity, wildlife conservation, and air quality. The vast majority of land enrolled in the CRP enters the program through a competitive general sign-up where the USDA ranks landowners' applications based on an Environmental Benefits Index (EBI) that awards points for wildlife, water quality, erosion control, and air quality benefits and the cost effectiveness of achieving those benefits. Thus, unlike EQIP, decisions made at the federal level, rather than at the state or local level, drive enrollment in the general sign-up.

The CRP's general sign-up has produced some substantial conservation successes. For example, in the late 1980s, farmers enrolled more than 8 million acres in the prairie pothole region of the northern Great Plains, a region containing a critical nesting habitat for a large percentage of North American ducks. The restoration of grasslands in the region under the CRP has helped to dramatically increase duck populations.

The landscape-level success in the Great Plains, however, has rarely been repeated elsewhere. In many regions, use of the EBI results in a shotgun approach to land enrollment in the program, reducing the potential benefits for wildlife populations achievable from targeted enrollments. Even when there are large concentrations of CRP lands in specific regions, the conservation practices undertaken through the program, such as the planting of nonnative grasses, may be inappropriate or counterproductive. For example, lands in the southern United States that could be reforested are being planted with nonnative fescue grasses, while in the grassland-dominated plains states, trees that hinder the restoration of native ecosystems are being planted.

Other lands have been planted to cover types, which, although native, have limited environmental benefits. For instance, hundreds of thousands of acres of dense loblolly pine plantations have been planted in the southern United States in recent decades. Those plantations produce ample supplies of pulpwood (potentially reducing regional pine pulpwood prices and thereby harming non-CRP landowners), but are a far cry from the biologically diverse, fire-maintained longleaf pine forests that once dominated much of the region. Recently, the CRP has offered increased incentives for reforestation of longleaf, and 200,000 acres have been planted, although loblolly pine is also still planted. As in this case, if the EBI were improved to prioritize restoration of rare native ecosystems, such as longleaf pine, then the program's wildlife conservation benefits could be enhanced significantly without sacrificing other goals of the program.

Improving the performance of the general sign-up will require overhauling the EBI. In particular, the EBI should award contracts to landowners who "plant the right things in the right places." The EBI should take into account the locational characteristics of lands, such as their occurrence within important watersheds, their proximity to other CRP lands, and their proximity to lands, held by public, private, or nonprofit entities, protected through other means. Finally, the EBI should give priority to landowners who agree to restore and manage rare native ecosystems—and the CRP should provide enhanced financial incentives for doing so.

Landowners can also enroll in the CRP outside of the general sign-up. Initiated in 1996, the CRP continuous enrollment program allows automatic enrollment of lands that serve important environmental functions, such as riparian buffers, filter strips, or grass waterways. Lands eligible for the continuous program do not have to compete in the general sign-up. In addition to cost share and rental payments, landowners can also receive enhanced incentive payments for enrolling lands and for carrying out conservation practices that produce significant environmental benefits. Four million acres are set aside under the CRP for the continuous program.

In 2003, the Bush administration authorized 1 million acres to be set aside in the continuous program for restoration of riverine floodplains, wetlands, and bottomland hardwood forests. Landowner participation has been tepid, particularly in the bottomland hardwood forest program, because of high crop prices and the refusal of the USDA to offer a full range of incentive payments to landowners. In 2004, the Bush administration announced a continuous enrollment program of 250,000 acres to benefit the bobwhite quail and other upland birds. Future continuous enrollment programs could be targeted to a number of other rare ecosystems and species. In addition, unlike the general sign-up, the continuous program and the additional financial incentives it can offer could promote more complex and intensive restoration activities required for some rare ecosystems.

Throughout the coming decades, the USDA should expand the continuous program by shifting a larger proportion of the CRP's 39-million-acre cap to it and by utilizing the enhanced incentives offered under the program to participating landowners. Doing so would significantly increase the environmental benefits of the CRP.

A second targeted use of the CRP, the Conservation Reserve Enhancement Program (CREP), began in 1997 with an effort in Maryland to restore riparian areas on farms for the benefit of the Chesapeake Bay. Under the CREP, states develop a program to address water quality, erosion, and wildlife habitat issues of state and national concern. The USDA provides 80 percent of the funding, with a nonfederal entity (typically the state) providing the remainder. States may automatically enroll up to 100,000 acres under the plan. Also, like the continuous program, the CREP focuses CRP dollars on specific environmental concerns, allowing for landscape-level conservation efforts in a way that the general sign-up does not. The CREP also provides the flexibility to address local needs—for example, allowing wider buffers necessary for wildlife corridors in Minnesota while focusing incentives in Maryland on efforts to address the looming threat of land development. To date, the USDA has approved twenty-nine CREPs in twenty-five states, thereby authorizing some 1.56 million acres for enrollment, and has enrolled 571,921 acres. As with the continuous program, the USDA should allocate more acreage to the CREPs throughout the coming decades as a means of increasing the environmental benefits from CRP lands.

The need for a more targeted CRP is evident in the USDA's own recent Environmental Impact Statement (EIS) for the program. An examination of the distribution of CRP contracts contained in the EIS shows that there are many areas with rare plants and animals that receive little attention from the program (see figures 12.2 and 12.3).[4] Of course, this is due in large part to the location of marginal cropland. Still, improving the EBI in the general sign-up and shifting a higher proportion of CRP acreage into the CREP and continuous enrollment would increase the program's environmental benefits by focusing CRP contracts on more sensitive lands with greater geographic diversity.

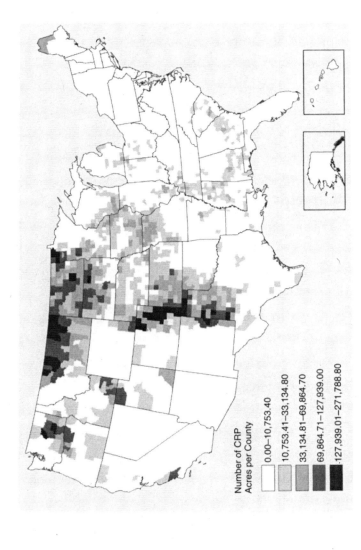

Number of CRP
Acres per County

0.00–10,753.40

10,753.41–33,134.80

33,134.81–69,864.70

69,864.71–127,939.00

127,939.01–271,788.80

Figure 12.2.

Distribution of acres enrolled in the Conservation Reserve Program by county. (Map developed by Peter Black, *Environmental Defense*.)

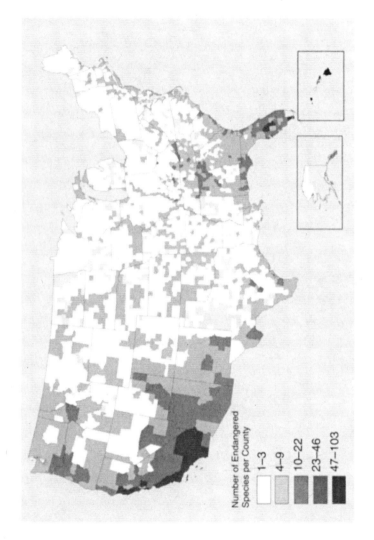

Figure 12.3.

Distribution of endangered species by county. (Map developed by Peter Black, Environmental Defense.)

The Conservation Security Program: Toward Green Payments

Both the EQIP and the CRP programs fund particular conservation practices on a portion of a landowner's land. One downside of such an approach is that it does not reward the landowner who is already implementing such practices. Moreover, a holistic approach would seek to improve the environmental performance of a landowner's entire operation and not just one aspect of it. Indeed, there is growing interest in so-called green payment programs that reward landowners for producing environmental services: for example, the 2002 Farm Bill authorizes the new Conservation Security Program (CSP), a nascent green payment program. Some observers believe that green payments could one day replace commodity support programs, so the CSP is attracting considerable attention.

Like commodity programs, the CSP is an entitlement program under which all eligible farmers and ranchers can participate if they meet the program's minimum criteria. As designed, the scope of this program could be enormous: in the United States, there are two million potentially eligible farmers and ranchers who own nine hundred million acres of land. For both practical and budgetary reasons (Congress, in fact, capped spending on the CSP in 2004 and 2005), the USDA has narrowed the program significantly in the near term to focus on a small number of watersheds. Given growing budget deficits, it is likely that the USDA, out of concern for the program's total cost, will continue to look for ways to limit landowner participation. One means to limit the total program cost is to require that program participants meet high environmental standards.

Most important of all, the aim of the CSP is not just to provide incentives for the adoption of new conservation practices, but also to reward good stewards for their existing management. The basic idea, as stated by the USDA, is to "reward the best and motivate the rest." This movement away from simply funding conservation practices and toward basing payments on measurable improvements in environmental management across a landholding is a dramatic change from other Farm Bill programs. Although very appealing, it will also be challenging to implement.

Rewarding existing stewardship requires measuring and comparing the environmental services produced by one landowner to those produced by others. As the program is currently being implemented, landowners enrolling in the CSP will develop conservation security plans corresponding to three different levels (or tiers) of stewardship commitment. To be eligible for program payments, tier one participants are required to meet a minimum level of commitment; tier three participants are required to prepare a comprehensive conservation security plan addressing all resources of concern on the landowner's entire operation. As landowners move from tier one to tier three, the financial incentives also increase. The USDA has proposed using management intensity levels as a means of assessing a landowner's operation and determining the payments that the landowner should receive.

In 2004, the program's first year of implementation, the CSP was administered based on rules adopted by the USDA on an interim basis. Permanent implementation rules are due out in 2005. The program will continue to evolve throughout the coming years, which is important because, although the CSP is the 2002 Farm Bill's most innovative new program, the USDA and Congress will have limited experience to draw on to make changes during reauthorization of the Farm Bill in 2007. Still, although many questions around implementation of the program remain, many are looking to the CSP as a potentially trailblazing program. Growing questions regarding traditional commodity support programs may move agricultural policy toward green payment programs that reward landowners not for how much corn, soybeans, cotton, rice, or wheat they grow, but for the environmental benefits produced while growing these and other products.

The 2007 Farm Bill

In 2007, Congress will again rewrite the nation's agricultural policies when the current Farm Bill expires. The next Farm Bill will see continued efforts by the conservation community to focus its conservation programs on the most pressing environmental issues and to use those programs to reward landowners for higher levels of environmental stewardship. No doubt, environmental, conservation, and hunting groups will also press for increased funding for conservation programs.

But there's also a larger struggle surrounding the role of conservation programs in the Farm Bill. Ultimately, conservation programs and crop subsidies compete for the USDA's overall Farm Bill budget. At present, commodity programs clearly dominate, even though they are under increasing scrutiny. Although the U.S. Congress voted to phase out traditional subsidies in 1996, lawmakers reinstated and then actually *enlarged* subsidies when market prices for commodities fell in 1998. As a result, the federal government now spends about $20 billion annually on crop subsidies to farmers. Fiscal conservatives in Congress are increasingly concerned about the costs of support programs, especially in light of projected federal deficits. There is growing concern from protrade lawmakers about the trade impacts of U.S. farm subsidies and the growing potential of retaliatory tariffs on U.S. goods. The agricultural policies of the United States also have a significant negative economic impact on farmers in developing countries, who cannot compete with highly subsidized farmers.

Of course, the environmental repercussions of commodity programs are well documented and include the loss of native grasslands, forests, and other ecosystems; soil erosion; and the overuse of fertilizers—a practice that causes eutrophication of streams and rivers and is implicated in the creation of a so-called dead zone in the Gulf of Mexico. Farm support programs also raise significant equity issues across different size operations, different crops, and different regions. From 1995 through 2003, the top 10 percent of subsidy recipients collected 72 percent of total subsidy payments (see table 12.1).[5] As a result, despite the rhetoric of those who support traditional crop payments, subsidies do not generally benefit small farmers and may, in fact, be hurting them. There are also regional tensions at play in the Farm Bill debate, because agricultural dollars continue to flow overwhelmingly to a few states that grow the bulk of subsidized commodities (e.g., corn, wheat, rice, soybeans, and cotton).

Conservation programs, on the other hand, are a means for states that grow fewer subsidized commodities to receive money for their farmers and ranchers (not to mention forest landowners who are cut out of the Farm Bill almost entirely) who don't grow the large commodity crops. Increasing funds for well-designed conservation programs leads to greater regional equity in the Farm Bill and greater equity among different types of landowners (that is, those who don't grow traditional commodities).

Table 12.1.

Concentration of Total USDA Subsidy Payments from 1995 to 2003

Percent of Recipients	Percent of Payments	Number of Recipients	Total Payments 1995–2003	Payment per Recipient
Top 1%	23%	30,502	$30,545,197,439	$1,001,416
Top 2%	34%	61,004	$45,114,923,422	$739,540
Top 5%	55%	152,511	$71,664,948,825	$469,900
Top 10%	72%	305,023	$94,503,069,015	$309,823
Top 20%	87%	610,046	$114,431,349,923	$187,578

Source

Environmental Working Group, summarized from www.ewg.org/farm/.

If the range of concerns confronting traditional farm payment programs results in Congress making significant changes to them in the 2007 Farm Bill, then it is quite possible that the CSP, or some green payment program like it, could help fill the void left by receding subsidy payments. Like crop subsidies, the CSP is an entitlement program and could thereby help to support farmers, albeit by rewarding them for environmental stewardship rather than crop production. Unlike traditional subsidies, green payment programs, if properly designed, should be trade-neutral and environmentally beneficial. Congress could also expand conservation programs such as the EQIP and the CRP to make up for at least a portion of reduced crop subsidies. This, too, could be a boon to conservation, but only if the USDA has the resources to adequately implement those programs in a way that improves their environmental performance. One should not underestimate, however, the political wherewithal of the proponents of traditional commodity programs. Reforming agricultural policy in the United States will be a challenge. Yet a more environmentally friendly Farm Bill would benefit more farmers, with more diverse operations, in more regions of the country.

The pending struggle over Farm Bill dollars could not be more important, given the central role of private land conservation in achieving U.S. environmental goals. There are thousands of U.S. farmers who, like the Markhams, are willing, given the right incentives, to manage their lands in ways that produce significant environmental benefits—benefits that accrue to all.

Notes

[1] John Markham is a fictitious name chosen to protect the identity of an actual Utah rancher.

[2] Aldo Leopold, "Conservation Economics," first published in 1934 in *Journal of Forestry*, reprinted in Susan Flader, ed., *The River of the Mother of God and Other Essays by Aldo Leopold* (Madison: University of Wisconsin Press, 1991).

[3] The U.S. Fish and Wildlife Service's safe harbor program has proven successful in allaying landowner fears regarding restoring habitat for endangered species. For more information, see www.environmentaldefense.org/go/conservationincentives.

[4] See United States Department of Agriculture, Farm Service Agency, *Conservation Reserve Program: Final Programmatic Environmental Impact Statement* (January 2003), chapter 2, pages 33, 40, 64–66, available at www.fsa.usda.gov/dafp/cepd/epb/pdf/Final_PEIS_03/CRP%20Final%20PEIS%20Jan%202003/Summary.pdf.

[5] Environmental Working Group, "Farm Subsidy Database," available at www.ewg.org/farm/progdetail.php?fips=00000&progcode=total&page=conc.

Bibliography

American Association of Fundraising Council. *Giving USA 2003: The Annual Report on Philanthropy*. Indianapolis: The Center on Philanthropy at Indiana University, 2003.

American Farmland Trust. *Protecting Our Most Valuable Resources: Results from a National Public Opinion Poll, 2001*. Washington, D.C.: American Farmland Trust, 2001.

Barile, Suzy. "State's Environmental Mitigation Takes a Proactive Turn." *Raleigh (N.C.) Triangle Business Journal*, February 20, 2004.

Bauer, Marybeth, Jessica Fox, and Michael Bean. "Landowners Bank on Conservation." *Environmental Law Review* 34 (August 2004): 10720–10721.

Blackstone, Nathaniel Brewster. *The Biography of The Reverend William Blackstone and Ancestors and Descendents*. 1974. Available at http://www.dangel.net/AMERICA/Blackstone/REV.WM.BLACKSTONE.html.

Blair, Tony. "A Year of Huge Challenges." *The Economist* 374:8407 (January 1–7, 2005): 44.

Bloomberg.com. "Commodity Strategists: Wheat May Rally, Bank Says." January 25, 2005. Available at http://www.bloomberg.com/apps/news?pid=10000081&sid=ayJRU7fG0qZU&refer=australia.

The Bond Buyer. "The Bond Buyer's 2nd Annual Deal of the Year Awards." *A Bond Buyer Supplement* (January 2004): 24.

Bradley, Ruth. "Saving a Unique Landscape." *bUSisness Chile*, AmCham Chile (the Chilean American Chamber of Commerce) (November 2004). Available at http://www.amchamchile.cl/UserAmcham/business_cover_story.html.

Brenner, Elsa. "Signs of a Comeback in Downtrodden Beacon." *New York Times,* late edition (final), section 11 (Real Estate Desk: SQUARE FEET/Dutchess County), Sept. 12, 2004, page 13.

Bryer, Mark T., Kathleen Maybury, Jonathan S. Adams, and Dennis H. Grossman. "More Than the Sum of the Parts: Diversity and Status of Ecological Systems." In *Precious Heritage: The Status of Biodiversity in the United States*, edited by Bruce A. Stein, Lynn S. Kutner, and Jonathan S. Adams, 201–238. New York: Oxford University Press, 2000.

Bushnell, C. S. Letter to Abraham Lincoln. October 8, 1863. (Recommendations for directors of Union Pacific Railroad.) Library of Congress collection. Available at http://www.cprr.org/Museum/Lincoln_Papers_LOC.html.

Charles Stewart Mott Foundation. "Revolving Loan Fund to Protect Shorelines of the Great Lakes Basin." January 24, 2002. Available at www.mott.org/news/pr-detail.asp?newsid=14.

Chesapeake Bay Foundation. "Take Action: 2005 Legislative Agenda." Available at http://www.cbf.org/site/PageServer?pagename=action_action_network_center_05_agenda_md.

The Conservation Fund. "Great Lakes Revolving Fund." Available at www.conservationfund.org/?article=2465&back=true.

———. "News Release: Revolving Fund Makes Loan, Receives $2 Million Grant." May 31, 2002. Available at www.conservationfund.org/?article=2528.

———. "Northern Forest." Available at http://www.conservationfund.org/?article=2249&back=true.

Davenport, Charles. "Federal Taxes and Transferable State Tax Credits." *Tax Notes* 110:10 (December 8, 2003): 1213–1231.

Defenders of Wildlife. *Conservation in America: State Government Incentives for Habitat Restoration: A Status Report*. Washington, D.C.: Defenders of Wildlife, 2002.

Dix, John. Letter to Abraham Lincoln. November 23, 1863. U.S. Library of Congress. Available at http://memory.loc.gov/cgi-bin/query/r?ammem/mal:@field(DOCID%2B@lit(d2818400)).

Environmental Defense. "Environmental Defense Center for Conservation Incentives: Helping Landowners Conserve Wildlife and the Environment." Available at www.environmentaldefense.org/go/conservationincentives.

———. "Global Warming: Undo It." Available at http://www .environmentaldefense.org/home.cfm.

Environmental Working Group. "Farm Subsidy Database." Available at www.ewg.org/farm/progdetail.php?fips=00000&progcode= total&page=conc.

Fish and Wildlife Service, Director. "Memorandum: Guidance for the Establishment, Use, and Operation of Conservation Banks." May 2, 2003. Available at www.fws.gov/endangered/policies/ conservation-banking.pdf.

Florida Trend. "Swamp Repair." *Florida Trend.* June 9, 2000. Available at www.floridatrend.com.

Fox, Jessica, and A. Anamaria Nino-Murcia. "Status of Species Conservation Banking in the United States." *Conservation Biology.* August 2005, vol. 19, no. 4, pp. 996–1007.

Garcia, Robert, Erica S. Flores, and Elizabeth Pine. *Dreams of Fields: Soccer, Community and Equal Justice, Report on Sports in Urban Parks to the California Department of Parks and Recreation.* Santa Monica, Calif.: Center for Law in the Public Interest, December 2002. Available at http://www.clipi.org/images/Dreams_ of_Fields.pdf.

Gaylord and Dorothy Donnelley Foundation. "Conservation Loan Fund a Key Resource for Lowcountry Groups." Available at www.gddf .org/interest/articleDetail.asp?objectID=572.

General Electric. *Growing in an Uncertain World: General Electric 2003 Annual Report.* February 13, 2004. Available at http://www.ge .com/ar2003/tools_download.jsp.

Gilmore, Bill. "North Carolina's Ecosystem Enhancement Program: A New Approach to Mitigation." Paper presented at the National Mitigation Banking Conference, New Orleans, March 2004.

Goldman Sachs. "Our Firm, Our Culture, Social Responsibility: Tierra del Fuego." http://www.gs.com/our_firm/our_culture/social_ responsibility/tierradelfuego/.

Groves, Craig R., Lynn S. Kutner, David M. Stoms, Michael P. Murray, J. Michael Scott, Michael Schafale, Alan S. Weakly, and Robert L. Pressy. "Owning Up to Our Responsibilities: Who Owns Lands Important for Biodiversity." In *Precious Heritage: The Status of Biodiversity in the United States*, edited by Bruce A. Stein, Lynn S. Kutner, and Jonathan S. Adams, 275–300. New York: Oxford University Press, 2000.

Hambourg, Maria Morris. "Carleton Watkins: An Introduction." In *Carleton Watkins: The Art of Perception*, edited by Douglas R.

Nickel, 8–17. San Francisco: San Francisco Museum of Modern Art, 1999.

Hummon, Lisa, and Frank Casey. "Federal Conservation Incentives: Programs, Status, and Trends, 1996–2001." *2004 Conservation Economics Working Paper No. 1.* Washington, D.C.: Defenders of Wildlife, 2004.

Ingerson, Ann. *Conservation Capital: Sources of Public Funding for Land Conservation, Focus on the Eastern United States.* Washington, D.C.: The Wilderness Society, 2004. Available at http://www.wilderness.org/Library/Documents/ConservationCapital.cfm.

Jefferson, Thomas. Letter to William Caruthers. March 15, 1815. Cited in "Jefferson and the Natural Bridge." Available at www.monticello.org/reports/interests/natural_bridge.html.

———. Notes on the State of Virginia. 1781–1782. Available online at http://etext.lib.virginia.edu/etcbin/toccer-new2?id=JefVirg.sgm&images=images/modeng&data=/texts/english/modeng/parsed&tag=public&part=5&division=div1.

John, Joshua Scott. "All Aboard: The Role of the Railroads in Protecting, Promoting and Selling Yosemite and Yellowstone." Master's thesis, University of Virginia, 1996. Available at http://xroads.virginia.edu/~ma96/railroad/home.html.

Jordan, Louis. "Commodity Money: An Introduction." Coin and Currency Collection, Department of Special Collections, Hesburgh Library, University of Notre Dame. Available at http://www.coins.nd.edu/ColCoin/ColCoinIntros/Commodity.intro.html.

Land Trust Alliance. "Land Trust Gleanings." *Exchange* (Spring 2002). Available at www.lta.org/publications/exchange/exchange_21_02_08.pdf.

———. *Land Trust Standards and Practices* (rev. ed.).Washington, D.C.: Land Trust Alliance, 2004.

———. "The Norcross Wildlife Foundation Offers a No-Interest Loan Fund for Land Protection." *Resources for Land Trusts.* Available at www.lta.org/resources/norcross.htm.

———. *Voters Invest in Open Space: 2000 Referenda Results.* Washington, D.C.: Land Trust Alliance, 2001.

Leopold, Aldo. "Conservation Economics." In *The River of the Mother of God and Other Essays by Aldo Leopold*, edited by Susan Flader and J. Baird Callicot, 193–202. Madison: University of Wisconsin Press, 1991.

———. "Roadside Prairies." In *Aldo Leopold, For the Health of the Land: Previously Unpublished Essays and Other Writings*, edited by J. Baird Callicott and Eric T. Freyfogle, 139. Washington, D.C.: Island Press, 1999.

Levitt, James N., ed. *Conservation in the Internet Age.* Washington, D.C.: Island Press, 2002.

———. "Conservation Innovation in America: Past, Present and Future." *Occasional Paper Series* (OPS 02-03), Institute for Government Innovation, John F. Kennedy School of Government, Harvard University (December 2002): 1–28.

———. "Land and Biodiversity Conservation: A Leadership Dialogue." *Land Lines: The Newsletter of the Lincoln Institute of Land Policy* 14:3 (July 2002): 1–4.

———. "Landscape-Scale Conservation: Grappling with the Green Matrix." *Land Lines: The Newsletter of the Lincoln Institute of Land Policy* 16:1 (January 2004): 1–5.

Lima, Alfred J. "Open Space Through Limited Development." Paper presented at American Planning Association meeting, San Diego, Calif., 1997.

Lindstrom, C. Timothy, Attorney. "State Tax Incentives for Conservation Easements Can Benefit Everyone." *Journal of MultiState Taxation and Incentives* (November/December 2002): 20 ff.

Long Dock Beacon. "Master Plan: Overview" and "Master Plan: Site Map." Available at www.longdockbeacon.com.

Ludlow, Fitz-Hugh. "Seven Weeks in the Great Yo-Semite." *The Atlantic Monthly* 13 (June 1864): 739–754.

Maine Coast Heritage Trust. "Revolving Loan Fund Aids Land Conservation." *Land Trust News: The Newsletter of the Maine Land Trust Network* (Summer 2002). Available at www.mltn.org/news/ltn_summer_02.pdf.

Massachusetts Audubon Society. *Losing Ground: At What Cost?* (November 2003). Available at http://www.massaudubon.org/news/index.php?id=19&type=news.

McCormick, Steve. "Conservation at the Crossroads." Remarks by Steve McCormick, president and chief operating officer, The Nature Conservancy, at the Land Trust Alliance Rally, September 13, 2003, Sacramento, California. Available online at http://nature.org/pressroom/files/land_trust_alliance_speech.pdf.

Mellman Group and American Viewpoint. National poll (sample of 800) for the Trust for Public Land. June 1999.

Miller, Joe. "Lower Haw Reveals Treasures." *Raleigh-Durham News and Observer*, April 2, 2004.

National Mitigation Banking Association. "The Little Pine Island Wetland Restoration and Mitigation Bank, Lee County, Florida." Available

at http://www.mitigationbanking.org/PDFs/FL-MarinerLITTLE
PINEISLAND.pdf.

National Park Service, National Center for Recreation and Conservation.
"Land and Water Conservation Fund: Current Funding for
Grants." Last modified December 22, 2004. Available at
http://www.nps.gov/ncrc/programs/lwcf/funding.html.

National Wildlife Refuge Association. "Paul Kroegel and America's First
Wildlife Refuge." *Blue Goose Flyer* (Summer 2003). Available at
http://www.refugenet.org/New-Centennial/CentStory3.html.

Natural Bridge of Virginia, LLC. "The Natural Bridge of Virginia." Available at www.naturalbridgeva.com.

New Jersey Department of Environmental Protection. "Green Acres Program: County Open Space Tax Programs." Available at
www.state.nj.us/dep/greenacres/coprograms.htm.

———. "Green Acres Program: New Jersey Local Government Open
Space Funding Programs." Available at www.state.nj.us/dep/
greenacres/taxsummary.htm.

———. "Green Acres Program: Planning Incentive Land Acquisition
Application." Available at www.state.nj.us/dep/greenacres/
planincent.doc.

New Jersey Permanent Statute, Title 40:12-15.1. Trenton: New Jersey Office of Legislative Services.

NMBA News. "The Best of Mitigation Banking: Little Pine Island Mitigation Bank, A Public–Private Partnership." Spring 2004. Publication of the National Mitigation Banking Association. Available
at http://www.mitigationbanking.org/PDFs/NMBA_Spring04.pdf.

North Carolina Ecosystem Enhancement Program. "About EEP." Available at http://www.nceep.net/pages/abouteep.html.

———. "Progress Report to the EEP Liaison Council, 11/16/04." Available at www.nceep.net.

North Woods Conservancy. "Seven Mile Point." Available at www
.northwoodsconservancy.org/sevenmile.htm.

Noss, Reed, Edward T. LaRoe, and J. Michael Scott. "Endangered Ecosystems." In U.S. Department of the Interior, *Biological Report 28.*
Washington, D.C.: U.S. Department of the Interior, 1995.

Office of the Federal Register. *Federal Guidance for the Establishment,
Use and Operation of Mitigation Banks* 60 (November 28, 1995):
58605–58614.

Office of the Governor [of New York, George Pataki]. "Governor Announces Historic Conservation Deal Completed." July 1, 1999.
Available at http://www.state.ny.us/governor/press/year99/
july1_99.htm.

Open Space Institute. "The New Jersey Conservation Loan Fund: An Overview." Available at www.osiny.org/njclp.asp.

Ottaway, David B., and Joe Stephens. "Nonprofit Land Bank Amasses Billions." *Washington Post*, May 4, 2003.

Rocky Mountain Institute. "Electric Efficiency." Available at http://www.rmi.org/sitepages/pid321.php.

Roe, David. *Dynamos and Virgins*. New York: Random House, 1984.

Roosevelt, Theodore. *An Autobiography*. 1913. Included in Theodore Roosevelt. *The Rough Riders, An Autobiography*. New York: Library of America, 2004.

———. *A Book-Lover's Holidays in the Open*. 1916. Available online at http://bartleby.school.aol.com/57/10.html.

Runte, Alfred. *Trains of Discovery: Western Railroads and the National Parks*, Fourth Edition. Boulder, Colo.: Roberts Rienhart Publishers, 1998.

———. *Yosemite: The Embattled Wilderness*. Lincoln: University of Nebraska Press, 1990 (chapter 2, page 4 of 10 ff.). Available at http://www.cr.nps.gov/history/online_books/runte2/chap2.htm.

Sekercioglu, Çagan H., Gretchen C. Daily, and Paul R. Ehrlich. "Ecosystem Consequences of Bird Declines." *Proceedings of the National Academies of Science*. December 15, 2004. PNAS 2004 101. Abstract available at http://www.pnas.org/cgi/content/abstract/101/52/18042?maxtoshow=&HITS=10&hits=10&RESULTFORMAT=&fulltext=birds&searchid=1105371798451_4483&stored_search=&FIRSTINDEX=0&journalcode=pnas.

Shaffer, Mark J., Michael Scott, and Frank Casey. "Noah's Options: Initial Cost Estimates of a System of National Habitat Conservation Areas in the United States." *BioScience* 52 (May 2002): 439–443.

Small, Steven J. *The Federal Tax Law of Conservation Easements*. Washington, D.C.: Land Trust Alliance, 1989.

Staats, Eric. "Collier's Manager Looks to Trim Costs of Environmental Mitigation." *Naples (Fla.) Daily News*, September 27, 2004.

State of Florida, Department of Environmental Protection. "Development of the State-wide Uniform Wetland Mitigation Assessment Method." Available at http://www.dep.state.fl.us/water/wetlands/mitigation/uwmam2.htm.

Stein, Bruce A., Lynn S. Kutner, and Jonathan S. Adams, eds. *Precious Heritage: The Status of Biodiversity in the United States*. New York: Oxford University Press, 2000.

Texas Center for Policy Studies. "Chapter 3: Public Lands." In *The Texas Environmental Almanac*. Austin: Texas Center for Policy Studies,

1995. Available at http://www.texascenter.org/almanac/Land/
LANDCH3P2.HTML.

Thoreau, Henry David. *Faith in a Seed: The Dispersion of Seeds and Other Late Natural History Writings.* Edited by Bradley P. Dean. Washington, D.C.: Island Press, 1993.

Trust for Public Land and the Association of New Jersey Environmental Commissions. *A Handbook for Public Financing of Open Space in New Jersey.* Mendham: Association of New Jersey Environmental Commissions, 2001.

Trust for Public Land and Land Trust Alliance. *Americans Invest in Parks and Open Space: Land Vote 2003.* Washington, D.C.: Trust for Public Land and Land Trust Alliance, 2004. Available at http://www.tpl.org/tier3_cdl.cfm?content_item_id=12030&folder_id=2406.

United States Department of Agriculture, Farm Service Agency. "Conservation Reserve Program: Final Programmatic Environmental Impact Statement." January 2003. Chapter 2, pages 33, 40, 64–66. Available at www.fsa.usda.gov/dafp/cepd/epb/pdf/Final_PEIS_03/CRP%20Final%20PEIS%20Jan%202003/Summary.pdf.

———. "Conservation Reserve Program Overview." In *CRP: Planting for the Future.* Washington, D.C.: United States Department of Agriculture, 2004.

United States Department of Commerce, Bureau of Economic Analysis. "Historical Gross Domestic Product Estimates." Available at www.bea.gov/bea/A-Z/A-ZIndex_h.htm.

United States Department of Energy. "Measuring Energy Efficiency in the U.S. Economy: A Beginning." Available at www.eia.doe.gov/emeu/efficiency/contents.html.

United States Department of the Treasury. Internal Revenue Service. Internal Revenue Code section 170(h). Available at http://assembler.law.cornell.edu/uscode/html/uscode26/usc_sec_26_00000170———000-.html.

United States Environmental Protection Agency. "Municipal Solid Waste in the United States: 2000 Facts and Figures." Figure ES-5. Available at http://www.epa.gov/epaoswer/non-hw/muncpl/pubs/report-00.pdf.

———. "Municipal Waste in the United States." Available at http://www.epa.gov/epaoswer/non-hw/muncpl/pubs/msw-sum01.pdf.

United States Fish and Wildlife Service. "Pelican Island National Wildlife Refuge." Available at http://pelicanisland.fws.gov/history.html#immigrant.

———. "Species Information: Threatened and Endangered Plants and Animals." Available at http://endangered.fws.gov/wildlife.html.

United States General Accounting Office. "Wetlands Protection: Assessments Needed to Determine Effectiveness of In-Lieu Fee Mitigation." Report Number GAO-01-325. May 2001. Available at http://www.gao.gov/new.items/d01325.pdf.

Virginia Conservation Credit Pool, LLC. "Tax Credit Sellers Information Memorandum," "Credit Buyers Information Memorandum," and "State Conservation Income Tax Credits Side-by-Side." Available on request from Philip Hocker at phil@hockers.com.

Wells, Jeff. "Birds Are Losing Ground." *Seattle Post Intelligencer*, December 23, 2004. Available at http://seattlepi.nwsource.com/opinion/204869_bird23.html.

Whyte, William H. *The Last Landscape*. New York: Doubleday & Co., 1968.

Wilson, Edward O. "The Bottleneck." *Scientific American* 286:2 (February 2002): 82–91.

Wireback, Taft. "Workers Restoring Stream's Old Flow." *Greensboro (N.C.) News Record*, June 26, 2004.

About the Contributors

Robert Bonnie

Managing Director, Center for Conservation Incentives, Environmental Defense

E-mail: rbonnie@environmentaldefense.org

Robert Bonnie heads Environmental Defense's Center for Conservation Incentives in Washington, D.C. Bonnie has been involved in the development and implementation of a variety of incentives for the protection of endangered species and other wildlife on private lands, including safe harbor agreements, conservation banks, Farm Bill programs, and carbon sequestration. Bonnie earned his M.E.M. and M.F. from Duke University.

Frank Casey

Director, Conservation Economics Program, Defenders of Wildlife

E-mail: fcasey@defenders.org

Dr. Frank Casey is a natural resources economist and is the Director of the Conservation Economics Program (CEP) at Defenders of Wildlife. His primary efforts center on analyzing, evaluating, and promoting landowner incentive policies for wildlife habitat and biodiversity conservation on private agriculture and forestry lands. Casey directs a CEP team that identifies and estimates public and private expenditures and resources dedicated to the conservation of wildlife habitat, as well as the market and non-market benefits associated with conservation policies. He was heavily involved in the 2002 Farm Bill conservation title legislation and has been instrumental in helping to define performance indicators for wildlife habitat and biodiversity conservation on private agricultural lands. Casey serves as a board member of the National Campaign for Sustainable Agriculture, is on the National Policy Advisory Group for the Minnesota Land Stewardship Project, and is a member of the National Farmlands Working Group, which is developing national ecosystem indicators for the H. John Heinz III Center for Science, Economics, and Technology. Casey earned his M.S. in agricultural economics at Cornell University and his Ph.D. in food and resource economics from the University of Florida.

Story Clark

Independent Consultant
E-mail: storyclark@earthlink.net

Story Clark is a consultant specializing in land conservation strategy, stewardship, and financing. She has advised numerous conservation organizations, land trusts, and foundations in the Rocky Mountain region and nationally, and has been involved in land conservation and land use planning issues for twenty-five years. Before establishing her consulting business in 2000, Clark was senior director at the Jackson Hole Land Trust; was founding executive director of the Jackson Hole Conservation Alliance; and worked for the National Park Service, the Alaska Coalition, and Teton County, Wyoming (for the last, she was a county planner). In 1996, she received the National Park Foundation's Citizen Leadership Medal for continued leadership in the preservation and protection of the United States of America's scenic and historic heritage. Clark has a B.A. in creative writing and biology from Hampshire College.

Patrick Coady

Managing Director, Coady Diemar Partners
E-mail: coadyco@earthlink.net

Patrick (Pat) Coady is managing director of a Washington, D.C., investment banking firm Coady Diemar Partners, which raises private equity for companies and assists with mergers and acquisitions. In addition to a career in investment banking, other work has included assignments as chief financial officer. Between 1989 and 1993, Coady was U.S. executive director of the World Bank. Since 1993, Coady has been a senior fellow at Conservation International, where he has served on the Investment Committee of the Conservation International biodiversity investment fund. In 1994, Coady cofounded the Northern Virginia Conservation Trust, a land trust supported through a unique public–private partnership with Fairfax and Arlington counties and the city of Alexandria in the Washington, D.C., suburbs. Coady is a graduate of Massachusetts Institute of Technology and the Harvard Business School.

Ernest Cook

Senior Vice President, Trust for Public Land
E-mail: ernest.cook@tpl.org

Ernest Cook has directed growing Conservation Finance program of the Trust for Public Land (TPL) since 1994. During that time, TPL has helped pass legislation and ballot measures providing more than $25 billion in parks and open space capital funding. Cook also serves as president of the Conservation Campaign, TPL's 501(c)(4) affiliate, which lobbies and sponsors ballot measure campaigns for new park and conservation funds. He is the coauthor of *The Conservation Finance Handbook* and author of numerous articles and reports on land conservation. Cook holds a B.A. from Harvard and an M.P.A. from New York University.

Adam Davis

President, Solano Partners, Inc.
E-mail: adavis789@sbcglobal.net

Adam Davis is currently president and owner of Solano Partners, Inc., a consulting firm focused on environmental economics and conservation finance issues. Current clients include Environmental Banc & Exchange and the Katoomba Group, an international consortium of organizations working on market mechanisms for forest and ecosystem conservation. His work focuses on development of meaningful and cost-effective offsets for large corporations and the creation of an information service that tracks news and transactions in new ecosystem service-based markets (see www .ecosystemmarketplace.com). Davis's work was recently featured in *The New Economy of Nature*, by Daily and Ellison, and he received the 2002 Ecological Society of America corporate award for "his contribution to the understanding of connections between recycling, resource recovery and ecosystem health." Davis serves as a member of the advisory council for the Aldo Leopold Leadership

Program and as a collaborating scientist at the Stanford University Center for Conservation Biology. Prior to founding Solano Partners, Inc., Davis was director of the Environment Division for EPRIsolutions and a founding principal at Natural Strategies, Inc., a management consulting firm working with companies to integrate sustainability principles into business strategy. He also served for nearly ten years at Waste Management, Inc., the world's largest recycling and solid waste management company.

Philip M. Hocker

ConServCo/Conservation Service Company, LLC
E-mail: phil@hockers.com

Philip M. Hocker is a conservation consultant based in Alexandria, Virginia. Together with his wife, Jean Hocker, he operates ConServCo, the Conservation Service Company, LLC. One of ConServCo's recent projects was the enactment of legislation in 2002 to make Virginia's state income tax credit for land conservation donations directly transferable. Hocker has worked on easements and other land-protection transactions in Virginia, the District of Columbia, California, and Wyoming. He has been actively involved with environmental policy issues since the early 1970s, when he lived in Jackson Hole, Wyoming. He served as Wyoming chapter chair for the Sierra Club from 1978 to 1980, and then on the Sierra Club's national board of directors until 1986. In 1988, together with a group of distinguished conservationists, he founded Mineral Policy Center, a nonprofit organization based in Washington, D.C., to address environmental problems caused by mining and oilfield pollution. From 1988 to 1998, Hocker was president and executive director of the center. Hocker is an architect by training, holding degrees from Princeton and Harvard universities; he is licensed to practice in several states. He holds awards for his conservation work from the United States Forest Service, the Sierra Club, and the Syracuse University School of Forestry. When not working on conservation, he and his wife enjoy mountaineering and wilderness canoeing in the western United States and the Canadian Arctic.

James N. Levitt

Director, Program on Conservation Innovation at the Harvard Forest
E-mail: james_levitt@harvard.edu

James N. (Jim) Levitt is director of the Program on Conservation Innovation (the PCI) at the Harvard Forest, a Petersham,

Massachusetts–based research facility of Harvard University. He also serves as a fellow of the Ash Institute for Democratic Governance and Innovation at Harvard's Kennedy School of Government. His research interests are present-day and historical innovations in the field of land and biodiversity conservation that are characterized by novelty, significance, measurable effectiveness, transferability, and an ability to endure. Prior to coming to Harvard, Levitt advised Fortune 50–sized corporations in the communications, computing, and retailing industries regarding the development of new telecommunications networks, Internet-related services, and the emergence of electronic commerce markets. Levitt holds a B.A., cum laude, with distinction in anthropology, from Yale College and a master's in public and private management from the Yale School of Management.

Mary McBryde

Project Manager, The Lyme Timber Company
E-mail: mmcbryde@lymetimber.com

Mary McBryde is a project manager at The Lyme Timber Company, focusing primarily on the advisory arm of the company, LTC Conservation Advisory Services (LTCCAS). She advises foundations and family and corporate landowners on a variety of land conservation projects and is responsible for structuring and negotiating multiple land and conservation easement transactions. She also assists with the evaluation and analysis of conservation limited development projects and conservation finance projects, including the creation and implementation of revolving loan funds. She is former land protection assistant with the Jackson Hole Land Trust, where she implemented multiple land protection strategies, including the negotiation of conservation easements and the coordination of the conservation buyer program. McBryde received a B.A. from Southern Methodist University and an M.S. in forestry from the University of Washington.

Jeffery T. More

Partner, The Accord Group
E-mail: jmore@theaccordgroup.com

Jeffery T. More, partner with The Accord Group, currently serves as outside counsel and government affairs consultant to Ducks Unlimited (DU), the Theodore Roosevelt Conservation Partnership (TRCP), the Water Infrastructure Network (WIN), the Outdoor Industry Association (OIA), and the National Association of

Clean Water Agencies (NACWA). He is also a policy committee member for the Congressional Sportsmen Foundation. Prior to coming to The Accord Group, More served as associate counsel to the House Water Resources and Environment Subcommittee and staffed the Speakers Task Force on the Environment. He received his B.A. from Syracuse University and his J.D. from George Washington University. More also completed the Senior Managers in Government Program at Harvard University.

James D. Range

Senior Public Policy Advisor, Baker, Donelson, Bearman, Caldwell & Berkowitz, P.C.

Email: jrange@bakerdonelson.com

A lifelong conservationist, Jim Range was instrumental in the 1970s in marshalling through many of the nation's most important environmental laws. As minority counsel to the U.S. Senate Committee on Environment and Public Works under Senator Howard Baker, Range helped draft the 1977 Clean Water Act, the amendments that toughened the Clean Air Act, and the 1980 Superfund law. He went on to be chief counsel to Senator Baker when he became senate majority leader and then vice president of government affairs of Waste Management Inc., the world's largest waste management company.

Throughout, Range has served on the board of directors of a number of the nation's most respected and effective conservation groups. Recently he was named chair of the Theodore Roosevelt Conservation Partnership, an organization representing most of the nation's hunting, angling, and resource management organizations.

At Baker Donelson, Range represents the interests of companies and organizations on public policy issues concerning resource management, environmental pollution, endangered species, water quality and quantity, and agriculture. He holds a B.S. in biology, chemistry, and physics from Tulane University, an M.S. in aquatic biology from Tennessee Tech University, and a J.D. in natural resources law from the University of Miami School of Law.

Steve Rosenberg

Executive Director, The Scenic Hudson Land Trust

E-mail: srosenberg@scenichudson.org

As executive director of The Scenic Hudson Land Trust and director of the Land Preservation program at Scenic Hudson, Steve

Rosenberg oversees the protection of Hudson Valley lands for public enjoyment. He joined the organization in 1990, and since that time he has led the group in safeguarding thousands of acres of land and has helped create or improve many of Scenic Hudson's numerous parks and preserves along one hundred and sixty miles of the Hudson River. In addition, the program converts neglected urban waterfront sites into more publicly beneficial uses, preserves productive farmland, and protects views from historic sites. Prior to his tenure at Scenic Hudson, Rosenberg practiced land use planning and real estate law for eight years. He received his bachelor's degree in history and urban studies from Northwestern University and graduated with honors from George Washington University School of Law.

Kevin W. Schuyler

Vice President and Director of Finance and Investments, The Nature Conservancy
E-mail: kevin_schuyler@tnc.org

Kevin W. Schuyler is vice president and director of finance and investments for The Nature Conservancy (TNC). He joined TNC in 2001 as the director of business development for its Compatible Ventures Group. In 2002, he founded TNC's Business Consulting Group and served as its initial manager. Schuyler was appointed TNC's director of finance in 2003. In 2004, he assumed additional management responsibility for TNC's $1.3 billion endowment. In each of his roles, Schuyler's objective has been to support TNC's conservation work around the world through the application of innovative financial approaches and tools. Prior to joining TNC, Schuyler was a principal with Birdwood Capital, a boutique venture consulting and executive services firm he cofounded. From 1996 to 1998, Schuyler was an associate with McKinsey and Company management consultants in Atlanta, where he consulted to industry leaders in transportation, insurance, and energy. He began his career trading agricultural futures at the Chicago Board of Trade with the Louis Dreyfus Corporation. His work with Louis Dreyfus later included founding the Forest Products Trading Group. Under his leadership, the group became the largest volume trader of Forest Products futures at the Board of Trade in 1995. Schuyler graduated from Harvard College with a degree in economics. He earned an M.B.A. from the University of Virginia's Darden School of Business, where he was honored with the faculty award for academic excellence. In addition to his work in conservation, Schuyler is the second vice chairman of the board of The Haitian Project, a nonprofit organization working to bring social and economic justice to Haiti by providing educational opportunity in Haiti's poorest neighborhoods.

Peter R. Stein

General Partner, The Lyme Timber Company
E-mail: peterstein@lymetimber.com

Peter R. Stein is a general partner at The Lyme Timber Company in Hanover, New Hampshire, and is responsible for the design and management of large-scale timberland purchases and limited development projects in cooperation with regional and national land conservation organizations. In addition, he manages LTC Conservation Advisory Services, Lyme's consulting business, which helps individual, corporate, and family landowners to design and implement conservation land transactions. Prior to joining The Lyme Timber Company in 1990, Stein was senior vice president of the Trust for Public Land, where he directed its conservation real estate acquisition activities in the Northeast and Midwest. Current and past board memberships include Appalachian Mountain Club, Island Press, Hubbard Brook Research Foundation, Vermont Natural Resources Council, and Board Chair of Land Trust Alliance from 1993 through 1995. He is currently an adviser to the Doris Duke Charitable Foundation, The Orton Family Foundation, and a small group of individual philanthropists concerned with land conservation. Stein received a B.A., with highest honors, from the University of California at Santa Cruz in 1975 and a Loeb Fellowship in Advanced Environmental Studies, Harvard University, in 1981.

Ned Sullivan

President, Scenic Hudson
E-mail: nsullivan@scenichudson.org

Ned Sullivan, president of Scenic Hudson, joined the organization in 1999. Scenic Hudson, founded in 1964, is a nonprofit organization that employs land acquisition, planning, education, and environmental advocacy to preserve and restore the Hudson River and the majestic landscapes of the Hudson Valley as public and natural resources. Prior to coming to Scenic Hudson, he served as commissioner of Maine's Department of Environmental Protection, where, from 1995 to 1999, he managed a staff of four hundred and was responsible for statewide pollution control and prevention efforts and land use programs. He served as deputy commissioner of the New York State Department of Environmental Conservation from 1987 to 1995, overseeing the state's hazardous waste cleanup initiative, as well as air, water, and waste management programs. During this same period, he represented the commissioner as chair of the Environmental Facilities Corporation, a public-benefit corporation providing financing and technical assistance to businesses and government agencies in the state. Sullivan's career also includes time spent as a vice president and managing director at the Bank of Boston, where he assisted government and corporate clients in obtaining funding for major capital projects involving energy and environmental facilities and real estate. As financial adviser to the state's secretary of environmental affairs, he helped develop legislation to finance the multibillion-dollar Boston Harbor cleanup. Sullivan earned a bachelor's degree in political science and a coordinate degree in environmental studies from Williams College; he earned master's degrees from Yale University's School of Management and School of Forestry and Environmental Studies.

Steve Weems

Senior Vice President, Coastal Enterprises, Inc.
E-mail: steveweems@ceimaine.org

Steve Weems is managing director of CEI Capital Management LLC (CCML), a for-profit investment management subsidiary of Coastal Enterprises, Inc. (CEI) based in Wiscasset, Maine. CEI is a regional (multistate) community development corporation with a mission to help create economically and environmentally healthy communities in which all people, especially those with low incomes, can reach their full potential. Weems also is a senior vice president of CEI. Weems has a B.S.M.E. degree from Bucknell University, has an M.B.A. from Harvard Business School, and served as a captain in the U.S. Army. Since 1968, he has pursued a cross-pollinated career in the private, public, and nonprofit sectors including senior positions in small business ownership/management (at organic materials recycling and commercial modular space companies); consulting (at three business and economic development consulting entities); commercial banking (at a subsidiary of the Bank of Boston); corporate acquisitions and large-scale project development (at Browning-Ferris Industries); venture capital (as a founder of Maine's first institutional source of venture capital); economic development and development finance (with Maine state government and as a founder of the Maine Development Foundation, a legislatively created statewide development corporation); and environmental protection (at the Connecticut Department of Environmental Protection). Weems is a past elected official (at the municipal level) and is an amateur juggler. He has lived in Maine since 1975.

Matt Zieper

Research Director, Conservation Finance Program, The Trust for Public Land
E-mail: matt.zieper@tpl.org

As Research Director of the Conservation Finance Program at the Trust for Public Land, Matt Zieper leads a team of researchers whose work underpins TPL's ability to design ballot measures, shape legislation, and influence public policy. In its role as adviser to state and local elected officials and community leaders, TPL has helped pass 266 ballot measures since 1996, raising a total of $38 billion, including $21 billion for land conservation. Zieper leads TPL's efforts to publish Land Vote, an annual comprehensive review of conservation ballot measures. He also authored *Keeping Our Commitment*, a report outlining policies to protect 1 million acres in the Chesapeake Bay watershed. Prior to joining TPL, Zieper was a legislative aide in the Massachusetts Senate and a fiscal and economic policy consultant. Zieper is a graduate of Harvard University's John F. Kennedy School of Government and the University of Massachusetts Amherst.

Index

227

233